W9-ARW-693

The
EVERYTHING®
Low Cholesterol Book

Dear Reader:

You hold the key to your own health and well-being. My own loss of health at the age of twenty-nine ignited my passion for wellness. While pursuing a career as an attorney in a large New York City law firm, I became seriously ill. It took one and half years for me to rebuild my health. I came to some important realizations during this painful time. I realized that without health and vitality, without close connection to family, friends, and community, and without passionate love for my work and for my life, my life held little value, regardless of how many material possessions I might own.

For those reasons, I chose to become a health educator and promoter, to dedicate my life to learning and teaching people about the power of wellness, and to do all I can to help others create health and joy.

Heart disease is a potent killer that touches many lives. The disease process consists of many factors and slowly robs you of healthy circulation and your cells of nourishing oxygen and life. Remarkably, many choices you make daily greatly affect your odds of preventing this disease.

I hope this book provides you with the information and motivation you need to realize how much you can do to create well-being for yourself and those you love. Feel free to contact me at my Web site (✍*www.shirleyarcher. com*). I'm always happy to hear from my readers.

Sincerely yours in health and wellness,

Shirley Archer

The EVERYTHING® Series

Editorial

Publishing Director	Gary M. Krebs
Managing Editor	Kate McBride
Copy Chief	Laura MacLaughlin
Acquisitions Editor	Eric M. Hall
Technical Reviewer	Sandra K. Nissenberg, M.S., R.D.
Development Editor	Christina MacDonald
Production Editor	Jamie Wielgus

Production

Production Director	Susan Beale
Production Manager	Michelle Roy Kelly
Series Designers	Daria Perreault
	Colleen Cunningham
	John Paulhus
Cover Design	Paul Beatrice
	Matt LeBlanc
Layout and Graphics	Colleen Cunningham
	Rachael Eiben
	Michelle Roy Kelly
	John Paulhus
	Daria Perreault
	Erin Ring
Series Cover Artist	Barry Littmann

Visit the entire Everything® Series at www.everything.com

THE
EVERYTHING®
LOW
CHOLESTEROL
BOOK

Reduce your risks and ensure
a longer, healthier life

Shirley Archer

Adams Media
Avon, Massachusetts

This book is dedicated to all people whose lives are touched by heart disease in the most intimate ways. May we replace disease with health and use knowledge to promote well-being.

Copyright ©2005, F+W Publications, Inc. All rights reserved.
This book, or parts thereof, may not be reproduced in any form without permission from the publisher; exceptions are made for brief excerpts used in published reviews.

An Everything® Series Book.
Everything® and everything.com® are registered trademarks of F+W Publications, Inc.

Published by Adams Media, an F+W Publications Company
57 Littlefield Street, Avon, MA 02322 U.S.A.
www.adamsmedia.com

ISBN: 1-59337-146-2
Printed in the United States of America.

J I H G F E D C B

Library of Congress Cataloging-in-Publication Data
Archer, Shirley.
The everything low cholesterol book : reduce your risks and ensure a longer, healthier life / Shirley Archer.
p.   cm. -- (An everything series book)
ISBN 1-59337-146-2
1. Hypercholesterolemia--Popular works. 2. Low-cholesterol diet--Popular works.
3. Coronary heart disease--Risk factors--Popular works. I. Title. II. Series: Everything series.

RC632.H83A735 2004
613.2'84--dc22

2004013356

This publication is designed to provide accurate and authoritative information with regard to the subject matter covered. It is sold with the understanding that the publisher is not engaged in rendering legal, accounting, or other professional advice. If legal advice or other expert assistance is required, the services of a competent professional person should be sought.

—From a *Declaration of Principles* jointly adopted by a Committee of the American Bar Association and a Committee of Publishers and Associations

The Everything® Low Cholesterol Book is intended as a reference volume only, not as a medical manual. In light of the complex, individual, and specific nature of health problems, this book is not intended to replace professional medical advice. The ideas, procedures, and suggestions in this book are intended to supplement, not replace, the advice of a trained medical professional. Consult your physician before adopting the suggestions in this book, as well as about any condition that may require diagnosis or medical attention. The author and publisher disclaim any liability arising directly or indirectly from the use of this book.

Many of the designations used by manufacturers and sellers to distinguish their products are claimed as trademarks. Where those designations appear in this book and Adams Media was aware of a trademark claim, the designations have been printed with initial capital letters.

This book is available at quantity discounts for bulk purchases.
For information, call 1-800-872-5627.

Contents

Acknowledgments

I want to thank Carol Roth, my literary agent, for her faith in me. Many thanks to everyone at the Stanford Prevention Research Center for giving me the opportunity to learn so much about the value of healthy lifestyle habits and the power of prevention and for supporting my efforts to contribute my gifts as an educator and communicator. Particular thanks to Drs. Jack Farquhar, Christopher Gardner, and Bill Haskell for always patiently answering my questions, and to my colleagues in the Health Improvement Program for their support and camaraderie: Wes Alles, Joyce Hanna, Jerrie Thurman, Julie Anderson, Jane Rothstein, Sonia Halvorson, and many others at the center too numerous to name individually, but all equally special. Thanks to Laurie, Rita, Kay, Robin, and others for sharing their personal testimonials. Thanks to Dr. Kenneth Cooper for sharing his time and to the wonderful staff at the Cooper Institute for their help. Thanks to Warren Pinckert at Cholestech Corporation for his support. Thanks to Jeff Aroy at Berkeley Heart Lab, Inc. Special thanks to my dear sister Georgia Archer and Anthony Dominici for their love and thanks to Monica, Carol, and Joan for being kind readers.

Top Ten Things You Need to Know
about Your Cholesterol Levels

1. Your total cholesterol number only tells part of the story.

2. Fifty percent of people with coronary artery disease do not have high total blood cholesterol levels.

3. As many as 10 percent of people with high cholesterol levels cannot lower these levels without medical help, due to strong genetic factors.

4. Children can have unhealthy cholesterol levels that put them at greater risk for heart disease as adults.

5. Not all LDL cholesterol is equal—studies show that small, dense particle LDL is significantly more harmful than the larger, more fluffy LDL particles.

6. Your cholesterol levels reflect the type of lifestyle that you lead on most days.

7. For many people, eating nutritiously and being active regularly can lower cholesterol levels as much as taking prescription drugs.

8. Free-range beef from cows fed grass and eggs from chickens fed grain have lower saturated fat and cholesterol levels.

9. A daily diet of foods rich in soluble fiber can lower your cholesterol by as much as 5 percent.

10. No level of trans-fat consumption is beneficial for health.

Introduction

▶ How many of us have felt our hearts sink when we heard that someone we know, only in his or her forties or fifties, has died from an unexpected heart attack? It is a sobering, powerful event that prompts us all to take a moment to think. Yet the U.S. government estimates that more than half of American adults, or as many as 100 million, have high cholesterol levels that endanger their health. Nearly half of all American adults do not even know their cholesterol levels.

While heart disease is the result of multiple factors, the level of cholesterol in your bloodstream is one factor that you can manage effectively. A few simple steps can make the difference between the life and death of you and your loved ones. Is it worth your time and effort? If you value the days of your life, then your answer should be clear.

In 2004, the National Cholesterol Education Program (NCEP), which is sponsored by the U.S. government as part of the National Heart, Lung, and Blood Institute, issued the most recent update to its recommendations for national guidelines for cholesterol levels. These guidelines are based on a foundation of decades of research studies that have focused on trying to understand who is most likely to develop heart disease and why. The message is loud, clear, and true—achieving and maintaining healthy cholesterol levels can significantly reduce the risk of death and disability from heart disease.

The actual role of cholesterol in heart disease is complex. The process of atherosclerosis, also known as hardening of the arteries, can begin in childhood but does not lead to complications until older adulthood. This process involves inflammation in the lining of blood vessels that leaves vessels susceptible to surface accumulation of blood fats. Cholesterol is among those blood fats. Over time, a chemical process turns these fats into a substance called plaque. This plaque might clog or block the blood vessel, but it can also rupture and create a blood clot that can block another blood vessel. Whenever there is a blockage of blood flow, cells are deprived of essential nutrients and tissue dies. Sometimes the consequences are so severe that the result is death. In other cases, the victim becomes disabled.

Scientists continue to study all the mechanisms behind atherosclerosis, which include inflammation, oxidation, and blood fats. Because of genetic factors, some individuals are more likely than others to experience this process. Because of hormonal and other factors, the disease process occurs differently in men and women. And because of lifestyle factors, some of these mechanisms are accelerated or slowed. As scientists continue to put the puzzle pieces together, a fascinating image emerges—the overall picture of how the body maintains or loses a healthy circulatory system.

Although scientists are still working to complete the full picture, certain aspects of the disease process are clear. Scientists agree that cholesterol levels and heart disease are related. You can take steps to reduce your risks of experiencing this life-threatening disease by addressing lifestyle factors that impact your cholesterol levels. These lifestyle factors include what you eat, your level of activity, your weight, whether you smoke, whether you abuse alcohol or other drugs, and whether you manage stress effectively. You cannot change your genetic heritage, your gender, or your age, but you can certainly make careful choices about your day-to-day lifestyle.

Understanding the role of cholesterol in your life and learning how to manage it for your health, therefore, is powerful. You have the power to create a vibrant and healthy life for yourself and for your loved ones. You have the power to reduce your risk of disease, to increase the years of your life, and to improve the quality of your daily experiences. Why wait to enjoy better living? Take the time to learn the information in this book that will help empower you on the road to wellness for years of dynamic living. Get started today.

Lowering Cholesterol

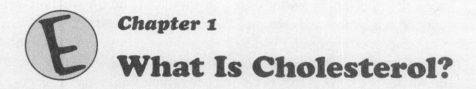

Chapter 1

What Is Cholesterol?

You don't need to be a scientist to understand what cholesterol is and how to effectively manage your cholesterol levels for better health. You do, however, need to take a moment to consider what is happening on the inside of your body to keep you alive. While most of us take for granted that we don't need to think about the constant maintenance of the body that we inhabit, these are miraculous ongoing processes of life. Cholesterol is an essential part of this life process.

Defining Cholesterol

Cholesterol is a necessary and natural part of each cell in the human body and in the bodies of other animals. Cholesterol helps to maintain the structure of the walls of cell membranes, and it also works to keep our brains healthy. The liver uses cholesterol as raw material in the creation of important hormones such as adrenalin and the sex hormones and to create digestive enzymes (such as bile acids that break down fats, among other things). Cholesterol is integral both to thinking and to sexual activity, as well as to other essential life processes. Cholesterol, therefore, is a subject that is definitely worthy of our close attention.

FACT

Most gallstones that are formed in the gall bladder are composed primarily of cholesterol. The liver responds to the presence of dietary fat by producing cholesterol to synthesize bile to digest the fats. If too much dietary fat is consumed, the liver may over-produce cholesterol, leading to formation of gallstones.

A healthy liver manufactures cholesterol, a waxy "lipid" (fat-like substance). In addition to being manufactured in the body, cholesterol gets into the bloodstream through the food that you eat. In particular, if you eat too much saturated fat, which is fat primarily from animal sources, the result is an elevated blood cholesterol level. The big picture, however, is not as simple as that. Many other factors play a role in the composition of cholesterol levels. Even if you are a vegetarian who eats no foods that contain cholesterol, you will have cholesterol in your body.

Factors Affecting Cholesterol

Total cholesterol is the sum total of all the cholesterol in your bloodstream at a given time. Different types of cholesterol, such as high-density lipoproteins (HDLs) and low-density lipoproteins (LDLs), make up the total amount. (Density refers to the weight of the lipoprotein.) Several factors affect the total cholesterol levels in your bloodstream. These factors include the following:

- **What you eat:** Foods that come from animals, such as meats and eggs, contain cholesterol. Foods high in saturated fats, such as meats and dairy products, are converted into cholesterol in your body. Processed foods that contain trans-fats are converted into LDL or "bad" cholesterol.

- **Whether you are overweight:** Excess consumption of dietary fat can lead to elevated cholesterol levels. People who lose as little as 10 percent of their total body weight have seen improvements in cholesterol levels.

- **Whether you smoke:** Smoking lowers levels of HDL, or "good" cholesterol.

- **Whether you consume alcohol:** For some people, moderate alcohol consumption raises levels of HDL, or good cholesterol. Excess consumption is, of course, not healthful.

- **Whether you are inactive or active regularly:** People who are physically active on a regular basis have higher levels of HDL, or good cholesterol. Inactivity leads to a relative increase in LDL, or bad cholesterol levels.

- **Whether you effectively manage stress in your life:** Research studies show that mental and emotional stress can adversely affect heart health.

- **Your family history of heart disease genetic predisposition:** Familial hypercholesterolemia strikes one in 500 children. The strongest risk factor for heart disease is hereditary. If a family member has had a heart attack or stroke before the age of fifty-five, your odds of having heart disease are much greater.

- **Your gender and age:** Before menopause, women have a natural advantage over men as female hormones help to maintain high levels of HDL. As the body grows older, the risk of heart disease increases as it typically takes years to develop to a life-threatening stage.

- **Your general state of health and well-being:** Several of the risk factors for heart disease are directly related to lifestyle habits that can be changed.

- **What type of medications you take:** For certain individuals, medications can help to effectively manage cholesterol levels. Always ask your health-care provider about any side effects of medications that you take and appropriate lifestyle changes that you can make to achieve similar goals. Also inform him or her about any dietary supplements you may be taking, so that you can protect yourself from adverse drug interactions.

All of these factors will be discussed in detail throughout this book, along with tips for reducing your cholesterol.

A Complicated Puzzle

According to National Cholesterol Education Program (NCEP) guidelines issued by the federal government and supported by leading researchers and the American Heart Association (AHA), desirable total cholesterol results should be lower than 200 mg/dL. Levels from 200 to 239 mg/dL are considered borderline high. Total cholesterol levels of 240 mg/dL and above are considered high.

Cholesterol and other fats are measured in milligrams per deciliter (mg/dL). Some European labs use a measuring system of millimoles per liter (mmol/L). To convert millimoles to deciliters, multiply the mmol/L figure by 38.67.

Your total cholesterol levels, however, do not paint a complete picture of the health of your arteries. Because not all cholesterol is bad, you need to find out what type of cholesterol you have. Remember that cholesterol is essential to the health of every cell in your body and to the production of your sex hormones. Good cholesterol, or HDL, actually helps to maintain healthy cholesterol levels. To fully understand the health of your arteries and what is flowing in your bloodstream, you also need to find out about the levels of other blood fats, known as triglycerides.

Half the people whose total cholesterol levels come within the "desirable" levels have heart disease, so simply achieving this target does not guarantee that you are not at risk of heart disease. To truly evaluate your risk, you need to take into account all of the risk factors that apply to you and pay particular attention if you have a family history of heart disease. Regardless of cholesterol levels, it is a good idea for everyone to observe healthy lifestyle habits, not only to lengthen your life but to increase the quality of those additional years.

The Body's Production and Transfer System

The major players in the cholesterol picture are the liver and the blood fats. To support bodily functions, the liver synthesizes cholesterol, lipoproteins, triglycerides, and phospholipids. The liver manufactures both LDL and HDL cholesterol, manages their release into the bloodstream, and collects them back from the bloodstream. Blood fats are the building blocks the liver uses to produce cholesterol.

The body uses LDL cholesterol to build cell membranes, create essential hormones, and to form digestive enzymes. This LDL cholesterol needs to be transported throughout the body. However, cholesterol is fatty and blood is watery; oil and water do not mix. This dilemma is resolved in the liver, where cholesterol is combined and coated with proteins to create lipoproteins. The protein coating enables fat to travel in the bloodstream. The various types of lipoproteins are outlined in the following chart.

Types of Lipoproteins		
Name	Type of Lipoprotein	Nickname
HDL	High-density lipoprotein	"Good" cholesterol
LDL	Low-density lipoprotein	"Bad" cholesterol
VLDL	Very low-density lipoprotein	—
SDLDL	Small, dense, low-density lipoprotein	—
Lp(a)	Apoliprotein (a) plus low-density lipoprotein	"Ugly" cholesterol

The Liver: Cholesterol Manufacturing Plant

To simplify how this cholesterol transportation process works in your body, imagine a pickup and delivery service to and from the liver, which is the cholesterol manufacturing plant. Imagine that the lipoproteins are like delivery trucks that carry packages of cholesterol in the bloodstream. The function of the HDL "delivery trucks" is to pick up excess LDL cholesterol "packages" from the bloodstream and return them to the liver for repackaging as needed.

Another type of lipoprotein, VLDL, or very low-density lipoprotein, acts as the delivery truck that transports the LDL cholesterol throughout the body and delivers it to all the cells. The cell receptors are the drop-off stops where the LDL deliveries are made. The VLDL delivery truck also carries blood fats called triglycerides. These fats are available for immediate use by the body as energy, or for storage in fat cells for later use.

In a healthy body, this efficient manufacturing, pickup, and delivery system maintains perfect balance. Cells pick up the LDLs that they need to perform their functions at the receptor stops. HDLs pick up excess LDLs that the cells don't need and deliver them back to the liver for repackaging. Trucks circulate constantly, at all hours of the day and night, providing energy for quick fuel and for minimal storage reserves. The liver manufacturing plant naturally manages the entire process.

FACT

The primary functions of the liver include metabolizing carbohydrates, proteins, and fats; storing and activating vitamins and minerals; forming and excreting bile to digest fats; converting ammonia to urea for elimination; metabolizing steroids; and acting as a filter by removing bacteria from blood. The liver also detoxifies substances such as drugs and alcohol.

Breakdown of the System

Modern living conditions, however, overload and strain the system. By eating too much and moving too little, people make it all too easy for this delicately balanced delivery, pickup, and storage system to break down. The efficiency begins to fail when more LDL packages are transported in the bloodstream than are needed by the body's tissues. This excess LDL cholesterol continues to circulate in the bloodstream, increasing fat levels in the bloodstream and contributing to congestion on the "roadways."

If this excess LDL occurs at the same time that too few HDL trucks are available to collect and deliver it back to the liver for recycling, then the LDL cholesterol starts to collect like piles of litter on the arterial walls in places where it finds areas of inflammation. Certain packages of this arterial litter become oxidized, and they begin the process that leads to the clogging up of the "roadways" or arteries. Over time, this collection of debris on the arterial walls leads to a complete blockage, which then prevents blood flow that delivers essential oxygen for survival to the body's tissues. The body's tissues begin to die. If this happens in the muscle tissues of the heart, the result is a heart attack that can lead to death.

The leading causes of the system breakdown are the following:

1. **Overproduction of LDL packages.** The liver produces too much LDL cholesterol for the body's needs and much more than the HDLs can pick up.
2. **Fleet reduction of HDL pickup trucks.** The liver does not produce or release enough HDLs into the bloodstream to pick up the excess LDLs.
3. **Breakdown of liver management dispatch system.** The liver does not correctly signal to the body that it needs to pick up more LDLs.
4. **Damage to roadways.** Inflammation is present in the interior walls of the arteries.
5. **Transformation of LDL packages into litter.** Free radicals (independent and unstable oxygen molecules in the body) attach to certain LDL packages and "oxidize" them, causing them to become large and sticky and attach to blood vessel walls.

ALERT!

According to the American Heart Association, nearly 2,600 people in America die of cardiovascular disease each day, an average of one death every thirty-three seconds. Approximately 150,000 Americans killed by cardiovascular disease each year are under age sixty-five.

Scientists worldwide continue to conduct research so they can thoroughly understand the roles of the different types of lipoproteins and blood fats in the mechanisms behind heart disease. Evidence from research suggests that there are seven LDL subtypes and five HDL subtypes. Some of these subtypes are more harmful and others are more beneficial to health. For LDL cholesterol, particle size plays a significant role in the risk picture. People with higher numbers of the small dense LDL particles, rather than the large fluffy LDL particles, have a significantly higher risk of heart attack.

What Is Plaque?

Plaque is composed of oxidized LDLs and calcium in the blood-stream, as well as other cellular debris, or "litter," that gets caught in the fatty ("lipid") deposits. As the deposit grows larger, it hardens due to the increase in the amount of calcium. Plaque is living and growing. It has an outer layer of scar tissue that covers the calcium and fats, as well as the white blood cells that responded to the damaged arterial wall within.

Eventually the buildup of plaque can decrease or block blood flow to the heart or to the brain, starving these organs of essential oxygen and causing chest pains, a heart attack, or a stroke. This plaque buildup is known as atherosclerosis and is one of the most common types of heart disease. Plaque can begin to accumulate in childhood and develops so slowly in our bodies that its presence often grows without any signs to make us aware of it.

The Endothelial Lining

The endothelium, or endothelial lining, is the tissue that lines the inside of our blood vessels, through which our nutrients travel in the bloodstream. Evidence from research studies tells us that when this inner lining of the vessel walls becomes inflamed, cells stick to it and begin the formation of plaque. Scientists have been conducting research on how to maintain the health of the endothelial lining to prevent the initial formation of plaque.

FACT

Heart diseases are the number-one killer of women in America. Heart diseases kill more than half a million women each year—approximately one death per minute. The American Heart Association reports that heart diseases claim more women's lives than the next seven causes of death combined.

HDL Cholesterol

High-density lipoprotein (HDL) cholesterol, or the pickup truck fleet, is known as the "good" cholesterol. When you understand how the liver's manufacturing and transport system works, it's easy to see why the HDLs are considered good—because HDLs help clear the excess LDL choles-terol from your arteries. For a healthy heart and circulatory system, your HDL cholesterol levels should be higher than 40 mg/dL. The higher the level of your HDLs, the better it is for your health. People who have low levels of HDL cholesterol are at higher risk for heart disease.

According to the NCEP guidelines, an HDL level of 60 mg/dL is con-sidered a negative risk factor. A negative risk factor is like a bonus point that can negate or counteract another risk factor (such as having excess weight) when you are calculating your total risk score. Since knowing the amount of your HDL cholesterol is an important aspect of assessing your overall risk of heart disease, it's a good idea to have your HDL cholesterol levels measured when you have your total cholesterol checked.

LDL Cholesterol

Low-density lipoprotein (LDL) cholesterol is known as the "bad" cho-lesterol; however, LDL cholesterol is bad for your body only if you have too much in your bloodstream or you have too much of the particularly harmful type. LDL cholesterol is an essential building block for cell membranes and the substance from which hormones, including cortisol and testosterone, are manufactured. The amount of LDL cholesterol that exceeds what your body needs, however, flows through your blood-stream and increases the likelihood of the formation of plaque that can block blood flow.

FACT

The cost of cardiovascular disease and stroke in the United States in 2003 was estimated at $351.8 billion, including $209.3 billion in direct costs and $142.5 billion in indirect costs, according to the Centers for Disease Control.

NCEP guidelines recommend that near-optimal levels for LDL are under 130 mg/dL. If you are at risk for heart disease due to other risk fac-tors, then the recommended level for LDLs is under 100 mg/dL. If you are at "very high" risk, the guidelines recommend aggressively lowering LDL to less than 70 mg/dL.

Total Cholesterol

A healthy total cholesterol level includes different forms of cholesterol: LDL, the bad cholesterol that builds up in our arteries, and HDL, the good cholesterol that collects bad cholesterol from the blood vessels. If you have a lower level of cholesterol, you reduce the likelihood that you will have heart disease. If your total cholesterol level is very high (above 240), you need to talk to your health-care provider about how to lower it. If your cholesterol levels are only slightly elevated, you can take many steps on your own as outlined in this book to lower it to an ideal, healthy level.

The Ratio of Total Cholesterol to HDL Levels

One method to predict your risk of heart disease is to look at the ratio of total cholesterol to the level of HDLs or good cholesterol at the time of your test. High levels of HDL in your bloodstream are good for your health. To calculate your ratio, divide your total cholesterol number by your HDL cholesterol. For men, a ratio of 4.5 to 1 or less is desirable. For women, the desired ratio is 4.0 to 1 or less. (See Chapter 5 for more information on figuring your ratio.)

ALERT!

According to the U.S. government, approximately 105 million Americans, or more than 50 percent of American adults, have total cholesterol levels of 200 mg/dL or higher. This level indicates increased cardiovascular risk. More than half of these Americans are unaware that they have high cholesterol. Be sure to get yourself tested.

Keep in mind, however, that this ratio is used as a rough predictor of risk, not to determine therapy. Your health-care provider should advise treatment to improve your overall blood lipid profile based on knowledge of levels of LDL and HDL cholesterol and triglycerides. It is not enough to simply know total cholesterol and HDL levels, especially for planning treatment, as it does not provide a complete picture of the health of the circulatory system.

Triglycerides (TRGs)

Triglycerides, also referred to as TRGs, are another type of fat that circulates in your bloodstream in the same way as HDL and LDL cholesterol. TRGs are composed of a sticky substance (called glycerol) and fatty acids. They can provide your body with a source of energy if needed. Triglyceride levels spike immediately after you eat and decrease slowly as the body processes nutrients from food that has been consumed. If muscles are working and active, the triglycerides can provide needed fuel. If the muscle cells do not use the circulating triglycerides to create energy, the TRGs are eventually deposited in the body's fat stores.

Since eating affects TRG levels, you should fast for at least nine to twelve hours before you have a lipid profile test. After you undertake this nine- to twelve-hour period without eating or drinking, the levels of TRG that are circulating in your bloodstream will more accurately reflect how much of these fats are consistently present in your blood.

A desirable level of TRG is less than 150 mg/dL. People who are overweight, who drink alcohol excessively, who are diabetic, or who have other disorders are prone to have elevated triglyceride levels. Women tend to have higher triglyceride levels than men.

Evidence from research shows that the risk of heart disease increases when the triglyceride level is too high, particularly when a person simultaneously has low levels of HDL cholesterol. Triglyceride levels of 500 mg/dL or above are associated with the risk of pancreatitis, which can lead to pancreatic cancer. Treatment is indicated for triglyceride levels above 150 mg/dL.

NCEP Cholesterol and Triglyceride Level Guidelines	
Total Cholesterol Level	**Category**
Less than 180 mg/dL	Optimal
Less than 200 mg/dL	Desirable
200–239 mg/dL	Borderline high
240 mg/dL	High

NCEP Cholesterol and Triglyceride Level Guidelines *(continued)*	
LDL Cholesterol Level	**LDL Cholesterol Category**
Less than 100 mg/dL	Optimal
100–129 mg/dL	Near optimal/above optimal
130–159 mg/dL	Borderline high
160–189 mg/dL	High
190 mg/dL and above	Very high
HDL Cholesterol Level	**HDL Cholesterol Category**
Less than 40 mg/dL	Low
60 mg/dL and above	High
Triglyceride Level	**Triglyceride Category**
Less than 150 mg/dL	Normal
150–199 mg/dL	Borderline high
200–499 mg/dL	High
500 mg/dL and above	Very high

Source: NIH Publication Nos. 01-3305 and 01-3290

Frequently Asked Questions

If I can't live without cholesterol, why is high cholesterol a problem?

Too much cholesterol in the blood can lead to blockage of the arteries. Fat-like deposits may build up inside arteries that provide blood to the legs, blood to the brain, or blood to the heart.

When blood flow through a coronary artery (blood to the heart) is completely blocked, an area of the heart muscle does not receive the oxygenated blood it needs to survive. When this happens, a heart attack occurs. Plaque can also build up in the carotid arteries that supply blood to the brain. If this breaks free and a clot of it goes to the brain, it can cause a stroke. When plaque builds up in the blood vessels of the legs, it can cause leg pain, fatigue, cramping, or feelings of heaviness.

This condition is known as peripheral arterial disease. When plaque builds up in the arteries that supply blood to the male sex organs, erectile dysfunction or impotence can result.

When I test my cholesterol, what information do I need to get?

The federal government guidelines recommend that every person who is age twenty or older should have a fasting lipoprotein profile at least once every five years. This test measures total cholesterol, LDL cholesterol, HDL cholesterol, and triglycerides. All of this information is relevant to get a picture of the health of your circulatory system. For some individuals, an even more detailed breakdown of the sub-types of LDL and HDL cholesterol may be relevant.

FACT

People with very high cholesterol levels can reduce both their cholesterol and level of risk for a heart attack. According to the American Heart Association, drug therapy combined with lifestyle changes helps people with very high cholesterol reduce heart attacks by 34 percent and cardiac deaths by more than 40 percent.

What is the difference between good and bad cholesterol and triglycerides?

HDLs are known as the good type of cholesterol because their function is to gather excess LDL cholesterol in the body and return it to the liver. LDL cholesterol, although it serves a valuable purpose, is referred to as bad cholesterol because too much LDL cholesterol is harmful to the body. The reason excess LDL cholesterol is harmful is because it contributes to plaque formation on the inside of inflamed blood vessel walls.

Triglycerides are not similar to LDLs in terms of their function in the body, but they are similar in the way they cause harm to the body when present in excess. Like LDLs, triglycerides also travel through the bloodstream. Since triglycerides are a type of sticky blood fat, they also contribute to formation of plaque inside damaged blood vessel walls. Therefore, in general, most people want to increase HDL cholesterol levels and decrease LDL and triglyceride levels.

How can I increase my HDL cholesterol levels?

HDL cholesterol responds well to lifestyle changes. If you increase your physical activity each day or exercise regularly, it will stimulate the liver's production of HDLs. Losing excess weight can also improve your HDL profile. If you smoke cigarettes, you will increase your HDL levels simply by quitting your habit. If your HDLs are less than 35 mg/dL, you may need drug therapy. Be sure to ask your health-care provider what strategies are most suitable for you.

ALERT!

Evidence from some research suggests that rather than simply measuring total cholesterol levels, identifying the type of LDL and HDL particles provides an even more accurate assessment of the risk of coronary artery disease. This theory explains why some people who do not have high total cholesterol levels, but who do have high levels of small, dense LDL, have coronary artery disease.

How does being more active help to lower cholesterol?

Regular physical activity can increase your HDL cholesterol and reduce triglycerides. Since triglycerides are a blood fat, they are available to the body as a source of fuel for muscular activity. Therefore, people who are active can use up the triglycerides in their bloodstream as a source of energy.

Evidence from numerous research studies shows that moderate exercise, such as brisk walking, that adds up to a total of thirty minutes on most days of the week can improve your health. The great news is that you do not need to exercise vigorously or for hours at a time to achieve health benefits. In addition to burning up excess fats, moderate exercise also helps to reduce stress, which further enhances your well-being.

How does smoking affect cholesterol levels?

Cigarette smoke contains many toxic chemicals. These not only destroy lung tissue, they also contribute to plaque formation and adversely affect the nervous system, causing both heart rate and blood pressure to elevate. These chemicals contribute to reducing levels of good HDL cholesterol and accelerating the process of heart disease. While it is difficult to kick the smoking habit, the benefits of not smoking begin as soon as you quit.

If high cholesterol runs in my family, what, if anything, can I do to lower it?

Approximately 10 percent of American adults with high cholesterol are genetically predisposed to have this condition. If you have a family history of heart disease, it is important for you to work together with your health-care provider to monitor your heart health with routine checkups annually.

Lifestyle factors such as physical activity, proper nutrition, not smoking, and effective stress management still matter. For you, it is even more important to lead a healthful lifestyle. Even with a healthy lifestyle, your physician may still recommend drug therapy. With today's tools and knowledge, much can be done to manage the risks that you inherited. The information in this book is a great first step toward arming yourself with the necessary knowledge to empower yourself to positively manage your own health and well-being.

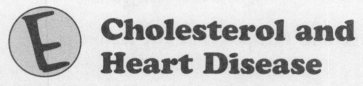

Chapter 2

Cholesterol and Heart Disease

In an instant, heart disease can tear a family apart. Abruptly, it can sever ties among spouses, parents and children, friends, neighbors, and other loved ones. The good news in this grim scenario is that with knowledge and with action, you can take significant steps toward reducing the heavy toll exacted by this disease. Understanding what heart disease is and how cholesterol contributes to it is an important first step.

What Is Heart Disease?

A healthy heart and circulatory system are something that many people take for granted—that is, until one day they experience chest pains or breathlessness and realize that something in the body is no longer working the way that it should. But what keeps a heart healthy? Or, what causes a heart to lose its ability to function properly?

The Structure and Function of the Heart

Before we can clearly understand what is going on when the heart dysfunctions, it's necessary to have a basic comprehension of its structure and function. The human heart lies in the upper left center of the chest, next to the lungs. It has four chambers: the right atrium and the left atrium on the top, and the right and left ventricles on the bottom. Blood flows into the right side of the heart and out of the left side. To guide the flow of blood in one constant direction, each chamber connects to the next one through valves that open when the heart contracts.

Blood that no longer contains oxygen enters the right side of the heart through a large vein called the vena cava. This deoxygenated blood flows into the right atrium. When the heart contracts, this blood flows through the tricuspid valve into the right ventricle. From the right ventricle, the blood enters the pulmonary artery via the pulmonary valve to become freshly oxygenated in the lungs. The newly oxygen-rich blood leaves the lungs and flows back to the heart's left atrium through the pulmonary vein. With the next contraction, the mitral valve opens and blood flows into the left ventricle, the strongest section of this miraculous muscular pump. When this section contracts, blood then rushes through the aortic valve into the aorta to repeat its journey around the body. This circulatory process continues automatically for as long as you live.

FACT

The circulatory system includes the heart, lungs, and all of the blood vessels. In the average person, these vessels would be 100,000 miles long if laid end-to-end. The heart pumps blood through these vessels to deliver oxygen and nutrients throughout the body and to remove carbon dioxide and other cellular waste products.

An electrical stimulus regulates the heartbeat. In the right atrium, a specialized group of cells—known as the sinoatrial node, the SA node, or the sinus node—triggers the electrical impulses that cause the chambers of the heart to contract and push the blood along its path. The rate of the electrical impulses is regulated, but it can vary depending on different chemical stimulators in the body. In this manner, a healthy heart can respond to different needs as required by the demands of life.

For example, when you are reclining on a couch in a primarily horizontal position, your heart does not have to work as hard to circulate blood around your body since it does not have to flow against gravity. When you stand up from the couch—let's say to get a drink from the refrigerator—your heart must work harder to pump blood against gravity and to your working muscles. In a person with a healthy heart, all of these adaptations occur effortlessly. We never pause to think about how our movements increase the demands on our circulatory system; we simply go and assume that our body will be able to respond smoothly and easily.

The function of the heart and the circulatory system is to keep blood flowing continuously at a consistent rate. This ensures delivery of essential oxygen and nutrients to the body's tissues. Other processes that occur simultaneously through the circulation include the removal of waste products from cells back to the lungs, liver, and kidneys for filtering. A healthy nervous system is also important to a healthy circulatory system, since it affects heart rate and vessel function.

A healthy heart is an electronically regulated muscular pump that is about the size of a fist. Each day and night, the average heart beats approximately 100,000 times and pumps 2,000 gallons of blood. Over a normal lifespan, the heart will beat more than 2.5 billion times.

What Can Go Wrong with the Heart?

Unfortunately, the heart doesn't always function perfectly. To comprehend the role of cholesterol, the process of atherosclerosis, and their impact on heart diseases, you need to be able to understand them in the context of the range of potential heart problems. There are several disorders that can have a negative effect on the circulatory process by reducing blood flow. Some of these disorders are genetic; others are either caused by or worsened by atherosclerosis that results from the presence of harmful types of cholesterol circulating in the bloodstream. The most common disorders are these:

- Arrhythmias, or malfunctions of the electrical system
- Congestive heart failure, or weakness of the muscular pump
- Congenital defects, such as a hole between the two atrial chambers (an atrial septal defect)
- Narrowing of the heart valves from calcification (stenosis) or from tumors in the heart
- Leaking valves, known as insufficiency, such as mitral valve prolapse
- Damage to the heart muscle itself from blockage of coronary arteries due to atherosclerosis

Each of these disorders results in a heart muscle that is not capable of pumping blood sufficiently. Atherosclerosis can be an indirect factor in arrhythmia and congestive heart failure and a direct factor in blockage of coronary arteries.

Signs and Symptoms of a Heart Attack

When circulatory disorders impair blood flow to the heart muscle itself, the person experiences mild to severe chest pain. This chest pain can develop into a full-blown heart attack. The odds of a heart attack occurring are high. Since a person with heart disease may have no external symptoms prior to a heart attack, it is important to be aware of the warning signs. Quick treatment in the event of an attack can make the difference between life and death.

Warning signs of a heart attack include the following:

- Uncomfortable pressure, fullness, squeezing, or pain in the center of your chest that lasts for more than a few minutes, or that recurs

- Pain that spreads from the chest to the shoulders, neck, jaw, or arms
- Chest discomfort combined with lightheadedness, fainting, sweating, nausea, or shortness of breath

Symptoms may range from severe to mild, or they may gradually worsen. For some people, symptoms come and go. The following are less common warning signs of a heart attack:

- Atypical (unusual) chest pain, stomach, or abdominal pain
- Nausea or dizziness
- Shortness of breath followed by difficult breathing
- Unexplained anxiety, weakness, or fatigue
- Heart palpitations, accompanied by a cold sweat or pale skin

What If You Experience Warning Signs?

If you experience any signs or symptoms of a heart attack, do not hesitate. Get medical help immediately. Every minute is important in a heart attack situation. Always keep emergency phone numbers in a convenient location near the telephone so no time will be wasted. Call 911 or your local emergency medical service (EMS) for an ambulance to take you to the hospital.

QUESTION?

Where can I find training classes in my area?
Your local fire department can provide you with valuable information on where to receive safety trainings in your neighborhood. In some communities, these training sessions are offered free of charge. Check your local newspapers, or contact your local fire department or emergency medical services for information.

Medical treatment, including clot-dissolving medicine, can save your life and reduce damage to the heart muscle, but only if treatment begins very soon after a heart attack occurs. Waiting, even if only for fifteen minutes, can result in damage to the heart muscle that could have been avoided with immediate treatment. EMS teams can begin administering care from the moment they arrive.

What If Someone Else Has Warning Signs?

It is very common for people to deny that they are having a heart attack. Often people think the pain and discomfort is indigestion and will go away. It is frightening for most people to admit that they may be having a heart attack. Almost anyone with a family member who has suffered from a heart attack will tell you that the family member's initial reaction was to deny or to minimize the seriousness of the symptoms.

Early care is critical to survival. Every second counts. The sooner a person who is having a heart attack arrives at the hospital, the better the chances are that he or she will live. Know the signs and symptoms of a heart attack, and when you see someone experience them, get that person to advanced health care as soon as possible. They may try to tell you they don't need to see a doctor, but don't take no for an answer. It's always better to be safe. Your efforts can make the difference between life and death.

Your Emergency Response Can Save a Life

You can make a difference in the event of a cardiac emergency if you have some basic training. Organizations such as the American Heart Association and American Red Cross offer training for laypeople. Each year, thousands of lives are saved by people who learned CPR and how to use automated external defibrillators (AEDs) and who were able to respond quickly to emergency situations.

Early CPR administered by a bystander is a valuable way of buying time by prolonging life until additional emergency assistance is available. Your knowledge of CPR can make the difference between life and death. Call your local Red Cross for information on CPR classes in your area.

A tragic incident occurred at a law firm during their annual holiday party. One of the attorneys collapsed from a heart attack in the midst of the festivities. None of the partygoers knew CPR. Although emergency assistance arrived, he died. Perhaps his life could have been saved if someone had taken emergency training. After the event, the firm initiated an internal CPR training program for its staff. It was an unfortunate case of learning a lesson the hard way.

Guidelines for CPR

If you don't know CPR already, take the time to learn it. The American Heart Association and International Liaison Committee on Resuscitation adopted new CPR guidelines in September of 2000. According to these guidelines, the first thing to do when you find an unresponsive adult is to call 911, then begin CPR. Exceptions to this rule include adult victims of submersion, trauma, and drug intoxication and infants and children up to age eight. In any of these cases, perform CPR before taking the time to dial 911. Children younger than age eight should receive about one minute of CPR before 911 is called.

ALERT!

If you feel that someone may have suffered a stroke, get the victim to a hospital as soon as possible. Be sure to call the hospital and let them know you are on the way.

If there are no signs of circulation—such as normal breathing, coughing, or movement—the guidelines recommend that you provide two breaths, known as rescue breaths. If there continue to be no signs of circulation or breathing after the rescue breaths have been provided, begin chest compressions. When there are one or two rescuers giving an adult CPR (that is, a victim age eight years or older), you should perform about 100 compressions per minute. For every fifteen compressions, give the victims two breaths. When giving CPR to a child or infant, you should still perform the same 100 compressions per minute, but give the victim one breath for every five compressions. Chest-compression-only CPR is recommended *only* when the rescuer is unwilling or unable to perform mouth-to-mouth rescue breathing.

Learn How to Use an AED

An AED is an external medical device that delivers an electrical shock to the heart to restore a normal heart rhythm in people who have suffered a specific type of cardiac arrest, known as sudden cardiac arrest (SCA). SCA is not the equivalent of a heart attack, nor are AEDs used to treat all heart conditions. Rather, AEDs are only indicated for the treatment of sudden cardiac arrest.

In the majority of cases, SCA is caused by ventricular fibrillation (VF), which is a complete lack of heartbeat that can be fatal within minutes. However, SCA can also result from ventricular tachycardia (VT), a rapid heartbeat that can occur after fever, exercise, or nervous excitement.

Sudden cardiac arrest can strike people of any age, race, or gender. For example, electrocution, drowning, choking, and trauma can all disturb the heart's normal rhythm. Although certain individuals are genetically predisposed to SCA, most people who have this condition have no prior symptoms or warning. Often, when you read about an apparently healthy young athlete collapsing during a game, SCA is the cause. Still, the majority of SCAs do occur in older adult males.

ALERT!

AEDs are not the recommended emergency treatment for every patient whose heart has stopped beating. In many cases, cardiopulmonary resuscitation (CPR) is the more appropriate response. Even when an AED is indicated, CPR is still the first line of treatment before a defibrillator is used. In other words, the use of an AED is not a substitute for performing CPR on victims of sudden cardiac arrest.

An AED is the appropriate emergency treatment in those cases when an electrical malfunction of the heart has stopped its normal rhythm. In these cases, a shock must be delivered via the AED within the first ten minutes of the SCA to restore a regular pulse.

Defibrillation can restore the heart's normal rhythm if it's done within minutes of the arrest. According to the American Heart Association, every minute that passes without defibrillation decreases the victim's chances of survival by 10 percent. This is significant when you consider how long it can take for emergency medical services (EMS) to respond to treat a victim of SCA.

According to researchers who evaluate public access defibrillation programs, the average EMS response time from call to shock interval in the United States is likely to be greater than five minutes. Response times vary greatly and can be longer in very urban settings with heavy traffic or in more isolated rural settings.

The American Heart Association recommends using a four-part "chain of survival" to maximize the effectiveness of emergency responsiveness to cardiac events. The four steps include early access (quickly calling 911); early CPR; early defibrillation; and early advanced cardiovascular care.

Effectiveness of AEDs

According to a recent study that looked at survival rates in Las Vegas casinos, which were among the first establishments to implement the use of AEDs, these devices have been demonstrated to be effective. The study, published in the October 2000 issue of the *New England Journal of Medicine*, found that the overall survival rate for patients with ventricular fibrillation (VF) was 53 percent. This finding is most impressive when you compare their success to victims who don't receive defibrillation. Most studies show survival rates for ventricular fibrillation/ventricular tachycardia to be about 10 percent. Having rapid access to an AED could improve survival rates by as much as 40 percent. In plain terms, that is four more lives saved for every ten people afflicted.

The American Heart Association recommends that AEDs be available wherever large numbers of people congregate. Such places include airports, convention centers, sports stadiums and arenas, large industrial buildings, high-rise offices, and large health and fitness facilities.

The Cholesterol/Heart Disease Connection

As you can see, heart disease comes in a variety of life-threatening forms. All heart diseases are referred to as cardiovascular diseases (CVDs). CVDs include high blood pressure, coronary heart disease, congestive heart failure, stroke, rheumatic heart disease, artery diseases, pulmonary heart disease, and congenital cardiovascular defects.

Coronary heart disease, also referred to as coronary artery disease (CAD), is the most common form and represents 54 percent of all cardiovascular diseases. Coronary artery disease includes angina pectoris, which is chest pain from narrowing of blood vessels, and myocardial infarction (MI), also known as a heart attack, from the complete blockage of blood supply to the heart.

It is possible for a person to have more than one type of cardiovascular disease at the same time. For example, a person may have both coronary artery disease and high blood pressure. Coronary artery disease is responsible for more than half of all cardiac events in men and women under age seventy-five. According to the National Heart, Lung, and Blood Institute's Framingham Heart Study, the lifetime risk of developing CAD after age forty is 49 percent for men and 32 percent for women.

FACT

According to government statistics, if all forms of major cardiovascular disease (CVD) were eliminated, life expectancy would rise by almost seven years. If all forms of cancer were eliminated, the gain would be three years. The probability at birth of eventually dying from major CVD is 47 percent. The chance of dying from cancer is 22 percent.

Scientists now know that atherosclerosis can start in childhood. Researchers have found the beginning of fatty streaks in the arteries of children as young as three years old. The average American has significant buildup in his or her arterial walls by middle age. In women, possibly because of the protective effects of estrogen, the thicker buildups do not begin to show up until after menopause.

Even without the impact of a stroke or heart attack, atherosclerosis advances the aging process. Healthy circulation in the body is the source of nutrition and life for the cells. As this circulation is slowly cut off, it impairs the functioning of your cells. Atherosclerosis does not need to be inevitable. With knowledge of the mechanisms that contribute to this disease, you can take steps to reduce your risks and to prolong your youthful vitality and energy.

Atherosclerosis and Coronary Artery Disease

The principle cause of coronary artery disease is atherosclerosis, or hardening of the arteries. Atherosclerosis comes from the root words "atheroma" and "sclerosis," which means "to harden." Atherosclerosis is a process that leads to a group of diseases characterized by the thickening of artery walls. The thickening results from a buildup of plaque on the arterial walls. Plaque is made up of various types of debris that collect on areas of inflammation on blood vessel walls, causing more and more narrowing of the passage through which blood can flow. (See Chapter 1 for more information on plaque buildup.)

ALERT!

According to the National Heart, Lung, and Blood Institute, heart attack risk for both men and women is highest when a person has a combination of low HDL levels and high total cholesterol levels. People with low levels of HDL are also at a high risk regardless of the level of their total cholesterol.

Plaque is formed in a variety of shapes and sizes. Small plaques accumulate throughout the arteries in the entire body and can be difficult to detect. Doctors can more easily discover the large, hardened plaques in the coronary arteries. These typically cause the chest pains associated with angina.

Small plaque buildups, however, are just as concerning as thick, hard plaques. Researchers now have determined that these smaller plaques are less solid on the outside and, consequently, less stable. These small, unstable plaques are much more likely to rupture and release the cholesterol mass into the bloodstream. This concentrated cholesterol contributes to formation of blood clots. If a small plaque buildup in the coronary arteries ruptures and forms a blood clot, it can trigger a heart attack.

As an initial assessment of your likelihood of having CAD, ask yourself the following questions:

- Have you ever had a heart attack?
- Have you had recurring chest pain that has been diagnosed as angina?
- Have you had heart surgery such as a bypass operation or angioplasty procedure?
- Have you ever had an angiogram that showed a blockage in your coronary arteries?

If you answered yes to any of these questions, you probably have CAD. Be sure to discuss strategies to manage your cholesterol levels with your health-care provider.

Atherosclerosis and Strokes

Cholesterol buildup that leads to plaque in the carotid artery is a cause of strokes. When this plaque breaks, debris and blood clots flow to the brain and cause either a reduction in blood flow or blockage of blood flow to parts of the brain. Just as in the case of a heart attack, it is important to take immediate action to restore complete blood flow to the brain.

Early warning signs and symptoms of stroke are set forth below. If you notice that you or someone close to you has any of the following signs, do not delay. Get emergency medical help immediately. Every minute is critical. Call 911 or contact your local emergency medical service without hesitation.

The most common warning signs of stroke include the following:

- Sudden weakness or numbness of the face, arm, or leg, especially on one side of the body
- Sudden confusion or trouble understanding or speaking
- Sudden trouble seeing in one or both eyes
- Sudden trouble walking, feelings of dizziness, or loss of balance or coordination
- Sudden, severe headaches with no known cause

A mild or mini-stroke, described as a transient ischemic attack (TIA), can end in a matter of minutes. The damage can include mild weakness or numbness in an arm or a leg, or slight difficulty with speech. In contrast, a severe stroke can result in extreme disability or death. According to the Centers for Disease Control, when considered separately from other cardiovascular diseases, stroke is the third leading cause of death.

FACT

Approximately 40,000 more women than men have strokes annually. Experts believe that this is because women tend to live longer than men, and the highest rates for stroke are among those in the oldest age groups.

Atherosclerosis and Peripheral Arterial Disease

Atherosclerosis not only affects the arteries that supply blood to the heart and to the brain, but it can also affect the vessels that supply blood to the legs. This condition is known as peripheral arterial disease (PAD). It leads to discomfort in the legs that can become more severe as time goes on. What is particularly worrisome about peripheral artery disease is that you are much more likely to have a heart attack or stroke if you have this condition.

Warning signs and symptoms of PAD include the following:

- Cramping, heaviness, fatigue, or aching of the buttocks, thighs, or calves when walking
- Leg pain that occurs when you walk uphill, carry heavy loads, or walk quickly
- Aching of the foot that worsens at night and is relieved by standing up or by allowing the foot to hang off the edge of the bed
- Leg pain that stops when you stand still or rest

Because the signs of peripheral arterial disease are subtle and not very dramatic, many people who experience these symptoms attribute them to the aging process. If you or anyone you know has any of these signs or symptoms, be sure to consult with a health-care professional.

Atherosclerosis and Erectile Dysfunction

Erectile dysfunction is often associated with atherosclerotic plaque buildup. Impotence can be an early warning sign of cardiovascular disease. According to the National Institute of Diabetes and Digestive and Kidney Diseases, about 5 percent of forty-year-old men and between 15 to 25 percent of sixty-five-year-old men experience erectile dysfunction. In addition, when smoking is part of the picture, the odds of erectile dysfunction increase even further. According to study results reported in 2003, male smokers had a 31-percent higher risk for erectile dysfunction when compared to nonsmokers. However, just as hardening of the arteries is not inevitable with aging, neither is the loss of potency. Maintaining health of the heart and circulatory system can also help to maintain this aspect of youthful vigor and vitality.

FACT

Erectile dysfunction affects 15 to 30 million American men, depending on exactly how it is defined. Approximately 70 percent of all cases are due to diseases such as atherosclerosis, vascular disease, diabetes, kidney disease, multiple sclerosis, neurological disease, and chronic alcoholism. Men of all ages can receive treatment for erectile dysfunction.

You Have the Power to Improve Your Health

Whether you are young or old, male or female, you can improve your health and reduce your risk of cardiovascular diseases by consistently monitoring and managing your cholesterol levels. While you cannot alter your heredity, you can make lifestyle changes that significantly lower risks, regardless of your genetic heritage. Even if you already have coronary artery disease, you can reap benefits by managing your cholesterol levels. Research evidence shows that decreasing your blood cholesterol levels can slow, stop, and even reverse plaque buildup over time. As you lower your LDL cholesterol levels and increase your HDL levels, you can reduce the cholesterol content in the unstable plaque that has built up in the arterial walls. Accordingly, you will reduce your future risks of having a heart attack.

Through effective cholesterol management, you can cut your risks of having a future heart attack and may even add valuable years to your life. At the same time, beyond extending your longevity, improving your lifestyle habits can also enrich the quality of those additional years of living. It is possible to become even healthier as you age; suffering years of disease, disability, and loss of vitality is not anyone's necessary fate. Adopting healthy habits extends your youthfulness and enhances your feelings of well-being. Cardiovascular diseases do not have to be such fearful killers. You can make a difference to improve your odds and to get even more enjoyment out of life.

Chapter 3

The Multifactorial Puzzle—Risk Factors for Heart Disease

Like most things in life, you are not completely in control of whether or not you will develop heart disease. At the same time, however, you are far from being totally helpless. There are many steps you can take to lessen your risk of developing heart disease. But before you can reduce your risks and improve your odds, you need to know what those risks are. Read on to learn more.

What Is a Risk Factor?

Heart disease is what is described as a multifactorial disease. This means that multiple factors contribute to the development and progression of the disease. One risky characteristic alone, such as your age, is generally not enough to trigger the disease. However, a combination of factors, such as age, inactivity, smoking, and improper nutrition, can easily support the progression of heart disease over time. The more risk factors that you possess, the greater your likelihood of having the disease. Fewer risk factors, on the other hand, mean less likelihood of having the disease.

Identifying Risk Factors

After many years of research, scientists have identified risk factors for heart disease. Investigators conducted a landmark long-term study observing over 4,000 male and female residents of Framingham, Massachusetts. This study is world-renowned for the size of its database. Researchers measured blood pressure, recorded cholesterol levels, and noted connections between the data and the participants who suffered from heart disease over the term of the study.

A clear relationship emerged among those who had heart attacks and those who also had high blood-cholesterol levels. Other causal factors also emerged. The sum total of research evidence from this and other studies provides us with the ability to assess risk by analyzing the presence or absence of these identifiable risk factors.

FACT

To determine your risk score according to the information gathered by the Framingham Study, use the online calculator at *www.nhlbi.nih.gov/ guidelines/cholesterol* (under the heading "Information for Patients"). Keep in mind that subjects in this study were primarily Caucasian, middle-aged, and without heart disease, so anyone who does not fit that profile will not be able to use this calculator to accurately assess a risk score.

Any condition that indicates the presence of atherosclerosis indicates a high risk of coronary artery disease. These conditions include symptomatic carotid artery disease, peripheral arterial disease, and abdominal aortic aneurysm. Researchers today also identify diabetes as a condition that creates a high risk of coronary artery disease. Diabetes is classified as carrying the equivalent risk of any of the other diseases that indicate the presence of heart disease.

Keep in mind that the basis for these risk factors is data from large population studies and is simply a reflection of profiles of those among the population who had a heart attack. Historically, however, research studies have not included in their database sufficient numbers of women, people from ethnic minorities, people from a variety of economic backgrounds, or people from a variety of lifestyles with different levels of access to health care. All of these factors, therefore, influence the applicability of these characteristic risk factors to any individual who may be different from those who have been studied.

The leading risk factors for heart disease are as follows:

- High total cholesterol and high LDL cholesterol
- Low HDL cholesterol
- Diabetes
- Cigarette smoking or inhaling secondary smoke
- Hypertension or high blood pressure
- Unmanaged stress
- Physical inactivity or a sedentary lifestyle
- Excess weight
- Family history of heart disease
- Age and gender

As you can see, this list includes several risk factors you can actively do something about. A few factors, such as your family history (or genetic predisposition) and your age and gender are things you cannot change or control. The good news, however, is that you can make a strong impact on your modifiable risk factors. The way you choose to live your life every day plays a very important role in reducing your risk of heart disease. What you do makes a difference.

Before you can take action, it helps to understand why these factors create risk and how they increase your chances of having a heart attack.

When you clearly see the relationship between your unhealthy habits and how they can cause your untimely death or disability or the loss of a loved one that is near and dear, it is easy to get motivated to improve your lifestyle and the lifestyle of your family.

It is well worth your time to assess where you stand today in terms of your risk for heart disease. With that information, you can get motivated to either keep up the great work or to make the changes that you need to lower your risks, as well as the risks of those that you love. Don't wait to get started. Get going right away toward creating a healthy lifestyle.

Diabetes as a Risk Factor

Diabetes is a condition characterized by the failure of insulin to perform its normal functions. In a healthy body, the pancreas produces the hormone insulin and releases it into the bloodstream. The body uses this insulin to convert sugar, starches, and other foods into energy. When the system is not functioning normally, the bloodstream is overloaded with excess sugar. Scientists have not yet identified the exact cause of diabetes, but they believe that genetics, excess weight, and inactivity all contribute to development of the disease.

Evidence from numerous research studies shows that people with diabetes mellitus have as much risk of having a heart attack as those who are already diagnosed with heart disease. To put this risk into statistical terms, people with diabetes have a 15- to 20-percent chance of having a heart attack within a ten-year period. This is the same level of risk as a person who is diagnosed with coronary artery disease. Furthermore, a person with diabetes has twice the likelihood of dying from a heart attack than a person who does not have diabetes.

Because of the increased risk of heart disease associated with diabetes, the federal government guidelines recommend that people who are diabetic pursue the same cholesterol goals as those who have heart disease. Adults age forty-five and over should be tested to determine whether they are diabetic. See Chapter 19 for more information on diabetes and its relationship to heart disease.

ALERT!

According to the American Diabetes Association, approximately 17 million Americans have diabetes. Health care professionals have diagnosed approximately 11.1 million of these people. As many as 5.9 million individuals, or one-third of the total people who have this condition, however, are not aware that they have it. Make sure to get yourself tested.

The Metabolic Syndrome

Researchers have identified a cluster of symptoms that includes abdominal obesity, high triglycerides, low HDL levels, high blood pressure, and a high fasting blood-glucose level as contributors to a higher risk for heart disease. Studies have substantiated that individuals who have a cluster of three or more of these factors together have a greater risk of heart disease than someone who may only have one or two of the risk factors.

This clustering of several risk factors is described as the "metabolic syndrome." The reason for this reference is that the metabolic syndrome focuses on risk factors that have a metabolic origin. Carrying excess weight and leading an inactive lifestyle increase the likelihood of developing the metabolic syndrome. Medical experts agree that when an individual has diabetes or has the cluster of factors that comprise the metabolic syndrome, he or she has a very high likelihood of having a heart attack. In addition to those conditions, there are several factors that can exacerbate the situation. See Chapter 19 for further information on the metabolic syndrome.

Cigarette Smoking and Secondhand Smoke

Smoking is a risk factor because smokers have twice the risk of developing heart disease as nonsmokers in the same condition. Also, a smoker who has a heart attack is more likely to die from it than a nonsmoker. Cigarette smoking is the greatest risk factor for sudden cardiac deaths. Smoking low-tar or low-nicotine cigarettes does not make any difference in reducing your risk of heart disease. Nonsmokers who are frequently exposed to secondhand smoke also have an increased risk of developing heart disease.

Smoking contributes to heart disease because the chemicals that are inhaled from cigarette smoke reduce the amount of the good HDL cholesterol in your bloodstream. In addition, nicotine increases the rate of the heartbeat and constricts arteries, which leads to higher levels of blood pressure and stress on the heart and circulatory system. Some researchers believe that this can also lead to damage to arterial walls, making them more susceptible to plaque formation. Carbon monoxide reduces the amount of oxygen available to your body by up to 15 percent. Not only does this starve the body's tissue of essential oxygen, it also reduces the amount of oxygen being delivered to fuel the heart muscle.

If you change this negative habit and quit smoking, you immediately begin to reduce your risk of heart disease. You also reduce your risks for lung cancer, lung disease, and other types of cancer. Your friends and loved ones reap the benefits of no longer being subject to secondhand smoke from you. See Chapter 17 for further information on the harmful effects of smoking and how to quit.

Increasing evidence shows that secondhand smoke can break down antioxidant defenses, leading to damage to the endothelial lining of blood vessels that represents the beginning of atherosclerosis. Studies show that oxidative stress is significantly higher in children exposed to secondhand smoke, even if exposure consists of less than twenty cigarettes (one pack) per day by one parent.

High Blood Pressure

High blood pressure, also referred to as hypertension, is a risk factor for heart disease and stroke. Approximately one in every four American adults has high blood pressure. If you include children aged six years and older, then one in every five Americans, or 50 million people, has high blood pressure. If untreated, high blood pressure can compromise the functioning of the heart and the circulatory system.

What Is High Blood Pressure?

High blood pressure occurs when the pressure of blood flowing through the blood vessels increases and remains elevated. This increase in pressure means that the blood flow is pushing against the arterial walls with a stronger than normal force. Over time, this increased pressure damages the arterial walls by causing them to become thicker and stiffer. The arterial walls lose elasticity. Research shows that damaged arterial walls are more likely to attract cholesterol and fats, which form plaque. This plaque formation leads to blockage of the arteries that can cause a heart attack or stroke.

In addition to contributing to arterial damage and consequent plaque formation, prolonged high blood pressure forces the heart to work harder and enlarge. Over time, the heart fails to function normally and cannot fully pump out all the blood it receives. This can cause fluids to back up into the lungs and can rob the rest of the body of the blood supply that it needs. This condition is known as congestive heart failure. If you have high blood pressure and you also have high cholesterol levels, your risk of having heart disease increases six times. If you have high blood pressure, high cholesterol levels, and you are also a smoker, your risk of having heart disease increases by a factor of twenty.

FACT

Blood pressure is measured in millimeters of mercury (mmHg) and consists of two numbers usually written one over the other. The top number reflects the systolic blood pressure reading—this is a measure of the pressure when your heart contracts, pumping the blood out. The bottom number reflects diastolic blood pressure. This reading measures the pressure when your heart rests, refilling with blood in between contractions.

Ideally, your blood pressure should be lower than 120 mmHg over 80 mmHg (usually spoken as "120 over 80" and written as 120/80). If either your systolic or your diastolic blood pressure reading is high, you may have high blood pressure. A high systolic blood pressure is a reading of 140 or above. A high diastolic blood pressure is a reading of 90 or above. It is important to pursue treatment if you have high blood pressure.

If high blood pressure is treated, the risk of heart disease and stroke is reduced. Blood pressure can be managed by losing as little as five to ten pounds of weight, exercising regularly, eating plenty of fruits, vegetables, and low or nonfat dairy products, and reducing stress.

ALERT!

According to the American Heart Association, of all the people with high blood pressure, only 27.4 percent are on an adequate therapy. If you have high blood pressure, discuss all treatment options, including lifestyle changes and drug therapy, with your health-care provider.

Foods that can increase blood pressure for people who are sensitive to salt are processed meats, cheeses, canned foods like soups and vegetables, salty crackers and snack foods, salad dressings and condiments like soy sauce or barbeque sauce, and any other foods prepared with salty seasonings. Caffeine and alcoholic beverages can elevate blood pressure in some people. Foods that can reduce blood pressure levels are fruits and vegetables that are rich in potassium. This can include any type of dried fruit as well as bananas and melons.

Blood Pressure Testing

High blood pressure is dangerous because it usually gives no warning signs or symptoms. Be sure to get your blood pressure checked regularly, at least every two years. To determine whether or not you have high blood pressure, you will need to have it checked on several occasions and at different times of the day. Some people simply become nervous when they are in the doctor's office, resulting in a higher reading. Your blood pressure naturally changes during the day and rises dramatically when you are anxious. Make sure that you have multiple tests before you accept a diagnosis of high blood pressure. See your health-care provider about getting regular blood pressure checks.

It is far better to keep your blood pressure from getting high in the first place. If you find that your blood pressure is not high, take steps to keep it that way. Keep your weight in a healthy range; aim to lose at least five to ten pounds if you are overweight; be more physically active; choose heart-healthy foods; and if you smoke, quit.

Excess Weight

Excess body weight is considered a risk factor because those who carry excess weight are at an increased risk of heart disease, high blood pressure, stroke, and diabetes, among other things. Carrying excess weight increases the strain on the heart and circulatory system, as well as on other body systems.

Just as the body needs a certain amount of LDL cholesterol to survive, it also needs a certain amount of body fat. However, excess body fat contributes to an increase in the natural production of higher levels of LDL cholesterol by the liver and to lower levels of HDL cholesterol. For whatever reason, the delicate balance of the body's production and collection system of cholesterol becomes disturbed when the body carries additional fat stores. While the exact amount of fat that represents an excessive amount seems to vary from one individual to another, there generally seems to be a point at which too much body fat starts to harm, rather than to support, optimum health.

Conversely, when a person sheds excess body fat, the body's natural balancing mechanisms can begin to function effectively again. By losing excess fat, a person can stimulate the liver to decrease the production of LDL cholesterol and to increase the production of HDL cholesterol. This change can actually start to restore health to the circulatory system.

The answer to the question of what is a healthy weight, however, is not a simple one. A healthy weight varies from one individual to another. An individual's healthy weight range can depend on a number of factors, including age, gender, ethnicity, body type, and personal situation, such as whether he or she is an elite athlete or pregnant or lactating.

Most people realize that being overweight can cause health problems, but it is just as important to understand that being significantly underweight can also be just as serious a problem. The bottom line is that too much weight or too little weight is not healthy—balance and moderation are the keys. See Chapter 14 for more information on determining what your healthy weight should be.

Lack of Physical Activity

Lack of exercise is an important risk factor that is largely within your control. People who are sedentary have twice the risk of heart disease than those who are active. The heart is a muscle. Like other muscles in the body, it becomes stronger with use. People are designed to be active, moving, living beings. Modern living conditions that include using cars and elevators, jobs that involve sitting at a desk working at a computer, and multiple other labor-saving devices have all but removed natural physical activity from our daily lives.

> The risk of being active is much smaller than the risk of being inactive. For that reason, the American College of Sports Medicine recommends that even people who are frail and/or elderly participate in some sort of regular physical activity.

Researchers from the National Institute on Aging have said that if exercise were a prescription drug, it would be the most widely prescribed medication. Adding some form of an endurance activity into your daily life conditions your heart, lungs, circulatory system, muscles, bones, brain, and nervous system. Being physically active reduces your risk of heart disease, and it reduces your risk of high blood pressure, diabetes, colon cancer, back pain, and cognitive disorders. Regular physical activity increases your levels of HDL or good cholesterol and lowers your level of total cholesterol.

The really great news is that research confirms that regular moderate-intensity exercise—at a minimum of thirty minutes a day on most days of the week—can have a powerful impact on improving your health. Moderate-intensity exercise includes activities like a brisk walk, fast enough that you break into a sweat but can still talk easily. To accumulate your thirty minutes of activity, you don't even have to do it all at once. People still enjoy improvements in health from as little as ten minutes of activity in three cumulative bouts over the course of the day. See Chapter 15 for everything you need to know to get going with your activity for health program.

High Total Cholesterol and High LDL Cholesterol

A high total cholesterol level or a high LDL (or bad cholesterol) level increases your risk of heart disease. As stated in Chapter 1, a total cholesterol level is considered high if it is greater than 200 mg/dL.

According to the most recent government guidelines, ideal LDL cholesterol levels depend on how many other risk factors that you have. For example, if you have one or no other risk factors, your LDL cholesterol level is considered high if it is greater than 160 mg/dL. It is considered "borderline high" if it is greater than 130 mg/dL. A total cholesterol greater than 240 mg/dL or an LDL cholesterol 160 mg/dL or greater are considered high risk.

ALERT!

Some people have high LDL cholesterol levels as a result of genetics or body chemistry, regardless of how hard they try to lower them. In these cases, drug therapy in combination with lifestyle changes may be the best treatment approach. Be sure to discuss all your options with your medical doctor if you think you may be one of these individuals.

If you have two or more risk factors, your LDL cholesterol level is considered high if it is equal to or greater than 130 mg/dL. If you have coronary artery disease or its equivalent (such as diabetes, peripheral arterial disease, symptomatic carotid artery disease, or abdominal aortic aneurysm), your LDL cholesterol level is considered high if it is greater than 100 mg/dL.

If your total blood cholesterol is in the borderline-high or high category, try to make some changes in your diet and increase your activity levels to lower your cholesterol. If you lower your cholesterol levels, you will reduce your risk of heart disease. Most coronary heart disease is caused by atherosclerosis, which occurs when cholesterol, fat, and other substances build up in the walls of the arteries that supply blood to the heart. Since atherosclerosis is a slow progressive disease, you may not experience any symptoms for many years. Lowering your total cholesterol level will slow plaque buildup in the arteries and reduce your risk of disability or of a future heart attack.

Low HDL Cholesterol

Low levels of HDL or good cholesterol are considered a risk factor, since HDL cholesterol helps to prevent the buildup of cholesterol in the arteries. If you recall the liver manufacturing plant and the HDL pickup truck analogy from Chapter 1, you will remember that the HDL cholesterol gathers up free-floating cholesterol in the arteries and returns it to the liver. Low HDL levels mean there are fewer "trucks" available to clean up the arteries. An HDL cholesterol level of less than 40 mg/dL is considered low.

Two steps you can take to raise levels of HDL cholesterol are to increase physical activity levels to a minimum of thirty minutes on most days of the week and, if you smoke, to quit.

If you elevate your HDL cholesterol level to 60 mg/dL or higher, it is so beneficial to your health that it is considered a "negative" risk factor. In other words, it serves to negate (cancel out) one of the other risk factors from your total count.

Unmanaged Stress

Strong research evidence exists to support the negative effects of prolonged stress on health. While the government does not include unmanaged stress as a specific risk factor for the new cholesterol management guidelines, numerous studies have demonstrated that chronic feelings of anger and hostility increase the risk of heart disease and hypertension.

Physical symptoms of stress include increased blood pressure and heart rate, chronic muscle tension, indigestion, irritability, anxiety, and altered sleeping habits, among other things. Reducing stress can minimize or eliminate these symptoms, which can improve your overall feelings of well-being. Furthermore, unless you manage the stress in your life, it is very difficult to successfully change any of your lifestyle habits.

The good news is that some health-enhancing activities, such as adding regular physical activity into your routine, also help to manage stress, improve heart health, and increase levels of good cholesterol—a win-win-win situation. Chapter 16 provides further information on managing stress.

Your Family History

Family history is an important consideration when determining your risk for heart disease. If you have a first-degree female relative (mother, sister, or daughter) under the age of sixty-five or a first-degree male relative (father, brother, son) under fifty-five who has heart disease, that is a risk factor for you. If your parents have had heart disease, then you are more likely to develop heart disease. Of course, no one can change their parents, but if you do have a family history of heart disease, it is even more important for you to assess your risk factors and to have annual check-ups. While genetics are powerful, they do not have to determine your fate. Take control of the factors that you can change.

QUESTION?

If my family has heart disease, what can I do to minimize risk?
Maintain healthy habits such as eating nutritious foods, maintaining a healthy weight, staying active on a regular basis, and managing stress. Be sure to check your cholesterol levels and blood pressure regularly.

Your Age and Gender

Men are at a greater risk than women of developing heart disease in middle age. From the age of forty-five, a man's risk of heart disease increases, and this risk continues to increase with age. By the age of sixty-five, half of all American men are likely to have coronary artery disease.

Women enjoy some protection from heart disease that may come from the hormone estrogen. Women who are fifty-five years of age and older, however, are at an increased risk of heart disease. As with men, this risk continues to increase with age. By the age of sixty-five, a third of all American women are likely to have coronary artery disease.

None of us can change our age, but we can improve our other health habits to create as healthy, vital, and enjoyable a life as possible. The good news is that by following healthy habits you can not only extend the years of life, but also add vitality to those later years. People who observe healthy habits when younger also tend to have much less disease and disability in their later years of life as well. Every person, male or female, old or young, can enjoy the benefits and rewards of a healthy lifestyle at any stage of life.

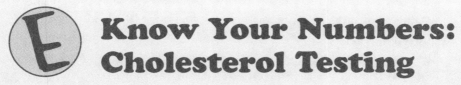

Chapter 4

Know Your Numbers: Cholesterol Testing

The reason for testing your cholesterol levels is to understand your risk for developing heart disease, stroke, or any of the other consequences of atherosclerosis. High blood-cholesterol has no visible symptoms. The only way to learn whether your cholesterol levels place you at risk for a heart attack or stroke is to measure your levels. You can get your cholesterol levels tested in your medical doctor's office, at a medical laboratory, or at public screenings.

When to Check Your Cholesterol Levels

Although cholesterol levels alone are not predictive of heart disease in all people, knowing your levels is a valuable first step toward understanding your risk status. When you know your cholesterol levels, as well as the status of your other risk factors, you gain valuable insight into the health of your current lifestyle and what you need to do to create and maintain your well-being. Furthermore, for those people who learn that they fall into high-risk categories, the sooner they begin a treatment plan to lower levels of bad cholesterol and increase levels of good cholesterol, the sooner they can start to reduce their risks of heart attack or stroke.

Cholesterol Testing for Healthy Adults

Federal government guidelines recommend that all Americans check their cholesterol levels with a complete fasting lipoprotein profile at the age of twenty. The measurements taken by this test include your levels of total cholesterol, HDL cholesterol, LDL cholesterol, and triglycerides. If test results indicate that all levels are in a healthy range, then government guidelines recommend retesting at a minimum of five-year intervals. The full lipoprotein profile test is preferred over a test that only provides data regarding total cholesterol and HDL levels. Since diabetes is considered to carry a risk equivalent to that of heart disease, it is also a good idea to have your blood glucose levels checked.

FACT

If you do not fast before testing your cholesterol, you can only measure total cholesterol and HDL levels. To receive more detailed information regarding your levels of LDL cholesterol and your triglycerides, fasting is necessary. If your test scores place you in a category for treatment, your health-care provider needs a complete, fasting, lipoprotein profile to plan your therapy.

Although federal government guidelines recommend cholesterol testing for adults at least every five years, if you have had a major change of lifestyle during that five-year period, your cholesterol levels may be different and, therefore, worth checking again before five full years elapse. For example, if you were a college student at age twenty and then became a working professional after graduation at age twenty-one or twenty-two, your physical activity levels, dietary choices, and stress levels may have changed significantly. All of these factors can impact your cholesterol levels. Therefore, it may be worth your time and effort to know your numbers as a measure of your health status in your new lifestyle.

Under current government guidelines, if you fall into a category that requires treatment for your cholesterol levels, you will have your cholesterol tested at much more frequent intervals to evaluate the success of the treatment program and to make any necessary adjustments. For example, if your health-care provider suggests that you adopt therapeutic lifestyle changes, the follow-up visit and test should be within six weeks. If your health-care provider suggests drug therapy, the initial follow-up visit and test should also be within six weeks. Subsequent visits for additional monitoring and adjustment of therapy should be scheduled at appropriate intervals depending on the nature of the individual therapy.

Cholesterol Testing for Children

Evidence from research shows that atherosclerosis can start in childhood. If heart disease runs in the family, children should have their cholesterol levels checked regularly. In families that are high risk, it's even more important that from two years of age onward, children follow a healthy lifestyle that includes a nutritious low-fat diet and regular physical activity.

Children from families with a high risk of heart disease can benefit from adopting healthy habits in their youth. These habits include eating a low-saturated fat, low-cholesterol, and low trans-fat diet, participating in regular physical activities, and keeping weight at healthy levels.

Dr. Kenneth H. Cooper, M.D., M.P.H., of the Cooper Institute in Dallas, Texas, recommends that children have a baseline cholesterol test around age five or six. In the future, if any issues come up, this baseline reading can serve as a reference point. If no other problems occur, Dr. Cooper recommends that the next childhood cholesterol test be conducted when the child becomes a teenager.

Cindy Zedeck, Program Director of the Stanford Pediatric Weight Control Program at the Stanford Prevention Research Center in Palo Alto, California, agrees that cholesterol testing for kids is a good practice to motivate families to establish healthy habits for children at an early age. She states:

> Many families with overweight children believe that the health risks from poor eating habits either will not occur to their child because their child will outgrow the overweight, or that the health risks are so far away that they will not worry about them now. Seeing the concrete result of high cholesterol may be just what it takes to motivate families to make changes now, reducing worse risk factors in the long run.
>
> Cholesterol testing could also be just the motivation for a child of healthy weight to improve eating and exercise habits. Many kids who are not "overweight" do not make healthy choices and feel that they can "get away" with eating whatever they want. Since thin people also have heart disease, perhaps a concrete result of high cholesterol would also motivate a thin child and family to make healthier eating and exercise choices. This would prevent both future disease and the risk of eventually becoming overweight. Since only half of adults who are overweight were overweight as children, this means that a lot of these thinner kids will become overweight in adulthood, if they don't change their unhealthy eating and exercise habits now.

Circumstances That Can Affect Your Test Results

Your general health also has an effect on your cholesterol test results. Do not go ahead with a scheduled cholesterol test if you have a cold or the flu. Cholesterol levels drop temporarily during periods of acute illness, immediately following a heart attack or stroke, or during acute stressors such as surgery or an accident. For a more accurate measure, medical experts recommend that you wait at least six weeks after any illness before checking your cholesterol levels.

Your cholesterol levels reflect your lifestyle and your genetics. The ideal time to obtain an accurate test is when you are observing your usual routine. Cholesterol levels may change daily in response to deviations from your normal physical activity and eating habits, particularly if you increase your fat intake. Rapid weight loss also impacts cholesterol levels. These fluctuations in cholesterol do not occur immediately, but there is a definite response. Experts estimate that cholesterol levels may change by as much as 10 percent from one month to another simply from normal variations in metabolism. Therefore, for the truest insight into your risk of heart disease on the basis of your cholesterol levels, schedule your test at a time when you are living your typical, routine lifestyle.

Current government guidelines suggest that the ideal total cholesterol level is 180 or below. Desirable levels are less than 200. Levels between 200 and 239 are considered borderline high. Levels greater than 239 are considered very high. Keep in mind, however, that total cholesterol does not tell the entire story.

Cholesterol Testing in Women

During pregnancy, women's cholesterol levels typically escalate. Unless your health-care provider advises you differently, an increase from your typical cholesterol levels at this time is not usually a cause for concern. Medical experts recommend that women wait at least until six weeks after delivery before checking cholesterol levels.

In some women, removal of the ovaries may trigger an increase in cholesterol levels. Menopausal women usually experience an increase in cholesterol levels that is thought to be related to reduced levels of estrogen. Be sure to discuss any changes in your typical cholesterol levels with your health-care provider. See Chapter 20 for more information about special considerations for women with high cholesterol.

Influence of Prescription Drugs

Certain prescription medications may also lead to an increase in cholesterol levels. These medications include the following:

- ACTH (adrenocorticotrophic hormone)
- Anabolic steroids
- Beta-adrenergic blocking agents (beta blockers)
- Corticosteroids
- Epinephrine
- Oral contraceptives
- Phenytoin
- Sulfonamides
- Thiazide diuretics
- Vitamin D

If you are taking any medications that have a potential adverse impact on your cholesterol levels, be sure to discuss this with your health-care provider. Make sure that you understand how you will monitor your cholesterol levels over time to ensure that they remain within a healthy range.

Your Blood Cholesterol Test

When you have your cholesterol tested, the test you should have is the full lipid profile. The results of this test include your levels of total cholesterol, HDL or good cholesterol, LDL or bad cholesterol, and triglycerides. For accurate results, you need to fast for nine to twelve hours before the test. That means you may have nothing to eat or drink but plain water during that time. It is important that you do not consume any alcoholic beverages, coffee, tea, or soda—only drink water.

QUESTION?

Why is it so important for me to fast before a lipid profile test?
The reason it is important not to eat for several hours before testing is that after a meal, triglycerides spike. Testing your triglyceride levels immediately after a meal would not give a clear reflection of the typical amount of triglycerides that tend to flow through your bloodstream at all times.

What to Expect

Since you need to obtain a fasting profile, schedule your test for first thing in the morning. Your health-care professional will take a blood sample, either from a vein or from a finger stick. After the health-care provider has collected the blood, he or she will either send it to a lab for analysis—if the test is being performed via a finger stick, a portable testing device will be used to analyze the sample.

If you are on any medications that affect cholesterol levels, such as those listed on page 52, work with your health-care provider to determine whether you should not take your prescription for a certain period of time before you take your cholesterol test.

Cholesterol Skin Testing

In 2002, the FDA approved a method of measuring cholesterol levels by testing the amount of cholesterol present in the skin. According to studies by the test manufacturer, International Medical Innovations, Inc., of Toronto, Canada, skin contains approximately 11 percent of all body cholesterol as measured by weight. As the severity of coronary artery disease increases, the levels of cholesterol present in skin also increase.

The test, however, is not designed as a screening device. It only detects cholesterol that is present in large quantities in the skin, a characteristic of people with severe coronary artery disease. The test is more valuable when used together with a blood cholesterol test to identify which people have the most severe arterial blockages.

According to the test's manufacturer, the skin test provides 4 to 15 percent more information about the risk of severe coronary artery disease than what is already available from blood cholesterol tests and an assessment of other risk factors.

FACT

Lipid is the chemical family name for fat. Its root is the Greek word *lipos,* meaning "fat." A blood lipid is a fat that circulates in the bloodstream. Cholesterol and triglycerides are both classified as blood lipids. A lipoprotein is a combination of fat surrounded by a protein to enable the fat to circulate.

Public Cholesterol Screenings

You may find public screenings for cholesterol at health fairs, your place of business, or at community events. Make sure that a reputable company is providing the screening and that they provide appropriate educational information, properly trained staff, and referral to health-care providers. Typically, technicians at screenings use a finger-stick sample and a portable testing device to measure test results. This test can still provide you with accurate and valuable information.

Cholestech Corporation offers a portable cholesterol testing system that is used in public screenings as well as in physician office settings. The Cholestech LDX system provides lab-accurate results in five minutes from only a single drop of blood. The Cholestech technology uses a variety of tests that range from a fasting, full-lipid profile and blood glucose levels to a simple, nonfasting, total cholesterol test. This technology facilitates quick results.

Share your test results with your health-care provider if you have your cholesterol tested at a public screening. Even if you are only able to take a nonfasting total cholesterol and HDL test, it can provide you with helpful information. If it is available, make sure that you still obtain the fasting, full lipoprotein profile. Keep in mind that learning the individual levels of LDL and HDL cholesterol and triglycerides gives you a much more accurate assessment of the health of your circulatory system. (See Chapter 5 or the chart in Chapter 1, pages 11–12, for information on what your score means.)

The Value of Public Screenings

The true value of public screenings for cholesterol is in raising awareness of the prevalence of the risk of heart disease among the public. Public screenings help people who have no idea whatsoever of what their heart health might be to realize that they are in need of further testing and evaluation. According to Claude Lenfant, director of the National Heart, Lung, and Blood Institute, "Americans at high risk for a heart attack are too often not identified and, so, don't receive sufficiently aggressive treatment. Yet, studies show conclusively that lowering the level of low-density lipoprotein, or LDL, the 'bad cholesterol,' can reduce the short-term risk for heart disease as much as 40 percent."

Public Screenings for Children

Both the federal government and the American Heart Association do not recommend mass public screenings of blood cholesterol for all children and adolescents. Health professionals are concerned that this type of mass screening would be costly and that it is likely to be inefficient. Children are often uncomfortable with needles and the sight of blood. Cholesterol testing for children is best conducted in the physician office setting.

According to the American Heart Association, about 10 percent of adolescents between the ages of twelve to nineteen years have total cholesterol levels higher than 200 mg/dL. This level is considered high risk.

Home Testing of Blood Cholesterol

At this time, home testing devices for cholesterol only measure total cholesterol and do not provide a breakdown of HDL cholesterol, LDL cholesterol, or triglycerides. Lifestream Technologies, Inc., based in Post Falls, Idaho, offers a cholesterol monitor for home use that allows you to test your total cholesterol levels. The Lifestream LSP system is not meant to replace the role of a medical professional. Instead, the device is designed to serve as an aid for those who want to monitor their cholesterol levels on a regular basis from the convenience of home.

Possible Future Tests

As scientific research continues to create a clearer picture of the mechanisms behind atherosclerosis, investigators are focusing more attention on other lipid-related risk factors. Studies continue to reveal more information about the subclasses of LDL and of HDL. As knowledge increases about the more exact role that each of these particles plays in the atherosclerotic process, scientists are developing tests that can identify risk with greater precision than simply looking at total LDL or HDL cholesterol levels. The focus of these studies includes the following particles, some of which are mentioned in Chapter 6:

- Small, very dense, low-density lipoprotein particles
- High apoliprotein B levels
- Low apoliprotein A-1 levels
- High lipoprotein a or Lp(a) levels
- High remnant lipoprotein cholesterol and triglyceride levels
- Low high-density lipoprotein 2b levels

Watch for results from future research trials and updates to guidelines that incorporate what is being learned about these particles. An understanding of the role of these markers and emerging risk factors may shed more light on why as many as 50 percent of people who do not have high total blood cholesterol levels develop atherosclerotic plaque that leads to heart disease and stroke.

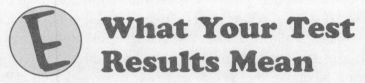

Chapter 5

What Your Test Results Mean

You've taken the first step and completed your cholesterol test. Now you've received a report with various figures, a ratio, and maybe even a risk interpretation. But it's not enough to simply know your numbers—you need to know what those numbers mean and whether you need to take action to change your numbers. This chapter gives you insight into how to interpret your results in each of the following categories: total cholesterol, LDL cholesterol, HDL cholesterol, triglycerides, and ratio of total cholesterol to HDL cholesterol.

Total Cholesterol Results

In general, the higher your total blood cholesterol level, the greater your risk of heart disease. For example, a person with a total cholesterol level of 240 mg/dL may have as much as twice the risk of heart disease as someone with a total cholesterol level of less than 200 mg/dL

Total cholesterol alone, however, does not tell the complete story, because heart disease risk is related to the composition of your total cholesterol. For example, if you have high total cholesterol due to a very high HDL cholesterol level, then that is a positive condition. On the other hand, if your total cholesterol is not high, but you have a high LDL level or a low HDL level, then that is a negative condition. First we will look at the guidelines for total cholesterol, and then we will drill down into each of the individual components.

Guidelines for Adults

The federal government and the American Heart Association recommend the following total cholesterol levels as a general guide for adults:

Classification of Total Cholesterol Levels for Adults	
Total Cholesterol Level	**Category**
Less than 200 mg/dL	Desirable
200–239 mg/dL	Borderline high
240 mg/dL and above	High

If your levels fall into the "desirable" category of less than 200 mg/dL, the preliminary assessment of your heart attack risk is considered to be low, assuming that you do not have any other risk factors. Keep in mind, however, that as many as 50 percent of people who do not have elevated lipid levels, and who therefore fall within the "desirable" category, still have heart disease. For a more complete picture of your potential risk, you need to check your other lipid levels and consider your lifestyle habits and genetic history.

Strong research evidence shows that high levels of total cholesterol are very predictive of future coronary events. Total cholesterol, however, is composed mostly of LDL particles. Therefore, leading experts believe that the strong relationship demonstrated in these studies between total cholesterol and heart disease is actually reflective of the fact that high LDL levels are a powerful predictive risk factor.

Those who have cholesterol levels between 200 to 239 mg/dL are considered to be borderline high risk. This categorization, however, is not necessarily cause for alarm. If total cholesterol levels are high because of high HDL levels of more than 60 mg/dL, it actually means that you have a reduced risk of heart disease, assuming that you have no other risk factors.

People with total cholesterol levels of 240 mg/dL are classified as "high risk." More tests need to be undertaken without delay to develop a therapeutic treatment approach. People in this category are at high risk of having a heart attack or stroke.

Children and Adolescents

Scientific studies show that atherosclerosis actually begins in childhood. The federal government and the American Heart Association recommend the following guidelines on blood cholesterol in children and adolescents from the age of two to nineteen years:

Classification of Total Cholesterol Levels for Children and Adolescents	
Total Cholesterol Level	**Category**
Less than 170 mg/dL	Acceptable
170–199 mg/dL	Borderline
200 mg/dL and above	High

Medical experts recommend cholesterol testing for children from families with a history of heart disease.

The majority of deaths from heart disease occur in older adults, simply because the disease has had more time to develop. Older adults include men aged sixty years and older and women aged seventy-five years and older. The challenge for older adults is that risk assessment by standard risk factors is less reliable, particularly as it is expressed as a percentage of risk over a ten-year period. This, however, does not mean that high total cholesterol levels in older adults should go untreated. Instead, we should keep in mind that elevated cholesterol levels in older adults simply do not have the same predictive power as they do for other adults.

FACT

Newborn infants have average levels of LDL cholesterol of only 30 mg/dL. Some scientists believe that this provides evidence that low levels of LDL cholesterol are safe. Other scientists believe there may be a point where too-low cholesterol is bad for health.

LDL Cholesterol Results

High levels of LDL cholesterol are known to be a major cause of heart disease. Federal government guidelines focus on reducing LDL levels as the primary means of providing therapy for people with high cholesterol. Strong research evidence supports the idea that reducing LDL levels results in reducing the risk of heart disease. However, before you assume that you have very high levels of LDL cholesterol based on the results of one test, make sure that you fasted for the recommended minimum of nine hours before you took your cholesterol test. If your LDL result was higher than 160 mg/dL and you are not certain you observed the fasting requirement closely, it's a good idea to repeat the test.

LDL Guidelines for Adults

The following table reflects the classification of LDL cholesterol levels that are recommended by both the federal government and the American Heart Association for adults.

Classification of LDL Cholesterol Levels for Adults	
LDL Cholesterol	**Category**
Less than 100 mg/dL	Optimal
100–129 mg/dL	Near optimal
130–159 mg/dL	Borderline
160–189 mg/dL	High
Above 189 mg/dL	Very high

Current treatment approaches for people with high total cholesterol levels are based on LDL levels, the presence of other risk factors, and the calculated percentage of short-term risk of having heart disease. (For a more detailed discussion of risk factors, see Chapter 3.)

People with elevated cholesterol levels are classified into four categories of risk for treatment. An existing diagnosis of coronary artery disease or an equivalent condition is a very important factor that affects the treatment goal for LDL-lowering therapy. If the following conditions are present, the individual is considered to fall into the highest category of risk and is therefore recommended to receive the most aggressive therapeutic treatment:

- Coronary artery disease
- Other forms of atherosclerosis, such as peripheral arterial disease, abdominal aortic aneurysm, and symptomatic carotid artery disease
- Diabetes
- Multiple risk factors that, according to the Framingham Risk Assessment (see Chapter 3) predict a ten-year risk of heart disease of greater than 20 percent

Research continues to show that excessive levels of LDL cholesterol are the most harmful to health. Furthermore, in people who have familial hypercholesterolemia and other genetic forms of heart disease, LDL levels are present in high levels, while other heart disease risk factors are not present. In contrast, people with very low levels of LDL typically enjoy longevity.

LDL Guidelines for Children and Adolescents

Similar to the guidelines for total cholesterol, the recommended levels of LDL cholesterol in children differ slightly from the guidelines for adults. The following chart sets forth how various levels of LDL cholesterol are categorized in children:

Classifications of LDL Cholesterol Levels in Children and Adolescents	
LDL Cholesterol Levels	**Category**
Less than 110 mg/dL	Acceptable
110–129 mg/dL	Borderline
Above 129 mg/dL	High

For children, the government guidelines recommend lifestyle changes as the first line of therapeutic intervention. These changes include improving eating habits and increasing physical activity. Experts disagree about the role of cholesterol-lowering drugs when children are concerned. See Chapter 20 for more information about children and high cholesterol.

Older Adults and LDL Cholesterol

Clinical studies show that older adults respond effectively to therapies targeting LDL cholesterol levels. The same recommendations for reducing LDL cholesterol levels that apply to young and middle-aged adults also apply to older adults. Recommended therapies include both changes in lifestyle habits and use of prescription drugs if indicated.

HDL Cholesterol Results

Levels of HDL, or good cholesterol, show an inverse relationship to heart disease risk. Unlike LDL cholesterol and triglycerides, where high numbers mean increased risk, higher levels of HDL cholesterol mean a lower risk of heart disease. In healthy individuals, HDL cholesterol represents approximately 20 to 30 percent of total cholesterol levels.

The reasons for HDL cholesterol's beneficial effect are not exactly clear. Some researchers believe HDL cholesterol actively reverses atherosclerosis by carrying cholesterol away from arterial walls.

FACT

Researchers have found that some individuals whose lower levels of HDL are due to genetic disorders also have a higher risk of heart disease. However, this is not true of all individuals with genetically induced low HDL levels.

Some scientists believe that there may be multiple subtypes of HDL cholesterol, just as there are multiple subtypes of LDL cholesterol, and that some subtypes of HDL have more beneficial characteristics than others. These scientists believe that HDL-2b, in particular, is important to the process of collecting excess LDL and returning it to the liver, thus maintaining healthy LDL levels.

HDL Cholesterol in Adults

A risk to health arises when HDL levels are too low. Evidence from studies shows that low HDL cholesterol is an independent risk factor for heart disease. This means that regardless of whether other risk factors are present, the risk of heart disease is higher for people with low HDL cholesterol. A 1-percent decrease in HDL levels is associated with a 2- to 3-percent increase in heart disease risk. The following chart sets forth the classification of HDL cholesterol levels as adopted by federal government guidelines and the American Heart Association:

Classification of HDL Cholesterol Levels for Adults		
HDL Cholesterol Levels	**Classification**	**Risk Category**
Less than 40 mg/dL	Low HDL cholesterol	High risk
40 to 59 mg/dL	Moderate HDL cholesterol	Higher levels are desirable
60 mg/dL and above	High LDL cholesterol	Negative risk factor

Interestingly, adult women tend to have higher HDL cholesterol levels than adult men. According to government estimates, approximately one-third of all adult men and one-fifth of adult women have low HDL cholesterol levels that put them at increased risk of heart disease. At 40 mg/dL, however, both men and women can be considered to have low HDL—there is no separate recommendation for women. Nor is there a separate recommendation regarding HDL levels for children.

Natural strategies to increase HDL cholesterol include losing weight, increasing activity, and quitting smoking. These natural strategies have no adverse side effects, as can be the case with some prescription drugs.

The question of whether increased HDL cholesterol levels reduce the risk of heart disease, independent of other factors, remains to be answered. Some medications that lower LDL cholesterol also raise HDL levels.

The Lipid Triad

Low HDL levels tend to occur in association with the presence of small, dense LDL particles (the worst type) and high levels of triglycerides. The relationship among these three types of lipids is known as the "lipid triad." Low HDL levels also tend to occur in conjunction with metabolic problems associated with insulin resistance. Many people who have the lipid triad also have Type 2 diabetes.

Several factors can lead to low HDL cholesterol levels. Many are variables related to lifestyle factors, and these can be changed by adopting healthy habits. These factors include high triglycerides; excess weight; lack of physical activity; cigarette smoking; very high carbohydrate intake levels (more than 60 percent of total calories per day); drugs such as beta-blockers, anabolic steroids, or progestational agents; and heredity.

Approximately 50 percent of people who have low HDL levels have a genetic basis for their condition. Some of these people have a type of low HDL cholesterol known as "isolated low HDL," so called because it does not appear as part of the lipid triad. The other 50 percent of people, however, can change their HDL levels by improving their lifestyle habits. It's easy to see why making an effort to eat more healthfully and to be active on a regular basis is truly worth your time and energy.

High HDL—A Negative Risk Factor

Research shows evidence connecting high HDL cholesterol levels with a lower risk level for heart disease. For this reason, high HDL levels are considered a negative risk factor. The use of this terminology can be confusing. Risk factors are known to be those conditions that increase the level of risk for heart disease. So what does it mean for a risk factor to be negative?

What this term refers to is the fact that high HDL cholesterol is such a positive condition that it actually "negates" one of the other risk factors. If you think of a regular risk factor as adding points to your risk score, a negative risk factor is one that gives you negative points, or subtracts points from your score. For this reason, high HDL levels are very important for maintaining a healthy heart and circulatory system.

FACT

Most people can improve their cholesterol profile by making lifestyle changes. Being physically active on a regular basis, not smoking, eating a balanced diet that's lower in unhealthy fats, and maintaining a healthy weight all raise HDL (good cholesterol) levels.

Triglyceride Results

Triglycerides are a form of fat. Triglycerides are present in most types of food and are the most common fat in the body. Triglycerides that float in the bloodstream provide fuel for energy. Those that are not used for fuel are stored in the body's fatty tissues. Recent research has made it clear that high triglyceride levels are a marker for increased risk of heart disease and are believed to be an independent risk factor. In addition, high triglycerides are usually present when other risk factors, such as diabetes and high LDL cholesterol, are present.

Classifications of Triglyceride Levels in Adults

As the role of triglycerides in the process of developing heart disease becomes clearer, experts support efforts to keep triglyceride levels low. The federal government and the American Heart Association have come up with the following guidelines regarding fasting blood levels of triglycerides in adults:

Classifications of Triglyceride Levels	
Triglyceride Level	Classification
Less than 150 mg/dL	Normal
150–199 mg/dL	Borderline high
200–499 mg/dL	High
Above 499 mg/dL	Very high

As with low HDL cholesterol levels, behavioral factors are the root cause of high triglyceride levels. Excess weight and lack of physical activity are the most common causes. However, any of the following can be a factor: cigarette smoking; excess alcohol consumption; very high carbohydrate intake levels (more than 60 percent of total calories per day); drugs such as beta-blockers, corticosteroids, estrogens, and protease inhibitors for HIV; heredity; or other diseases such as Type 2 diabetes, chronic renal failure, and nephrotic syndrome. People who do not have any of these factors generally have triglyceride levels of less than 100 mg/dL. The first course of action to lower triglyceride levels is to adopt lifestyle changes, including improved nutrition and increased physical activity.

Total Cholesterol and HDL Ratio

For a quick estimation of risk, you can calculate your total cholesterol and HDL ratio. To do this, divide your total cholesterol number by your HDL number. This method is based on the fact that high HDL levels relative to your total cholesterol are generally predictive of a lower risk of heart disease. While this estimate can give you a rough idea of your cholesterol level breakdown, it is not recommended as a test upon which to base therapeutic treatment.

Today, the American Heart Association recommends using absolute numbers for total blood cholesterol and HDL cholesterol levels. They are more useful to physicians than the cholesterol ratio in determining appropriate treatment for patients. If you're still interested in calculating your ratio, the classifications are as follows:

Classifications of Ratio of Total Cholesterol to HDL	
TC/HDL Ratio	Classification
3.5 to 1	Optimum
4.5 to 1	Desirable
5 to 1 and above	High

To apply the formula, let's take an example of a woman with a total cholesterol level of 200 and an HDL level of 50. Her ratio is calculated by dividing 200 by 50, to equal a ratio of 4 to 1. According to this rough measure, her cholesterol is in the desirable range, but for a more comprehensive understanding, it's necessary to look at the entire spectrum of blood lipid levels.

Keep in mind that all of these numbers are not your health. They are tools to give you a better picture of the composition of your blood, which ultimately affects the health of your arteries and your heart. The miracles of modern technology and the diligent pursuit of knowledge on the part of numerous researchers are beginning to unravel the progression of the deadly process of atherosclerosis. Yet in your hands, you hold much of the power to optimize your own health and to feel and be your best. Use your knowledge wisely. Your choices make all the difference between a better and longer life or an untimely death.

Chapter 6

Diagnostic Tests for Other Markers of Heart Disease

Typically, your health-care provider will include a cholesterol test as part of a routine physical checkup. In addition to blood lipid tests, medical professionals may use other tests to achieve a full picture of the health of the heart and circulatory system. This is particularly important if you have other risk factors, since 50 percent of people with "desirable" cholesterol levels still have heart disease.

Noninvasive Diagnostic Tests

Several of the tests doctors use to measure the function of the heart and the state of the arteries are noninvasive, meaning that they are done without entering the body or puncturing the skin. Instead, medical professionals use different types of technology to look at the heart and arteries and to measure how well they are functioning.

Stress Tests

In the stress test, you exercise on a treadmill or a stationary bicycle to put your heart under stress. As you are exercising, medical professionals will administer tests to measure your heart's response to the stress. One type of test is an electrocardiogram (EKG), which measures the electrical flow through your heart. The test is noninvasive and involves putting electrodes on your chest that are connected to a machine, the electrocardiograph. The electrocardiograph prints out a record of how the heart is beating and reveals any irregularities. As you exercise, the printout shows whether your heart is able to meet the extra demand placed on it by the exercise.

Another method of stress testing uses a radioactive tracer that is injected intravenously. The tracer flows through the arteries. Medical professionals use special cameras to view the tracer's passage as it reveals the extent of openness or blockage of various blood vessels.

ALERT!

Studies show that some diagnostic tests and procedures are not as accurate in women as in men. For example, an exercise stress test may show a false positive in a younger woman. Some doctors prefer other types of tests that are more diagnostically accurate for young women. If you are a woman, be sure to discuss these issues with your health-care provider.

Due to certain physical conditions, some individuals cannot undergo the rigors of a stress test. In these cases, doctors use medications to stress the heart as if it were exercising. They then follow the flow of the tracer and assess the health of the heart and its coronary arteries.

Echocardiogram

An echocardiogram, also known as an "echo" test or EKG, uses sound waves to take a dynamic picture of the heart as it beats. In most cases the test is noninvasive. A technician administers the test by placing a wand-like transducer on your ribs near the breastbone. This transducer transmits high frequency sound waves directed toward the heart. The EKG machine receives electrical impulses that reflect the echoes of the sound waves and converts them into a dynamic picture of the heart.

The cardiologist analyzes this moving picture of the heart to evaluate its functioning. Echocardiography reveals the shape and thickness of the walls in the heart's chambers and the large veins and arteries of the heart, among other things. This information is particularly helpful in assessing the risk of atherosclerosis and other heart problems.

Medical professionals also use echocardiography with stress tests, performing the EKG before exercise begins and immediately after it stops. If a patient is unable to exercise, drugs may be used to produce a stress response in the heart.

Cardiovascular Magnetic Resonance Imaging

Magnetic resonance imaging (MRI or NMR) is another noninvasive test. This test uses a magnet and radiofrequency waves to read signals from the body's cells to create an image of the interior of the body. MRI can provide detailed and accurate pictures of the size and thickness of the heart muscle. The test can also provide data about the amount of blood flow. To take the test, the patient lies on a mobile examination table that moves through a large magnetic tube.

The cardiologist analyzes the MRI images and data to evaluate the blood supply to the heart muscle and to assess the function of the blood vessels. Since these tests are highly dependent on operator analysis, be sure to choose a health-care provider with solid training and extensive experience who regularly performs these test analyses.

Ultrafast CT Scan or EBCT

The ultrafast CT scan, also called electron beam computed tomography (EBCT), is used to measure the amount of calcium deposited in your coronary arteries. The calcium content of arterial plaque increases as it ages and hardens. Therefore, larger and thicker buildups of plaque reveal a higher risk of complete arterial blockage in the near future. Being able to detect the amount of calcium allows medical professionals to determine the degree of risk for blockage of the arteries. The scanner is noninvasive and uses low-grade radiation to produce computer-generated pictures.

The tests described in this chapter can provide you with some insight into the true state of plaque buildup within your arteries. This information can help you to refine the degree of risk for an imminent heart attack. These test results also provide physicians with important data for planning effective therapy programs.

Medical experts derive multiple benefits from EBCT testing. With repeat evaluations, a cardiologist can track the rate of increase in calcification. This rate can provide further insight into the degree of risk of a heart attack. Other medical experts use the test in conjunction with tests such as the EKG and stress test to more accurately assess risk and to decide whether additional testing is required. Physicians also use test results to evaluate the effectiveness of treatment over time. Currently, EBCT is not covered by insurance.

Angiogram

An angiogram is an invasive test used to measure the degree of blockage in blood vessels. It is considered the "gold standard" when it comes to detecting narrowing of blood vessels. To perform an angiogram, the physician punctures a major artery and inserts a long plastic catheter up to a heart blood vessel. Then a dye known as a contrast agent is injected into the catheter to allow for observation of the heart blood vessels. The doctor observes the dye's progress on an X-ray machine to see how it flows through the vessels.

If the angiogram reveals a blockage, the doctor may perform an angioplasty, which involves clearing the blockage from the artery and then placing a hollow tube—called a stent—on the inside of the blood vessel to keep it open. If the blockage is so severe that the artery cannot be saved, bypass surgery may be required.

A challenge with angioplasty is that when the arterial blockage is cleared, it causes inflammation and swelling in the arterial walls, which can be just as obstructive as the plaque that had to be removed. This condition is called restenosis. Newer stents are drug-coated to prevent plaque from building back up into the artery or to keep tissue from growing into the inside of the stent.

Intravascular Ultrasound

Intravascular ultrasound (IVUS) uses sound waves to create a multidimensional image that shows the level of blood flow and plaque buildup inside the coronary artery. Medical professionals take images using a catheter with a transducer inside the artery itself. The transducer takes the images and transmits them to a viewing monitor. This can provide an extremely accurate view of the size of the vessel's opening and condition of the plaque and arterial walls.

FACT

Medical professionals can use intravascular ultrasound (IVUS) to plan or evaluate the success of an angioplasty and the placement of a stent. They can also use IVUS to plan or evaluate the success of a bypass surgery procedure.

Blood Test for CRP

The presence of higher-than-normal levels of C-reactive protein (CRP) in the bloodstream is evidence of an infectious or inflammatory disease in the body. Medical professionals frequently give CRP tests to patients after surgery to determine whether an infection is present. Health-care providers also use CRP tests to diagnose diseases, such as rheumatoid arthritis, and to evaluate the effectiveness of therapy. CRP is not indicative of the presence of a specific disease, simply that the body is fighting some form of infection or inflammation.

Strong evidence from research studies shows that CRP is also a marker for heart disease. In the noteworthy Nurses' Health Study conducted by researchers from Brigham and Women's Hospital and from Harvard Medical School on 40,000 healthy, postmenopausal women, levels of CRP were clearly linked to heart disease risk. Women with high CRP levels were five times more likely than women with low CRP levels to develop heart disease and seven times more likely to have a stroke or heart attack.

A "marker" for a disease is not a causal factor or an agent that makes a disease better or worse. The presence of the marker is simply evidence of the presence of the disease. In the case of CRP, high levels of CRP in the bloodstream indicate the presence of heart disease. Therapy, therefore, has nothing to do with eliminating the CRP but focuses instead on treating the underlying heart disease.

The reason that CRP levels can be a marker for heart disease is related to the fact that damage to, or inflammation of, the interior lining of the arteries (referred to as the endothelial lining) precedes the formation of plaque. In other words, plaque collects in locations where there is damage to arterial walls. CRP can be evidence of this damage. Leading researchers worldwide continue to study the question of why and how this inflammation occurs to the endothelial lining.

The hs-CRP Test

Given the strength of research evidence, some medical experts support the use of a high-sensitivity CRP (hs-CRP) test to measure the risk of a future heart attack or stroke. The value of the hs-CRP test is that it helps detect those individuals with low blood cholesterol levels who have high CRP levels and a high risk of heart attack. If you have low levels of CRP and healthy blood cholesterol levels, you can be that much more sure that your risk of heart attack and stroke is low. With a simple blood cholesterol test, you can be much less certain.

The CRP testing provides valuable insight into the long-term assessment of risk for heart disease. Some medical professionals believe this assessment is so valuable that everyone should have an hs-CRP test when they take a blood cholesterol test. This position is made even stronger given that the hs-CRP test is not expensive.

Interestingly, people with the highest hs-CRP results but no other risk factors—including high levels of cholesterol—have as much as two to four times the risk of developing blocked arteries than people at the low end of the hs-CRP results.

FACT

In January 2003, an expert panel appointed by the American Heart Association and the Centers for Disease Control and Prevention recommended use of an hs-CRP test for people who have a 10- to 20-percent risk of heart attack within ten years, which is considered an intermediate risk level.

The good news is that hs-CRP testing is likely to become even more accessible and affordable. The Cholestech Corporation, based in Hayward, California, offers a number of point-of-care diagnostic testing tools. One product in development is a finger stick hs-CRP test. When this test is released, it will be possible to get an accurate hs-CRP reading from as little as a single drop of blood in a matter of minutes.

Conditions That Affect the Test

If you are fortunate enough to be able to get an hs-CRP test, be certain to take it when there are no other conditions that may increase the level of inflammation in your body. For example, do not take this test when you have any kind of infection, if you are injured, or if you know you are experiencing any type of inflammation.

Since their levels will already be elevated, people who suffer inflammatory-type conditions such as lupus or arthritis cannot use the hs-CRP test to accurately measure their risk for heart disease. The ideal candidate for an hs-CRP test is someone who is otherwise healthy, with healthy blood cholesterol levels, who is also concerned that he or she may be at risk for heart disease due to the presence of other risk factors.

According to the American Heart Association and Centers for Disease Control, hs-CRP test results are expressed as milligrams per deciliter (mg/dL). Concentrations of less than 1.0 mg/L are low risk; 1.0 mg/dL to 3.0 mg/dL are average risk; and concentrations greater than 3.0 mg/dL are high risk. People in the high-risk group have approximately twice the risk for cardiovascular disease than those in the low-risk group.

Lp(a) Blood Test

When LDL cholesterol combines with a substance known as Apoliprotein (a), the result is a compound known as Lp(a), or "ugly" cholesterol. Lp(a) is called ugly cholesterol because evidence from some research studies shows that in high levels, it can increase a person's risk of heart attack or stroke, even if cholesterol levels are otherwise "desirable." Lp(a) is measured through a blood sample and can be tested as part of a lipoprotein panel.

Federal government guidelines describe Lp(a) as an emerging risk factor. Researchers believe that the presence of Lp(a) can increase the formation of blood clots and the formation of plaque by assisting LDL particles to attach to plaque buildups.

Genetics determines your levels of Lp(a) and even the size of the Lp(a) molecule itself. Lifestyle changes do not alter levels of Lp(a); instead, levels for most people tend to remain consistent over a lifetime except for women, who will experience a slight rise in levels with menopause. Some physicians request testing of Lp(a) for patients who have a strong family history of premature heart disease or hypercholesterolemia. It can be a valuable test, particularly when other types of cholesterol are at healthy levels, yet concern exists that heart disease is developing.

Physicians will typically order this test if a patient has had a heart attack or stroke, yet cholesterol levels fall within a "healthy" category.

Berkeley HeartLab, Inc., based in Burlingame, California, offers a number of advanced lipid tests—including a test for levels of Lp(a)—that provide quantitative determinations of lipoprotein subclasses. According to Jeffrey Aroy of Berkeley HeartLab, Inc., "the value of the quantitative measurements is that they go beyond simply noting whether levels are 'good' or 'bad.' Instead, these measurements not only provide guidance for therapeutic treatment, but also provide valuable insight into the success of therapy and the need for adjusting treatment approaches on an ongoing basis."

FACT

Approximately 50 percent of people who have heart attacks do not have elevated cholesterol levels. These individuals, however, typically have higher levels of CRP, Lp(a), Apo B, or homocysteine. As researchers continue to learn about the exact mechanisms of heart disease, more tests are developed to identify and measure these other risk factors and markers.

Treatment for elevated Lp(a) includes niacin therapy. Some experts believe that antioxidant therapy is also useful. People with high levels of Lp(a) benefit by concentrating their efforts on lowering LDL levels since at lower levels, it is harder for LDL particles to attach to plaque buildup. Lowering LDL levels ultimately lowers the level of risk.

According to a study published in the *New England Journal of Medicine* in November 2003, researchers found that elevated levels of Lp(a) among healthy men age sixty-five years and older are predictive of the risk of stroke and death. Study participants with the highest levels of Lp(a) were more likely to experience a stroke and were 76 percent more likely to die than men with the lowest levels. These researchers support the use of Lp(a) testing as a screening tool to measure the risk of stroke and heart disease in older men.

Apoliprotein B (Apo B) Blood Test

Evidence from research shows that small, dense LDL are more highly associated with atherosclerosis than large, "fluffy" LDL. Studies also show that Apoliprotein B (Apo B) is a potential marker for the precise levels of LDL or bad cholesterol circulating in the bloodstream.

What Is Apoliprotein B?

Apoliproteins are essential to the transport of blood lipids through the bloodstream and to the uptake of blood lipids into body cells. Apo B-100 is manufactured in the liver. It combines with very low-density lipoproteins (VLDL) to carry triglycerides and LDL cholesterol in the bloodstream. By measuring levels of Apo B, it is possible to measure the exact number of LDL particles.

Some researchers believe that measurements of Apo B may be better than LDL measurements when it comes to predicting the risk of heart disease. This is because levels of Apo B can be measured directly, while LDL cholesterol levels are often calculated indirectly from levels of total cholesterol. These indirect calculations tend to be less accurate as triglyceride levels increase. But experts believe that research evidence is not sufficient to support the superiority of Apo B over LDL cholesterol measures. Therefore, federal government guidelines do not yet recommend the Apo B measure as a factor in risk assessment. This may change as new tests continue to be developed and are more accurate and standardized.

Most LDL levels are calculated indirectly, by measuring the total weight of all LDL cholesterol present rather than by calculating the actual number of LDL particles. Tests that measure Apo B measure the exact number of LDL particles, providing insight into whether the LDL cholesterol is composed of the large, fluffy type or the small, dense type that is worse for health.

Research on Apo B

In October 2003, results from the Insulin Resistance Atherosclerosis Study were published in *Circulation: Journal of the American Heart Association*. Researchers used a number of tests to determine whether people should be put on therapy. Interestingly, researchers found that 19 percent of subjects would have received a different treatment recommendation if they had been tested for Apo B levels rather than for LDL levels. Investigators who conducted the study confirmed that LDL is still an important marker for heart disease risk. However, researchers believe that testing for Apo B levels provides even more valuable information. The test is inexpensive and does not require fasting.

Alice Lichtenstein, a spokesperson for the American Heart Association, said, "This is an important observation and needs to be considered carefully in light of prior data to determine whether current guidelines should be modified to recommend routinely measuring Apo B levels in high risk individuals." National government guidelines in Canada recommend use of the Apo B test. Watch for potential changes in government guidelines in the United States.

Homocysteine Blood Tests

Unlike the fatty particles discussed so far, like LDL cholesterol and triglycerides, homocysteine is an amino acid. Like those other particles, however, evidence from research studies shows that elevated levels of homocysteine in the blood are related to an increased risk of stroke, heart disease, and peripheral arterial disease. Blood levels of homocysteine escalate when the body lacks three B vitamins—folate, B_6, and B_{12}—that are essential to protein metabolism. Kidney disease can also lead to high homocysteine levels. Researchers continue to investigate the exact reason for elevated levels of homocysteine to be related to vascular problems.

Some researchers theorize that increased levels of homocysteine damage the endothelial lining within the blood vessels. This damage creates the conditions for cholesterol to build up into plaque. Homocysteine also contributes to plaque ruptures, which can lead to harmful blood clot formation.

Homocysteine is measured in micromoles. Experts consider 9 to 10 micromoles per liter (mol/L) to be normal. Studies suggest that 15 mol/L or higher indicates an increased risk for heart disease. People with high levels of homocysteine may have as much as four times the risk of heart disease as those with normal levels, contributing to the position among many medical experts that high homocysteine may be a marker for increased risk of heart disease.

Currently, the American Heart Association does not recommend population-wide screening of homocysteine levels, although more and more research supports the position that knowledge of homocysteine levels is an accurate predictor of risk. Federal government guidelines identify it as an emerging risk factor. Further research needs to be completed to understand whether lowering homocysteine levels confers benefits. The best strategy for maintaining healthy homocysteine levels is to ensure a balanced intake of foods rich in B vitamins or to take a B vitamin supplement.

FACT

Berkeley HeartLab includes homocysteine testing as part of its Advanced CVD Profile test. Currently, Medicare provides reimbursement for this profile for patients who have been diagnosed with conditions related to atherosclerosis.

Chapter 7

Creating Your Healthy Lifestyle

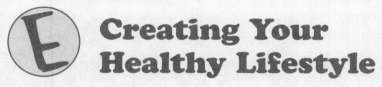

Creating your own health by adopting a healthy lifestyle is worth your time and will lengthen your life. In fact, according to the Centers for Disease Control, about half of all deaths in the United States are linked to behaviors that can be changed. By making healthy choices, you will live longer, enjoy a higher quality of life, feel better about yourself, have more energy, look better, and reduce your risks of disease.

The Power to Create Health

You've learned about cholesterol. You've learned about the risk factors. You've learned that you can take steps to improve your cholesterol levels and accordingly improve your overall health. In this chapter, we examine the importance of improving your health. This means understanding not only the individual pieces of the puzzle—like eating more veggies or walking daily—but also how to fit them all together over a lifetime. The power of the whole, an integrated wellness lifestyle, is much greater than the sum of the parts.

The purpose of this chapter, therefore, is to give you insight into what it means to create a healthy standard of living. You may not realize how easy it is, with our modern way of life, to experience an unhealthy existence. Regardless of how difficult the challenge, however, the rewards of healthy living are worth the commitment and effort.

Change never happens overnight. You will examine a psychological model of the process of change and learn tips on how you can stay motivated. The following chapters will provide more specific practical information on what to eat, what to do, and how to implement other strategies that enhance your wellness.

ALERT!

In today's environment, if you don't have an aggressive strategy for eating whole foods and incorporating physical activities, it is easy to gain weight. In other words, if you go through modern life passively and do what is easiest and most convenient, your choices are likely to be harmful to your long-term health.

What Science Can Teach Us

The great benefit of being alive today is that scientific research allows us to have an almost complete picture of the mechanisms behind cholesterol, atherosclerosis, and heart disease. Soon, researchers may even be able to identify the genetic markers for heart disease, so that testing can be done long before any symptoms ever manifest themselves. In the process of unraveling how our physical system develops disease, we also gain even more insight into how to prevent, or at least to deter, the disease processes. People even one generation before us did not have the depth of knowledge and understanding now available about the relationships between what we do and how our actions affect our health and longevity.

What You Can Do

What science cannot change is that when push comes to shove, you are the bottom line. In other words, just as money cannot buy happiness, it cannot buy health. Yes, money can buy access to the best health-care providers, to all the procedures and drugs that are available, and to minimally processed whole foods. But even the wealthiest person on the planet cannot simply buy his or her health. Health must be created.

The World Health Organization defines health as "a state of complete physical, social and mental well being, not merely the absence of disease or infirmity." This definition of health is very expansive. It supposes an optimal condition of being, rather than a minimal state of being disease-free. So instead of putting your focus on how to stop disease, consider for a moment the power of shifting your focus to how to create optimal health. You have the power to achieve it. All you need is the knowledge, which this book can help to provide, and the motivation, which comes from deep within yourself.

FACT

Health does not come in a bottle or pill. Your doctor cannot "make" you healthy. Only you can create your health on a daily, weekly, monthly, and yearly basis. Your health is a direct result of your way of living—eating, breathing, walking, sleeping, and embracing life.

The Hazards of Modern Living

One of the greatest ironies of modern living is that it is actually much easier to survive in a manner that contributes to poor health and chronic disease than it is to live a life of vibrant, vital health. The reasons for this are many and complex. Some of the factors of modern convenience are closely intertwined with the leading risk factors for heart disease.

Poor Eating Habits

The foods that are the easiest to obtain and the most plentiful are fast, high-fat, high-sugar, calorie-rich, highly refined processed foods. These foods are often nutrient poor, yet cheap and effortless to find. It takes more time and dedication to find and prepare natural, whole foods. But the rewards of eating such health-enhancing foods are clear. You will live longer and feel better.

What you eat has a powerful influence over whether you create a healthy blood lipid profile that includes low LDL cholesterol, high HDL cholesterol, and low triglyceride levels. Research supports that eating a primarily plant-based diet that consists of a large proportion of minimally processed (or whole) grains, vegetables, and fruits is essential to support optimal health.

The challenge of modern living is that it makes it very easy to overeat foods that do not support health and makes it very easy to reduce or practically eliminate all physical activity.

Lack of Exercise and Excess Weight

Technology has made our lives so easy that it takes perseverance to find opportunities to move. Modern innovations have created so many labor-saving devices that we have almost made the requirement to move obsolete. This is not good. To create optimum health, the human body needs to be physically active.

In the old days, people did not need to exercise because the tasks of daily living kept them active. In contrast, today we can drive to work or to run errands, sit in a chair to perform our jobs, shop and play games on our computers, use elevators and escalators to transport our bodies, and even use remote-control devices to operate the appliances in our homes. Physical education is no longer a required daily curriculum for many children, and stationary, technology-driven activities are often children's choice for play instead of physical outdoor games.

All of this technology means that something we used to take for granted, like walking around each day to complete our tasks or even to have fun and play, is no longer an essential part of our lives. Instead, we need to plan for movement. We need to brainstorm strategies to stay active. All of this inactivity has contributed to weight gain. When the inactivity is combined with easy-to-grab calorie-rich foods, even more weight gain is the result.

Exposure to Toxins

Another aspect of modern living that makes it difficult to support health is that we are exposed to environmental toxins, including numerous carcinogens. Cigarette smoke, air pollution, and other harmful chemicals in our air, water, and food supply undermine our well-being. They have also been proven in scientific studies to be harmful to both human health and to the environment.

ALERT!

Chemicals and other toxins in our water, air, buildings, and food supply are impossible to avoid completely. Although you cannot totally control the environment you live in, you can do your part to work actively toward your health. Your personal efforts to promote your own health can make a powerful difference in spite of your environment.

Mental Stress

One of the most prominent features of modern living is the difficulty of escaping the mental stresses of daily life. Technology continues to drive the pace of work and living to faster and faster speeds. The cost of living, the pressure of competition for material wealth, and the challenge of balancing family, professional, and community ties all contribute to increasing daily pressures. Finding time to relax, unwind, and savor simple pleasures becomes a rare treat.

In addition to the specific stress-related disorders that this daily pressure causes, stress makes it all the more challenging to actively pursue healthy eating and activity habits. At the end of a long, hard day, it's much easier to grab a fast snack, sit on the couch, and do what you need to do to get through the rest of the day. It takes much more discipline and motivation to spend time meal-planning, shopping carefully, strategizing on how to be more active, and creating time to relax in refreshing and restorative ways.

So what do you do? Start educating yourself about what a healthy lifestyle requires and the rewards and benefits of the extra effort that it is going to take. Start acknowledging that, all things being equal, it is more difficult to live a life that nurtures and supports your health. Be patient and gentle with yourself, and congratulate yourself for taking any time and making any effort in the direction you want to go.

Every step that you take toward positive living is good and valuable. Appreciate that it is challenging to create your healthy life, but know it is more than worthwhile to get pleasure from many years of feeling great, having energy, enjoying life, and being at your best.

The Process of Change

As you get ready to embark on your own path toward healthful living, it is useful to familiarize yourself with the process of change. In the field of behavioral medicine, researchers are examining how to support the process of change toward more positive habits. As it became more and more evident that people have all the information that they need to know that they should be eating more fruits and vegetables and exercising more regularly, the question for scientists then became, "Why aren't more people doing it?" Researchers realized that changing behaviors is a very difficult task, and they sought to understand how to improve the process to maximize people's odds of success.

A leading behavioral scientist, James Prochaska, Ph.D., along with Carlo DiClemente, Ph.D., developed a psychological model for behavioral change that divides the course of action into five stages of readiness that are very useful for analysis. Understanding this progression can help you to be successful in achieving your goal to living a healthier lifestyle. The five stages include precontemplation, contemplation, preparation, action, and maintenance.

These phases are meant to describe the process of becoming more ready for change and, therefore, of being more likely to succeed. In other words, you must become truly ready and motivated to change a behavior first, before you start to take action. And, if the process is cultivated in that order—motivation first, action second—the odds of ultimate success in achieving the lifestyle changes are much higher.

FACT

Not all people follow a linear path on the road to change. For example, a person may progress to the action stage and then return to the contemplation stage. What is important is that you continue to try—don't let your setbacks become permanent.

Precontemplation

Congratulations! Anyone who is reading this book has already progressed beyond the precontemplation stage. A person in the precontemplation stage is not making any behavioral changes and does not intend to make any changes. A person at this stage is not motivated and does not have the tools and information necessary to make a positive change. This person feels that it is easier to stay in his or her situation and even risk poor health and a shorter life than it is to make any changes. You may have friends or loved ones who are at this level.

Contemplation

In the contemplation stage, a person knows that it is better to live a healthier lifestyle. Although the person is thinking about it, he or she has not yet taken any action toward making this change a reality. During this stage, a person is engaged in information-gathering and weighing the pros and cons of taking any action. This person has not yet made any commitment to change but is instead just thinking about it. This, however, is a very important stage.

If you feel that you are in the contemplation stage, then you are doing exactly the right thing by reading and learning more about the benefits of making positive modifications toward a healthier lifestyle.

QUESTION?

How can I help friends or loved ones who are in the contemplation stage?

The best way to provide support is to share information about specific benefits that come with adopting healthier behaviors. For example, tell them that a person who starts a moderate exercise program will sleep better at night and have more energy during the day. These are usually benefits everyone can relate to and wants to enjoy.

Preparation

People who are in the preparation stage have already started taking small steps toward acquiring new, healthy habits. For example, if a person wants to be more active, she has gone out and bought a new pair of walking shoes. Or, if a person wants to eat more healthfully, he has purchased a book such as this one, full of heart-healthy recipes and tips for incorporating better snacking habits.

The best way to help someone who is in the preparation phase is to provide support and encouragement to continue to take action. Keep visual cues and props in obvious places. For example, post pictures of fruits, vegetables, and whole grains on the refrigerator or pictures of fit and healthy role models. Keep workout equipment, such as shoes, both at home and in the office as reminders. Persist in learning about all the benefits that can be derived from eating nutritious foods, staying active, managing stress, and feeling your best.

Action

In the action stage, things start to get exciting. This is the first six-month period of starting up a new exercise program, following a new eating pattern, or of integrating new methods of relaxation into your day. Studies show that it typically takes two months to develop a new habit, and that as many as 50 percent of people who start a new program drop out within the first six months. Strategies to make it through the first six months include eliciting support from friends, family, and coworkers or keeping useful reminders to continue doing your new routines and practices in places that you look frequently.

Maintenance

The ideal conclusion to a concentrated effort in making a behavioral change is to reach the maintenance phase. In the example of incorporating regular activity, a person gets to the maintenance phase when she has been exercising regularly for at least six months. The odds of giving up this new habit after that length of time are low. The behavior becomes self-motivating because it is easy to feel the benefits and rewards of the healthy activity. It's still important to incorporate fun and different activities to keep motivation levels high, but the longer the behavior is continued the less and less likely it is going to be dropped.

Dealing with Relapse

As the saying goes, humans are creatures of habit. Change is not easy. Relapsing is a normal part of the process. In fact, studies show that people who ultimately succeed in quitting smoking usually have tried to quit at least three times.

Approach the process of change as a learning experience. With every step forward, figure out what worked. With every step backward, rather than beating yourself up, try to determine why that backward step occurred. If you approach transformation of your habits as a journey and as a self-learning adventure, you are likely to be more successful. Remember to forgive yourself and keep right on going.

Your new health practices, such as eating a piece of fruit for breakfast or completing a set of push-ups in the morning, are not burdensome "problems" or "prescriptive medicines." View them as solutions that will improve your life, not another duty to add to your list of chores.

Find ways to incorporate healthy habits that work for you so that you will continue to do them. For example, if you don't care for raisins, don't plan to eat them on your oatmeal every morning for breakfast. It will feel like taking a nasty medicine that you hate. Instead, find something that you like to eat that is also good for you and plan to include more of it in your diet.

If you find that you need someone to help keep you accountable with your diet or in a regular exercise program, consult a registered dietitian or hire a personal trainer to work with on a regular basis. Don't set yourself up to fail. Set yourself up to win. Don't punish yourself. Reward yourself. Find solutions that work and make you feel good about you.

Believe in Yourself

Another important concept that researchers have determined is fundamental to successful change is how much you believe in your own ability to achieve it. Self-confidence is important. The more you believe that you can be successful, the more likely you will be successful. In contrast, if you see yourself as a person who simply can't eat nutritious foods or who can't possibly find time to move around more during the day, then it will be true for you. Your perception of yourself is powerful.

Furthermore, the power of your belief in yourself is behavior-specific. For example, you may be very confident that you can walk at least thirty minutes a day on most days of the week. At the same time, you may be very unsure of the fact that you can eat more vegetables and less candy every day. You need to build your confidence in each particular area that you want to succeed. Also, you need to believe that you can achieve the goals that you set for yourself.

ALERT!

Studies show that if you engage in behaviors that promote health, you can add as much as twenty years to the length of your life. This holds true even if you start incorporating more healthy behaviors at the age of fifty.

Identify Your Priorities

Here's an interesting exercise that helps you to get in touch with what really matters in your life. Take a few moments to write down the top five things that are important to you. Examples of items you may want to include might be your family, health, community, profession, a hobby, political causes, or volunteer work. Then, on the same piece of paper, list the top five activities that take up most of your time in an average day. Note the percentage of your waking time that they require.

Take a moment to compare how you spend your time each day with what you value most importantly in your life. Have you found a good match? Or have you realized that you are neglecting some things that are very important to you? Once you increase your awareness of the way you are spending your time versus the way you *want* to spend your time, you can start making a difference. As you bring your unconscious habits and behavior patterns out into the open, you can begin realistically to assess small steps that you can take toward your new goals.

For example, if you realize that you are spending three hours each day watching television and no time walking or participating in any other type of moderate physical activity, you can see that there is some time in your day that you can carve out to use for exercising. If you really can't give up your television time, then consider ways to do some exercises as you watch your favorite programs. Then, try to do this at least four days a week.

Enjoy the Rewards of Your Effort

Last, but certainly not least, remember to reward yourself for your good behavior. For example, promise yourself that if you stick to your new eating plan or exercise schedule for four consecutive weeks, you will reward yourself with a nice massage, or buy yourself some new exercise clothing.

Living in a time when we can strive to optimize our health is truly a privilege. When you move about, be aware of the joy of experiencing the sensation of your muscles in action. As you eat a dish of fresh foods, savor the flavors, colors, aroma, and textures that whole foods add to your dining pleasure. And as you feel stronger, more energetic, and simply more alive, know that it is the direct result of your efforts to create a healthy life. You can do it—just keep believing in yourself and in your worth—because you *are* worth it.

Chapter 8

Healthy Nutrition to Improve Cholesterol Levels

What you put in your body directly creates your health. Dietary factors are associated with four of the ten leading causes of death in the United States: coronary heart disease, stroke, Type 2 diabetes, and certain cancers. The foods you eat can increase or decrease your risk of heart disease, disability, and death. A diet that contributes to atherosclerosis is a major, modifiable risk factor, which means that you can make a powerful difference simply by choosing good foods.

Dietary Guidelines for Better Health

In 2000, the American Heart Association issued dietary guidelines to help people follow eating and lifestyle habits to reduce the risk of cardiovascular disease. (These guidelines replace the organization's old "Step 1" and "Step 2" dietary recommendations.) In the 2000 guidelines, the American Heart Association strongly endorses "consumption of a diet that contains a variety of foods from all the food categories and emphasizes fruits and vegetables; fat-free and low-fat dairy products; cereal and grain products; legumes and nuts; and fish, poultry, and lean meats." Researchers agree that food-based guidelines are more practical and easier to understand than those that focus on counting calories, fat, or cholesterol.

FACT

The six major food groups include milk, yogurt, and cheese; meats, poultry, fish, dry beans, eggs, and nuts; vegetables; fruits; bread, cereal, rice, and pasta; and fats, oils, and sweets. Within each food group, the goal is to select a variety of foods to ensure that you get all the essential nutrients that you need.

The American Heart Association guidelines recommend the following foods:

✓ Five servings of fruits and vegetables a day

✓ Six servings of grains a day

✓ Two servings of fatty fish per week

✓ Include fat-free and low-fat dairy products

✓ Include legumes (beans)

✓ Include poultry

✓ Include lean meats

These guidelines are meant to emphasize the importance of choosing an overall balanced diet with foods from all major food groups, especially fruits, vegetables, and grains. In addition to including the recommended number of servings of the first three types of foods, include balanced amounts of the other foods listed in your meal choices.

The above guidelines are appropriate for everyone age two years and older. Laying the foundation for healthy eating patterns in children is critically important in helping them build healthy habits and in preventing the development of diseases later in life.

Benefits of a Dietary Pattern for Health

After years of research, specialists are fitting together the puzzle pieces of what constitutes an eating pattern ideally suited to optimizing health. When scientists first began investigating the causes of heart disease, fats were identified as an enemy. However, as more and more research studies have determined, the picture is more complex than that. A diet that is higher in fat is actually the primary eating pattern of some of the people with the lowest rates of heart disease. The difference is that the fats include heart-protective vegetable fats. Recognizing the benefits of this style of eating, known as the "Mediterranean diet," represents a landmark change in the thinking about dietary effects on blood lipids. Researchers today support the concept that a primarily plant-based diet, including vegetable oils and fatty fish, is optimal for supporting health.

The Mediterranean Diet

Researchers became intrigued by the diet of southern Europeans (those who live near the Mediterranean) when they realized that people from this area enjoyed a very low incidence of heart disease and tended to live longer than North Americans and northern Europeans. The Mediterranean diet is characterized by a high intake of fruits and vegetables, nuts and cereals, and olive oil. In addition, fish and dairy products and wine with meals are regular features. In contrast, the amount of meat and poultry consumed is minimal.

Studies have shown that people placed on a Mediterranean diet can lower their chances of having another heart attack by as much as 67 percent. In another study published in the *New England Journal of Medicine* in 2003, investigators evaluated 22,000 Greek adults over approximately four years and rated the degree to which the participants followed a Mediterranean diet. Scientists found that people who followed the Mediterranean diet closely were 33 percent less likely to die from heart disease and 24 percent less likely to die from cancer when compared to those who did not adhere to a Mediterranean diet. Clearly, these dietary measures had a strong impact on the subjects' risk of heart disease.

Lessons learned from the Mediterranean diet and other healthy eating patterns in various cultures have changed the focus from particular nutrients (such as fat) to an approach that embraces a generalized pattern of food choices.

These studies confirm the power of dietary influences on heart health. What is even more interesting is that when the dietary components are examined, researchers have found that there is no single element that creates the health-enhancing effects. Instead, it's the combination of the foods in the dietary pattern as a whole.

The Dietary Approaches to Stop Hypertension (DASH) Diet

The DASH Study is another significant investigation that supports the value of a diet emphasizing plant-based foods as a way of reducing the risks of high blood pressure, a form of heart disease. Researchers divided study participants into three groups: a control group; a group that ate a lot of fruits and vegetables; and a combination diet group that ate a lot of fruits and vegetables along with low-fat dairy products.

Investigators found that reductions in blood pressure among the combination diet group were as strong as any single medication. While participants in the fruit and veggie group did experience modest blood pressure reductions, it was not nearly as significant as those who also got calcium and other minerals from the dairy products. Members of the combination diet group also reduced their LDL cholesterol levels 9 percent more than people in the control group. In other words, the risk of heart disease could be reduced through dietary factors alone—not through supplements or any individual magic food, but rather through a dietary pattern that focused on a variety of whole, fresh foods that included calcium-rich foods.

Risks of Animal-Based and Processed Foods

To achieve healthy cholesterol levels, the first course of action is to avoid foods with components that elevate LDL cholesterol. This priority comes from the evidence that high total cholesterol and high LDL cholesterol levels increase the risk for heart disease and stroke and that lowering LDL cholesterol levels reduces these risks.

FACT

Food components from animal-based and processed foods that you should limit or avoid include the following: saturated fatty acids, trans-unsaturated fatty acids, and (to a lesser extent) cholesterol.

Saturated Fatty Acids

There is a direct relationship between the increased intake of saturated fatty acids, often called saturated fats, and an increase in LDL cholesterol levels. Saturated fatty acids are found in animal-based foods such as meats and dairy products. Steaks and chops, hamburger, sausage, processed meats such as lunchmeat, hot dogs, or salami, and fatty cuts of meat are all common sources of saturated fats, as is the skin on poultry. Dairy products that are rich in saturated fat include cheese, butter, whole milk, 2-percent milk, ice cream, cream, and whole-milk yogurt. Plant-based foods do not contain any saturated fat.

For those who do not have heart disease or high levels of LDL cholesterol, the American Heart Association recommends that saturated fat intake represent less than 10 percent of total calories per day. For those who know they have cardiovascular disease or who do have high LDL cholesterol, the recommendation for daily consumption of saturated fat is much lower, less than 7 percent of total calories. If you have a known disease or health condition, be sure to work closely with your health-care provider or a registered dietitian to create individualized nutritional guidelines for your personal situation.

The following steps show an example of how a person without high cholesterol levels might determine their recommended daily amount of saturated fat. In this example, assume a daily recommended intake of calories, based on activity and metabolic needs, of roughly 2,000 calories per day.

1. Calculate the total number of calories from saturated fat, at less than 10 percent of total calories per day, as follows:

   $$10 \text{ percent (or .10) x 2,000 calories} = 200$$

2. Next, calculate the total grams of saturated fat, at less than 10 percent of total calories per day, with the following formula:

   $$200 \text{ calories from saturated fat} \div 9 \text{ calories per gram} = 22.22$$

This person should consume less than 22 grams of total saturated fat per day.

The following steps show how to determine calories and grams for a diet with less than 7 percent of saturated fat. This example would apply to a person with cardiovascular disease or high cholesterol levels and again assumes a diet of 2,000 calories per day.

1. Calculate the total number of calories from saturated fat, at less than 7 percent of total calories per day, as follows:

   $$7 \text{ percent (or .07) x 2,000 calories} = 140$$

2. Next, calculate the total grams of saturated fat, at less than 7 percent of total calories per day, with the following formula:

   $$140 \text{ calories from saturated fat} \div 9 \text{ calories per gram} = 15.55$$

This person should consume less than 16 grams of total saturated fat per day.

To see how those figures apply to a serving of real food, here's the breakdown for a cheeseburger. A three-ounce hamburger patty has approximately 7 grams of saturated fat. A one-ounce piece of cheddar cheese has 6 grams of saturated fat. One tablespoon of mayonnaise has approximately 2 grams of saturated fat. So far, this hamburger contains 15 grams of saturated fat, and we're not even finished putting it together! When you break down the numbers, it's easy to see how saturated fat grams add up quickly if you eat a lot of meat and dairy foods.

ALERT!

The current consumption of saturated fats in the average American diet is 13 percent of total calories, in excess of the current recommendations for health.

Since it is difficult or nearly impossible to analyze every bite of food that you put in your mouth, a good rule of thumb for limiting saturated fats in your diet is simply to reduce the amount of animal-based foods that you eat. See Chapter 9 for specific strategies to help reduce your intake of animal-based foods. When you choose more plant-based foods, you will naturally eat less animal-based foods. Plus, living without all those calculations is certainly easier and makes mealtime a lot more pleasant.

Trans-unsaturated Fatty Acids

Trans-unsaturated fatty acids, often referred to as trans-fats, are more harmful to your health than saturated fats. As with saturated fats, there is a direct relationship between an increased intake of trans-fats and an increase in LDL cholesterol levels. Additionally, a direct relationship exists between increased consumption of trans-fats and a reduction in HDL levels. Therefore, a diet high in trans-fats does double damage, first by increasing your levels of bad cholesterol and second by simultaneously reducing your levels of good cholesterol.

Trans-fats are primarily found in commercially processed foods such as pies, doughnuts, cookies, chips, candy, pastries, shortening, and fried fast foods. Food manufacturers create trans-fats through a process called hydrogenation that converts otherwise liquid oils into a more solid substance. This hydrogenation is useful to food manufacturers because it increases the shelf life of foods, adds form to otherwise liquid substances, and adds flavor. Studies, however, have confirmed that there is no level of consumption of trans-fats that is considered to be safe.

According to a report by the Institute of Medicine, a nonprofit organization chartered by the National Academy of Sciences, there is a direct relationship between the consumption of trans-fatty acids and an increase in total cholesterol and LDL levels. This means that consuming trans-fatty acids increases the risk of coronary heart disease and should therefore be avoided. However, the National Academy of Sciences recognizes that it is almost impossible to completely avoid trans-fatty acids in foods available to us today, and recommends that trans-fatty acid consumption be as low as possible as part of a nutritious diet.

Research supporting the fact that there are no safe levels of trans-fats in the diet is so strong that the U.S. Food and Drug Administration has instituted a food labeling requirement for trans-fats that will be effective in 2006. Food manufacturers will be required to list the amount of trans-fats per serving in any food product.

FACT

In 2006, updated food labels will spell out the amount of trans-fats in addition to the total fats and saturated fats that are already listed. The labeling rules, however, do not require that trace amounts of trans-fat, considered to be less than 0.5 grams per serving, be listed on the label.

The good news is that food manufacturers are getting involved and responding to the evidence that these fats are so harmful to health. PepsiCo, one of the world's largest producers of commercial foods and beverages, has undertaken an initiative to eliminate trans-fats from its snack products, which include popular lines such as Frito-Lay chips, Doritos, Lays, Ruffles, Cheetos, and Cracker Jack snacks, among others.

Kenneth Cooper, M.D., M.P.H., founder of the Cooper Clinic in Dallas, Texas, and father of the "aerobics" movement, has been working together with PepsiCo. "Trans-fats have been found to increase the most harmful type of LDL cholesterol, the small dense particle LDL, and there is a direct increase in the risk of heart attack with the increased consumption of trans-fats," says Dr. Cooper. "We must attack all trans-fats in the diet. These products will hit the markets in 2004 and reduce the intake of trans-fats around the world by millions of pounds annually."

As food manufacturers and distributors become more aware that we care about the health of our food choices, more healthful products will be made available. Vote with your dollars, and choose health and vitality. The length and quality of your life depend on it.

For the healthiest choices, instead of choosing snack foods with or without trans-fats, choose minimally processed, whole-food snacks. This choice ensures that you will receive fiber, vitamins, minerals, and nutrients that all enhance health.

Cholesterol from Animal-Based Foods

Just as the cells in the human body contain cholesterol, so do the cells of all other animals. Plants and plant-based foods, however, contain no cholesterol. A good rule of thumb to remember is that many foods that are high in saturated fats are also high in cholesterol. Cholesterol-rich foods include organ meats (such as liver), certain shellfish, poultry, dairy products, and eggs. A recent study, however, showed that consumption of one egg per day by a person who does not have known cardiovascular disease or elevated lipid levels did not contribute to elevated blood cholesterol levels.

Eating foods high in cholesterol can increase LDL cholesterol levels, but not nearly as much as eating foods high in saturated fats and trans-fats can. In other words, you will improve your cholesterol levels more by cutting down on foods high in saturated and trans-fats than by reducing consumption of foods that contain cholesterol.

The American Heart Association guidelines recommend an average daily consumption of dietary cholesterol of less than 300 mg for healthy people. For people who know they have cardiovascular disease, diabetes, or elevated lipid levels, the recommendation is less than 200 mg. Currently, the average daily consumption of dietary cholesterol in the United States today is 256 mg. The amount consumed among men is slightly higher, at 331 mg, than it is for women, at 213 mg. Therefore, the current average consumption of cholesterol-rich foods among healthy Americans is at appropriate levels to support health.

Foods to Choose for a Healthy Heart	
Foods to Choose More Often	**Foods to Choose Less Often**
Breads and Cereals (6 servings or less per day, adjusted to caloric needs)	
Whole-grain breads, cereals, and pasta	Bakery products made with refined flour (doughnuts, croissants, sweet rolls, Danish)
Brown rice	Cakes, pies, coffee cakes, cookies
Potatoes	biscuits, butter rolls, muffins
Dry beans and peas	—
Whole-grain crackers	Processed and refined grain-based snacks (chips, cheese puffs, snack mix, regular crackers, buttered popcorn)
Vegetables (3–5 servings per day)	
Fresh, frozen, or canned vegetables without added fat, sauce, or salt	Vegetables fried or prepared with butter, cheese, or cream sauce
Fruits (2–4 servings per day)	
Fresh, frozen, canned, dried fruits, without added sugars	Canned fruits packed in heavy syrups
Dairy Products (2–3 servings per day)	
Fat-free, ½-percent, 1-percent milk, buttermilk, yogurt, cottage cheese	Whole milk, 2-percent milk, whole-milk whole-milk yogurt
Fat-free and low-fat cheese	Regular ice cream, cream, cheese
Eggs* (no more than 2 egg yolks per week)	
Egg whites or egg substitute	Egg yolks, whole eggs

Foods to Choose for a Healthy Heart *(continued)*	
Foods to Choose More Often	**Foods to Choose Less Often**
Meat, Poultry, Fish (5 ounces or less per day)	
Lean cuts of vegetarian-fed meats	Higher-fat meat cuts from animals fed animal-based foods
Loin, leg, round	Ribs, T-bone steak, bacon
Extra-lean hamburger	Regular hamburger
Cold cuts made with lean meat or soy protein	Cold cuts, salami, bologna, hot dogs, sausage
Skinless grain-fed poultry	Poultry with skin
—	Organ meats (liver, brains, sweetbreads)
Wild fish	Fried fish
Fats and Oils (amount adjusted to caloric needs)	
Unsaturated oils	Coconut oil
Soft or liquid margarines	Stick margarine
Vegetable oil spreads	Butter, shortening
Salad dressings, seeds, and nuts	—

*Recommendation for people with elevated lipid levels

Benefits of Plant-Based and Whole Foods

Nutrition experts believe that the best way to achieve a healthy diet is to think in terms of what types of food to eat, rather than what to eliminate. They recommend that you keep in mind that the healthiest diet consists primarily of whole foods from plants, which will lead you to eat lots of grains, nuts, seeds, fruits, and vegetables. Focusing on a plant-based diet does not mean that you have to become a vegetarian. It simply means that the ideal diet to enhance health contains more plant-based than animal-based foods.

Fruits and Vegetables

Studies show that dietary patterns that include a high consumption of fruits and vegetables are associated with lower risks of developing heart disease, stroke, and hypertension. Unlike many high-fat and high-sugar processed foods, fresh fruits and vegetables are nutrient-dense and low in calories. Fruits and vegetables are also high in water content. This helps to maintain adequate hydration levels and contributes to feelings of fullness. This type of eating pattern will provide you with plenty of healthy fiber, essential nutrients, and beneficial phytochemicals and antioxidants.

Phytochemicals are chemicals that give plants colors and assist in keeping the plants healthy. In the same way that they fight disease, oxidation, and inflammation in plants, they can also further human health. Different phytochemicals support heart health through different protective actions. Antioxidants such as certain vitamins, carotenoids, and flavanoids, prevent oxidation and decrease the likelihood of oxidized LDL cholesterol sticking to arterial walls. Recall that when LDL cholesterol is oxidized, it forms arterial plaque (as described in Chapter 1). Vitamins C and E are rich sources of antioxidants. Furthermore, it is preferred to obtain these antioxidants from foods, rather than from supplements.

FACT

Food sources of vitamin C include citrus fruits, tomatoes, kiwi, and broccoli. Vitamin E–rich foods include whole grains, nuts, seeds, avocados, and vegetable oils. Selenium, an antioxidant mineral, is found in grains, seeds, and seafood.

Vegetables and fruits are also a rich source of the B vitamin complex. Folate in particular is essential to health, as it helps to prevent high levels of harmful homocysteine from circulating in the bloodstream and damaging arterial health. Eating foods rich in folate prevents high levels of homocysteine. While it is not yet proven by research that treating elevated homocysteine levels reduces the risk of heart disease, we do know that elevated levels are a marker for increased risk. Foods rich in folate include beans, asparagus, fresh leafy greens, and oranges. Many breakfast cereals are also fortified with B vitamins, including folate, which means that the vitamins have been added to the product during processing.

Other minerals play a valuable role in regulating blood pressure and in keeping blood vessels healthy. Remember that another part of the atherosclerosis picture is that the walls of the blood vessel need to be inflamed or damaged before any arterial plaque can attach to it. Minerals such as calcium, magnesium, and potassium can help to keep these vessel walls healthy. As studies have shown, people who have healthier blood pressure levels tend to eat a diet full of fruits and vegetables that are rich in these nutrients. Food sources of calcium, magnesium, and potassium include artichokes, cantaloupes, broccoli, bananas, cauliflower, bell peppers, and many others.

For maximal nutritional value, be sure to choose food with a variety of flavors and colors. Deep, dark leafy greens and bright yellow and orange vegetables are rich in cancer-fighting antioxidants, as well as essential nutrients.

Whole Grains

Whole grains provide fiber, vitamins, complex carbohydrates, and minerals. Studies show that people who consume more whole grains have a lower risk of heart disease. A whole grain still contains the outer shell, or bran, of the grain and the germ, which would turn into a seedling. Whole grains are superior to processed grains because many nutrients are lost during refining.

When you purchase grain products, look for the terms "whole," "whole wheat," or "whole grain" before the name of the grain in the list of ingredients to ensure that you are getting the best nutritional value for your money. If you must eat processed grains, then be sure to choose those that have been enriched, particularly with B vitamins, to replace those lost during refining.

Diets high in simple carbohydrates, such as white flours and pasta, can lead to elevated triglyceride levels and reduced levels of HDL or good cholesterol. This increases risks for cardiovascular health and explains why dietary recommendations are changing that severely limit fat intake and emphasize high carbohydrates. Importantly, this adverse effect does not occur when the carbohydrates in the diet come from complex carbohydrate sources such as whole grains. Therefore, you should eat whole grains for optimal health and avoid highly refined grains as much as possible.

Since grains are rich in fiber and low in fat, they also contribute to a healthy, lower-calorie diet. Therefore, when you eat the recommended amounts of grains, you feel full without having consumed excess calories. This contrasts greatly to the typical highly processed and refined foods that are quickly digested, high in calories, and do not provide the same feelings of satiety.

Nutrients Found in Whole Foods

When you choose plant-based and whole foods, there are several important nutrients that become part of your diet. These include soluble fiber found in plant-based foods, omega-3 fatty acids found in fish, as well as other important nutrients.

Soluble Fiber

A huge variety of grains contribute to health, not only as a source of vitamins and minerals, but also as a valuable source of complex carbohydrates and soluble fiber. Whole wheat, whole oats, barley, rye, oat bran, rice bran, corn bran, and psyllium seeds all contain soluble fiber. Certain fruits, such as apples, prunes, pears, and oranges, also contain soluble fiber.

Studies show that eating foods that contain soluble fiber can reduce LDL cholesterol levels. In fact, increasing soluble fiber by only 5 to 10 grams per day is shown to reduce LDL cholesterol by as much as 5 percent. Even more significant reductions in cholesterol level can be achieved by increasing the daily intake to 10 to 25 grams per day. Because of this benefit to cholesterol levels, federal government guidelines recommend the use of dietary sources of soluble fiber as a therapeutic option to enhance the reduction of LDL cholesterol for people with high LDL levels.

The reason that soluble fiber helps to lower LDL cholesterol is that it acts much in the same way as prescription bile acid sequestrants. (See

Chapter 18 for more information.) In the intestines, soluble fiber binds with cholesterol, making it unable to be absorbed by the body. The cholesterol is then excreted, forcing the liver to dip into its cholesterol reserves to manufacture more bile acids for digestion, resulting in an overall reduction in cholesterol in the body.

FACT

Eating soluble-fiber–rich foods such as oat products, psyllium seeds, pectin (in apples and other fruit) and guar gum reduces LDL cholesterol, particularly in people with high cholesterol. Studies show that for about each gram of soluble fiber eaten daily, LDL cholesterol drops an average of 2.2 mg/dL. Furthermore, high-fiber diets do not reduce HDL cholesterol or elevate triglycerides.

Omega-3 Polyunsaturated Fatty Acids

Numerous studies indicate the benefit to increasing foods rich in omega-3 fatty acids in the diet in terms of reducing the risk of heart disease. Deep-water fish such as salmon, tuna, herring, and mackerel are particularly good dietary sources of omega-3 fatty acids. The American Heart Association guidelines recommend at least two servings of fish per week. Other plant-based sources include flaxseed and flaxseed oil, canola oil, soybean oil, and nuts.

Studies show that consumption of foods rich in omega-3 fatty acids offers multiple benefits for heart health. Positive effects include reducing triglyceride levels, reducing risk of sudden death, reducing blood-clotting tendencies, improving blood vessel dilation, and lowering the risk of arrhythmia (irregular heartbeat). Another benefit of consuming fish is that fish is a good source of protein that does not contain harmful saturated animal fats. Fish oil also seems to alleviate inflammation and is recommended for people who suffer from joint pain related to arthritis. The reasons behind why these fats produce such beneficial results are unclear.

Eating fish is preferred to consuming fish oil capsules; however, concerns exist about high levels of mercury in fish in today's food supply, making filtered and monitored fish oil capsules a viable alternative.

Other concerns about carcinogens in farmed fish lead some experts to suggest that wild fish may be more healthful.

Soy Protein

Multiple studies show that soy protein, taken daily as part of a diet that is low in saturated animal fats, can lower levels of total cholesterol and LDL cholesterol in people who have high cholesterol levels. The reasons for this result, however, are unclear. A review article of thirty-one studies on soy and cholesterol published in the *New England Journal of Medicine* concluded, "Eating soy in place of animal protein lowers high cholesterol, which may reduce one's risk of heart disease by 10 to 30 percent." Based on these studies, the FDA has approved a health claim on food labels that consuming 25 grams of soy protein daily reduces the risk of heart disease, primarily due to its effect on blood cholesterol.

ALERT!

The beneficial effects of soy protein can be destroyed during food processing. When you purchase soy, read the label carefully. Some food manufacturers wash soybeans in ethanol, and that process removes the beneficial components (the isoflavones) from the soy. Make sure the food producer notes that the soy has been processed with water or in a manner that preserves the original nutrients.

The reason that dietary soy protein is beneficial to health may be that soy is rich in phytoestrogen isoflavones, or plant estrogens, that can have a heart-protective effect similar to human estrogen. The presence of this nutritional quality, however, depends on how the soybean product is processed. Do not purchase products that have been prepared by ethanol washing, as that removes all of the beneficial isoflavones. Instead, choose soy products that have been processed with water.

Soybeans are a good source of vitamins, minerals, protein, and unsaturated fat, and they contain no cholesterol. An additional benefit of consuming soy foods that are rich in soy protein is that these foods can serve to meet protein needs and replace consumption of animal food products that are rich in saturated fats. Nutritionists advise that until we fully understand the health potential of soy protein, it is better to choose soy foods than soy supplements, which only contain part of the soybean, not all the components.

Plant Stanols and Sterols

Studies have revealed even more benefits of plant-based foods by demonstrating the dietary effects of plant sterols. Plant stanols and sterols are components that are isolated from the oil of soybeans and of tall pine trees. They are phytochemicals, or chemicals from plants. These are then added as a supplement to certain foods.

Cholesterol is an animal sterol that serves as an integral part of the structure of cell membranes in animals; plant sterols serve the same role in the cell membranes of plants. Because of their structural similarity to cholesterol, plant sterols and stanols will bind with cholesterol during the digestive process. But their subtle differences from cholesterol keep plant sterols from being easily absorbed through the human intestine. Therefore, if a plant sterol binds with cholesterol, it effectively blocks the absorption of that cholesterol through the intestine and promotes its excretion from the body, thus lowering cholesterol levels that circulate in the bloodstream.

Foods on the market today that incorporate these substances include certain margarines, such as Take Control and Benecol, and more recently, Minute Maid orange juice. This practice has given rise to a whole new category of foods known as "functional foods," or foods that have a medical effect. Christopher Gardner, Ph.D., Nutrition Studies Director at the Stanford Prevention Research Center, points out, however, that we need to think carefully about whether to add individual foods into our diet:

> The potential benefits of this phytochemical must be considered in the context of how it is taken. For example, simply adding margarine to your diet will increase energy intake, lead to weight gain, and eventually more problems than benefits. On the other hand, if an equivalent amount of butter is replaced with these margarines, there is a good likelihood of a net benefit. If you were planning on cutting back on having broccoli for dinner, and were going to replace it with margarine, you'd again be worse off than when you started. The potential benefit, therefore, depends on the context.

Research-based evidence shows that consumption of 2 to 3 grams of plant sterols per day can lower LDL cholesterol by 6 to 15 percent without changing HDL cholesterol or triglyceride levels, although results vary among different individuals. Older adults typically experience more lowering of LDL cholesterol than younger people. To maximize the beneficial LDL lowering effect, the ideal amount of plant sterols in the diet is 2 grams per day.

FACT

Some studies suggest that over periods of at least a year, plant stanol ester spreads are somewhat more effective than plant sterol spreads. In short term studies, both spreads lower cholesterol similarly.

Based on current research, the FDA has authorized the use of a health claim on food labels stating that consuming products that contain plant sterols or stanols reduces cholesterol levels. More research, however, is needed to examine the long-term effect of consumption. Among the concerns related to use of these components is that the sterols and stanols not only block the absorption of cholesterol, but they also seem to reduce absorption of beneficial carotenoids and some fat-soluble vitamins. It is not clear yet whether this can have any adverse effects.

Because of the strength of their positive impact on blood cholesterol, however, federal government guidelines recommend that only people who need to lower their levels of LDL cholesterol for therapeutic reasons should use these products. Consult with your health-care provider if you have any questions about whether foods supplemented with this product would be beneficial to your personal situation.

Monounsaturated Vegetable Fats

Research shows that a diet that includes monounsaturated fats reduces total cholesterol and LDL cholesterol levels and has no effect on good cholesterol levels. Nor does consuming foods rich in monounsaturated fats raise triglycerides. This heart-protective effect of monounsaturated fats is believed to partly explain why people who follow a Mediterranean diet that is rich in olive oil live long and healthy lives.

Monounsaturated fats are liquid at room temperature and include fats from vegetables and nuts. Foods that are rich in monounsaturated fats include nuts, avocados, and plant oils such as olive, canola, and peanut.

Monounsaturated fats found in plant-based foods can replace saturated fats, according to recommendations endorsed by the American Heart Association. The recommended amount of consumption of these plant-based fats can be up to 20 percent of the total calories in the diet.

Polyunsaturated Vegetable Fats

Evidence from research demonstrates that a diet that includes foods rich in polyunsaturated fats reduces LDL cholesterol levels and increases HDL cholesterol levels. Other studies have shown that substituting poly-unsaturated fat reduces the risk of heart disease.

Foods that contain polyunsaturated fatty acids include nuts and seeds and also certain plant oils such as corn, safflower, and soybean. Nuts, seeds, and even fish contain polyunsaturated oils. The American Heart Association endorses guidelines to replace saturated fats with poly-unsaturated fats up to a total of 10 percent of total calories.

Chapter 9

Strategies for Heart-Healthy Eating

Knowing what foods are good for you is only half the story; figuring out how to eat them regularly is the challenging part. Changing your routine is never easy, but you can do it if you keep taking small steady steps. The tips in this chapter will help you to move toward a healthier pattern of eating. Once you start feeling the benefits of enjoying more fresh, wholesome foods, your new habits will be self-reinforcing. Enjoy the process as you travel toward a healthier you.

Eat Healthful Plant-Based Foods

A nutritious diet is one of the single most important keys to creating your long-term health. Poor nutrition is one of the leading causes of heart disease. The old adage, "You are what you eat," is actually quite truthful. Your body derives its nutrients, its building blocks for cellular repair and growth, and its fuel for all activities directly from the food that you consume.

The connection between food and your blood cholesterol levels is direct and powerful. Overconsumption of saturated fats, trans-fats, and cholesterol-rich foods leads to overproduction of LDL cholesterol in the liver and to the release of excess amounts of triglycerides into the bloodstream. Saturated fats and cholesterol are only present in animal foods. Trans-fats are only present in processed, commercial foods (as described in Chapter 8).

When you alter your eating habits to include more plant-based foods and fewer animal based and processed foods, you take a powerful step toward improving the health of your bloodstream. Studies have shown that nutritional factors alone can reduce total blood cholesterol by as much as 30 percent in individuals with high levels of cholesterol. This change is almost as powerful as the best prescription medications. The significant difference is that improvements in nutrition do not have the same risk of adverse side effects as taking a long-term prescriptive drug. Furthermore, it is much more affordable.

FACT

In a Harvard study, increasing cholesterol intake by 200 mg for every 1000 calories in the diet, the rough equivalent of one egg a day, did not appreciably increase the risk for heart disease among over 80,000 healthy female nurses. For those who have diabetes, however, no more than two to three eggs a week are recommended.

Numerous nutritional studies demonstrate that plant-based foods enhance our health, particularly cardiovascular health. The human animal cannot exist without plant foods. While it is possible to live healthfully over a lifetime without any consumption of meat, it is not possible to survive without eating plant-based foods.

Moving away from Meats and Animal Fats

Although researchers have determined that a varied diet of whole fresh foods is the most beneficial to health, you can still enjoy meat as part of a heart-healthy diet. You just need to use it carefully. What you need to focus on is creating dishes from lean cuts of meats and enjoying meats as more of a side dish than a main course. Purchase meats that have been fed grass diets, also called "free range," rather than animal fats and animal by-products.

If you eat a typical fast-food diet, it is challenging to convert to a diet of whole fresh foods. The rest of this chapter will provide you with specific strategies for making this transition as smooth as possible. Keep in mind that a dietary pattern is not a medical prescription. Should you require personal dietary assistance to meet individual needs, have your physician refer you to a registered dietitian in your area. What you eat affects your life in a very intimate way. You need to be able to enjoy your meals and snacks and not feel deprived or punished. Take the time that you need to incorporate healthier foods that you enjoy in order to create lasting changes.

Reducing Saturated Fat in Meats

Eating saturated fats increases the amounts of harmful LDL cholesterol. At the same time, avoiding these foods completely in your diet can help to lower harmful LDL cholesterol levels and reduce your risk of heart disease.

When you prepare meats, try to do so in a manner that reduces rather than increases the amount of fat. For example, baste with wines or marinades and season with herbs; grill or broil meats instead of frying or breading; sauté or brown meats in pans sprayed with vegetable oils. If you are adding meat to other dishes, such as spaghetti, brown it first and pour off the fat before you add it to the sauce. Here are some more preparation tips to reduce saturated fats in meats:

- Trim excess fat from meats.
- Avoid purchasing meats that are marbled with fat.
- Remove skin from poultry.

- Broil, grill, roast, or bake meats on racks that allow fats to drain off.
- Skim fats from tops of stews or casseroles.
- Limit or avoid organ meats, such as livers, brains, sweetbreads, and kidneys.
- Limit or avoid processed meats, such as lunchmeat, salami, bologna, pepperoni, or sausage.
- Serve smaller portions of higher-fat meats.

These preparation tips will not only reduce the harmful saturated fats in your diet, they will also lower the total fat that you consume, which will help you to manage your weight successfully.

Cows are naturally grass-eating animals. Meat from grass-fed cattle has about one-half to one-third the fat as meat from grain-fed cattle. Grass-fed beef is lower in calories, and higher in vitamin E, omega-3 fatty acids, and conjugated linoleic acid, another health-enhancing fatty acid. Ask your grocer for grass-fed or free-range beef.

Lowering Saturated Fats from Dairy Products

While dairy products are a valuable source of calcium and protein, they are not the only sources of these important nutrients. Keep in mind that eating lots of full-fat dairy products increases the levels of saturated fat in your diet, which directly increases your levels of LDL or bad cholesterol. You can still enjoy dairy foods. Simply choose low- or nonfat versions to promote health, and choose milk from dairy cows that have been fed grass diets.

Cheese, in particular, is a very high-fat food, even higher than beef. While an occasional treat of creamy cheeses is not going to harm your overall health, indulging in them regularly will increase your risk of heart disease. Here are some practical tips on lowering the amount of saturated dairy fat in your diet:

- Choose nonfat, ½-percent, or 1-percent milk, preferably from grass-fed cows.

- Select nonfat or low-fat yogurt, sour cream, and cottage and cream cheese.
- Use lower fat cheeses for cooking, such as part-skim mozzarella, ricotta, or Parmesan.
- Enjoy rich, creamy, and hard cheeses on special occasions, not daily.
- Limit the use of butter, and use sparingly.

Check that dairy products come from cows fed grasses and grains rather than meat by-products. Look for other sources of calcium in your diet. Vegetables such as broccoli, chard, greens, and artichokes are all great sources of dietary calcium, as well as calcium-fortified orange juice and some whole-grain cereals. Check the labels.

Avoiding Trans-Fats

Keep in mind that there is no level of consumption of trans-fats that is not harmful to health. These fats increase your LDL cholesterol and decrease your HDL cholesterol levels. Trans-fats are found naturally in some dairy and meat products but most trans-fats in the food supply have been created artificially through a process called hydrogenation. This converts a liquid fat to a solid.

QUESTION?

Why do food manufacturers use hydrogenation?
The benefits to food manufacturers of converting vegetable oils to a solid state is that it gives form to otherwise shapeless foods so that they can be eaten more easily by hand. The process preserves products and extends the shelf life, and it adds flavor. However, manufacturers will soon have to start accounting for the resulting harmful trans-fats on the label.

Trans-fats are abundant in processed foods such as cereals, chips, crackers, stick margarine, shortening, lard, and fast fried foods. Remember that trans-fats can be manufactured from vegetable oils, so simply because a food manufacturer indicates that something is prepared with vegetable oil does not mean that it is trans-fat free.

When reading food labels on items, look for ingredients such as hydrogenated or partially hydrogenated oils. If they are listed, try to avoid using these foods. If you must buy a product with such an ingredient, ensure that the hydrogenated ingredient appears at the end of the ingredient list, indicating that it is present in very low quantities.

While it is likely to be impossible to completely eliminate trans-fats from your diet, you can take the following positive steps to reduce the amounts you consume:

- Avoid or reduce intake of commercially prepared baked goods such as cakes and cookies, snack foods, processed foods, and fast foods.
- Select liquid vegetable oils that contain no trans-fats.
- Read margarine labels carefully, and avoid those that contain hydrogenated oils.
- Avoid cooking with lard, shortening, or stick margarine; use vegetable sprays or tub margarine made without trans-fats.

For everything that you remove from your diet, you need to introduce something else to replace it. Start by making small changes in your eating habits. Over time, move slowly away from a diet that revolves around animal-based foods, such as meat and dairy products, toward a diet that consists primarily of plant-based foods and fish.

Reduce Intake of Dietary Cholesterol

Dietary cholesterol does not elevate blood cholesterol levels as much as saturated fat. For most people, excess dietary cholesterol is not an issue. The largest source of dietary cholesterol in America is eggs. Studies show that in healthy individuals, consuming one egg per day did not lead to elevated cholesterol levels. If, however, you think that you may be overeating cholesterol, here are some tips on how to reduce your dietary intake:

- Do not eat more than one egg per day, or eat one egg yolk with two egg whites.
- Purchase eggs from chickens raised on a vegetarian diet rather than animal fats and animal by-products.

- Read egg carton labels and compare brands to purchase the most nutritious eggs.
- Cook with egg whites only, use egg substitutes, or use one egg yolk for every two egg whites.
- Limit intake of shellfish high in cholesterol, such as shrimp, abalone, crayfish, and squid. (Other forms of shellfish are not excessively high in cholesterol and provide valuable nutrients.)

Increasing Vegetables and Fruits

As you reduce the amount of meat you consume, gradually increase the amount of vegetables. Over time, your taste buds will evolve, and you will enjoy more of the subtle flavors of vegetables and fruits. Your meals will be equally tasty, more colorful, and will include more fiber and plant-based nutrients. This not only reduces your risk of heart disease but also reduces your risk for certain types of cancer.

Try to incorporate fruits or vegetables at every meal and as snacks. Reduce the amount of meat or chicken in typical combination dishes. For example, in spaghetti, reduce the amount of beef or substitute ground turkey. Then increase the vegetable content in your sauces by adding more mushrooms, green peppers, celery, and carrots.

Here are some more tips on how to include more vegetables in your daily diet:

- At breakfast, slice half a banana or toss some berries or raisins on your cereal.
- Add frozen fruits such as berries or peaches to hot cereals.
- For a mid-morning snack, try chopped carrots and celery with a glass of fresh vegetable juice.
- At meals, serve larger portions of vegetables, or prepare multiple vegetable dishes, and have meat as a side dish.
- Prepare meats with fruit toppings or marinades instead of butter.
- Enjoy fruit-based desserts such as poached pears, baked apples, or fresh fruit sorbets.

- Buy packaged, prewashed, and sliced veggies to pack as snacks or to eat at lunch.
- Eat fresh whole fruits that are in season as snacks.
- Add vegetables such as peas or beans into rice or pasta dishes.
- Incorporate multiple vegetables into salads in addition to lettuce.
- Enjoy a smoothie made with fruits or vegetables as a snack.

Keep in mind that all these fruits and vegetables add up to less weight, less disease, less disability, more energy, and a healthy, glowing appearance.

Fruits and vegetables are a great source of fiber, and they contain both soluble and insoluble fiber. Soluble fiber that's part of a healthy diet can reduce blood cholesterol levels. Some fruits and vegetables that contain soluble fiber, in addition to numerous other beneficial nutrients, include apples with peels, oranges, figs, prunes, peas, broccoli, and carrots.

Enjoying Whole Grains

Whole-grain foods are minimally processed and therefore rich in vitamins, minerals, and fiber. Grains include whole wheat, brown rice, barley, rye, oatmeal, and corn. Whole grains provide complex carbohydrates that are essential for energy and vitamins A and E, magnesium, calcium, and other important nutrients. These fiber-rich foods contain both soluble and insoluble fiber, but mostly contain insoluble fiber, which aids digestion, keeps your colon healthy, and makes you feel full, helping with weight management. Processed grains, in contrast, are simple carbohydrates and have lost many of the nutrients and the fiber.

Oatmeal that contains oat bran is a rich source of soluble fiber that can help to lower cholesterol levels. Food manufacturers often remove the oat bran in the instant-cook varieties. Be sure to purchase whole oats or oat bran to obtain the cholesterol-lowering results.

Ideally, you should eat six servings of grains per day. Here are some tips to add more whole grains into your daily diet:

- Include a grain-based food at every meal.
- Try whole-grain rolls, breadsticks, and muffins for snacks.
- Purchase whole-grain crackers for meals or snacks.
- Enjoy rice cakes or popcorn that does not include trans-fats for snacks.
- Prepare desserts with fruits and whole grains, such as apple crisp.
- Sprinkle wheat germ into your cereals or smoothies.
- Use whole-grain tortillas or pita breads to make healthy chips for dips or salsas.

FACT

Whole oats are a rich source of soluble fiber. Studies show that consuming 10 to 25 grams of soluble fiber per day can lower cholesterol by 10 percent. Portions that contain as little as 5 to 10 grams of soluble fiber can lower LDL cholesterol by as much as 5 percent. Three-quarters of a cup of uncooked oatmeal or half a cup of oat bran contains 3 grams of soluble fiber.

Increasing Good Fats—Vegetable Oils, Nuts, and Fish

Research shows that the type of fats that you eat strongly affect your cholesterol levels. While saturated and trans-fats increase your LDL or bad cholesterol, unsaturated fats (including monounsaturated fats and polyunsaturated fats) actually reduce levels of bad cholesterol and increase levels of good cholesterol. Unsaturated fats are found in plant-based products such as most vegetable oils, nuts, seeds, and whole grains. The one nonplant source of these good fats is deep-water or fatty fish, which is a rich source of polyunsaturated fat.

Dietary fat is not the "enemy." Clearly, heart-protective unsaturated fats play an important part in a healthy diet. The key is to try to be careful what *type* of fat you eat—reduce saturated fats, eliminate trans-fats, and then replace those fats with unsaturated fats in the diet. Historically, dietary guidelines have recommended a fat intake of between 20 and 30 percent. However, with this new knowledge of the benefits of unsaturated fats, this recommendation is now increased to up to 30-percent fat intake by experts who recommend consumption of heart-healthy fats.

Here are some tips on how to incorporate unsaturated fats into your daily diet:

- Cook with unsaturated liquid vegetable oils such as olive, canola, or safflower oil.
- Buy tub or liquid margarines with an unsaturated vegetable oil, such as soybean oil, as the first ingredient.
- Throw a few nuts or sesame seeds into your morning cereal
- Spread natural peanut butter on celery sticks or green peppers for a healthy snack.
- Dip bread in limited amounts of olive oil instead of spreading on butter.

Polyunsaturated fats are oils that remain liquid regardless of temperature. Corn, safflower, sunflower, sesame, cottonseed, and soybean oils are all polyunsaturated fats. Deep-water fish also contains polyunsaturated fat.

Monounsaturated fats are oils that solidify at cold temperatures. Olive, canola, peanut, most other nuts, and avocado oils are all monounsaturated fats. Foods that contain monounsaturated fats include almonds, cashews, peanuts, and walnuts.

Omega-3 Fatty Acids

Another important heart health benefit is found in polyunsaturated fats that include omega-3 (linolenic) and omega-6 (linoleic) fatty acids. Researchers have found that omega-3 fatty acids have an anti-inflammatory effect. They also reduce the likelihood of forming blood clots, help blood vessels to relax or dilate, and can lower levels of LDL cholesterol. The primary source of omega-3 fatty acids is fish. Fish that come from cold, deep water are the best source of omega-3s. The American Heart Association recommends eating fatty fish at least twice a week. More recent information, however, about high mercury levels in fish and high carcinogen levels in farmed fish have caused concern, so be careful about the fish you buy. Wild fish are often safer than farmed fish.

Flaxseed and Flaxseed Oil

Flaxseed also contains high levels of omega-3 fatty acids, and does not present the same mercury or carcinogenic concerns as fish. Using flaxseed, however, requires some care. Flaxseed must be ground up in order for the body to absorb the oils, and it cannot be cooked as heat will destroy the oils.

You can also take fish oil supplements. A dose of about 4 grams of fish oil is considered beneficial. Finding high-quality supplements, however, is always a concern. Search for those from highly reputable producers that affirm that the oils have been filtered for toxins such as mercury.

If you decide to add flaxseed into your diet, be sure to grind them before you eat them. Ground flaxseed can be sprinkled on cereal. Remember to store flaxseed in the refrigerator so the oil does not go rancid. If you purchase flaxseed oil, you can use it in salad dressings or on pasta, but do not cook with it. Based on results from research studies, the best amount to consume to achieve cholesterol-lowering results is 50 grams per day.

Raise a Glass to the Benefits of Moderate Drinking

Excessive drinking of alcohol is never a good practice. Heavy drinking can lead to high blood pressure and heart rhythm problems, as well as liver damage. For women, studies show that alcohol intake increases the risk of breast cancer. According to government statistics, up to 10 percent of U.S. adults misuse alcohol. Abstention from alcohol is the best practice for people who cannot enjoy it in moderation.

For those, however, who can enjoy alcoholic beverages in moderation, studies show that alcohol consumption is associated with a lower risk of death from heart disease. The amount of alcohol that confers this benefit is in the low to moderate range. A moderate amount is defined as no more than one drink per day for women and no more than two drinks per day for men. The reason for the difference between men and women is that men are generally assumed to be larger. Four to five drinks per day are considered excessive or heavy drinking.

Interestingly, research shows that moderate alcohol drinking confers moderate benefits upon young, middle-aged, and older adults. Scientists have not identified the precise reasons why moderate alcohol consumption reduces the risk of heart disease. Some experts theorize that it may be because it increases HDL cholesterol. Furthermore, the benefits occur regardless of which alcoholic beverage is consumed. It is simply the ethanol in the alcohol that provides the positive results.

FACT

One drink is equal to five ounces of wine, twelve ounces of beer, or an ounce and a half of eighty-proof whiskey. For heart health benefits, consume drinks with meals. No one should begin drinking alcoholic beverages if they do not already drink alcohol.

For wine enthusiasts, the news is even better. In addition to the HDL-raising benefits of alcohol, red wine also contains phytochemicals. These are plant-based chemicals that provide health benefits when consumed. The grape skins used in making red wine are full of compounds known as flavonoids. Flavonoids are known to help prevent LDL cholesterol from oxidizing and turning into the kind of litter that may adhere to arterial walls. Flavonoids also prevent blood clots, further reducing risk of a heart attack or stroke.

How to Read Food Labels

Eating right can help you to feel better, have more energy, manage your weight more effectively, and help you to live a longer life with less risk of disability and disease. You know that you want to decrease the saturated fats, trans-fats, and simple sugars in your diet and increase the mono- and polyunsaturated fats, whole foods, and complex carbohydrates.

But where do you begin? First, you need to understand how to read food labels. Next, you need some tips for navigating the aisles of your favorite grocery store.

What to Look For

The FDA regulates food labels. Labels must include not only a list of nutrients but also a list of ingredients. These are both sources of valuable information. In the nutrient list, the important items to check include the total fats and the breakdown of the types of fats included, as well as the total carbohydrates and breakdown of fiber and sugar.

In the total fat section, check to see how much saturated fat and total fat are listed. Starting in the year 2006, food manufacturers will also need to list trans-fats. Some food producers have already started including this information on their labels. Remember, "bad" fats that you should limit or avoid include saturated fat, trans-fat, and—to a limited extent—cholesterol. "Good" fats that you should include are monounsaturated and polyunsaturated fats.

ALERT!

Keep in mind that food manufacturers do not need to list trans-fats if the total amount equals 0.5 grams per serving or less. This explains the labels you find that say "no trans-fats" and at the same time list hydrogenated vegetable oil on their ingredient list.

In the carbohydrate section of the label, check how much dietary fiber and sugar is in the product. Select foods that are higher in dietary fiber and as low as possible in sugar. When making a buying decision, compare products to find those that contain good fats instead of bad fats and that are high in fiber and whole grains.

Understanding the List of Ingredients

The ingredient list also provides a wealth of valuable information. Ingredients are listed in order of magnitude, with the items used in larger amounts listed first and smallest amounts at the end. Try to choose foods that feature the fat and oil ingredients toward the end of the list.

Choose products that list the specific type of vegetable oil—soybean oil, for example—rather than labels that use a generic "vegetable oil" listing. Often when manufacturers use the term "vegetable oil," the product includes tropical oils such as palm or coconut that contain saturated fats, rather than the healthier monounsaturated and polyunsaturated fats. To avoid trans-fats, stay away from products that say hydrogenated or partially hydrogenated vegetable oils.

When it comes to grain products, choose products with the words "whole," "whole wheat," or "whole grain" in front of the grain ingredient, as well as terms like "bran" or "germ." Sometimes food manufacturers will use enriched flour and dye it a brown color to make it appear like a whole grain. If the ingredient list shows enriched flour as the main ingredient, the grains are highly processed. These are not whole grains, and the product is likely to be high in sugar and low in fiber. Read carefully.

Take Your Time

Be prepared to spend a little more time on your grocery shopping to allow you to read labels. However, once you have selected foods you like that prominently feature healthful ingredients, you can return to your faster style of moving through aisles and throwing items in your shopping basket. As you work your way through the fine print on labels, keep in mind that you are what you eat. This task of careful shopping, while tedious and time-consuming at first, will pay great dividends to your better health in the long run.

Your Shopping List

An important strategy that can go a long way toward improving your food choices is to prepare a shopping list before you go to the store. This helps you to resist the newest, flashiest, and trendiest food products that are designed to catch your eye.

Note that the outer edges of the store tend to have the healthiest foods. These include the fresh fruits and vegetables, meats, breads, and dairy products. The inner aisles are filled with processed foods and ready-to-eat preparations that are full of saturated and trans-fats, sugar, and salt. Keep in mind that you want to select a balance of foods from each of the food groups.

From the bread and cereal group, remember to choose whole grain products like breads and muffins. You can also buy whole-grain pita bread, pasta, and rice cakes. Choose whole-grain flour for baking and items such as brown or wild rice and whole corn or flour tortillas. Select whole-grain, unsweetened cereals such as Kashi, or whole-grain hot cereals like oatmeal.

As a careful shopper, over time you may become familiar with which food manufacturers create the healthier foods that you want. You can gravitate toward those brands with more assurance that you are selecting items that will both taste good and be good for you.

From the fruit and vegetable group, select a variety of fresh foods. Today's frozen and canned vegetables can have as much nutritional value as fresh vegetables. If you're busy, you may be concerned that stocking up on fresh fruits and vegetables is wasteful. Go ahead and buy frozen products. If you buy canned vegetables, either go with a low-sodium variety or rinse the vegetables before serving. Canned fruits should be packed in juice, not syrup.

Another time-saver are packaged, prewashed, presliced vegetables. These are ideal for snacks and salads. They may cost slightly more, but if they help you to incorporate more vegetables into your diet, you will save more in the long run from your health dividends as you age. Fruit and vegetable juices are also good selections, especially if you can find fresh juices. Also be sure the fruit juice you buy is either 100-percent fruit juice or juice and water.

When choosing dairy and meat, remember the guidelines you learned earlier in this chapter. Look for low- or nonfat milk, cheese, and yogurt and lean cuts of meat. You can also select alternative sources of protein such as beans, lentils, tofu, and other soy products.

Meal Planning for Health

Maintaining healthy nutrition does require some planning. However, with a minimal amount of organization, you can keep health-enhancing foods in your refrigerator and cupboards. Now let's look at how you can use these tips to plan healthy meals. Incorporate even a handful of these suggestions into your daily life, and before you realize it, you will have shifted to a healthier overall eating pattern.

QUESTION?

Which types of cooking oils should I buy?
Choose either monounsaturated vegetable oils, which include olive, canola, peanut, avocado, almond, hazelnut, and pecan, or polyunsaturated vegetable oils, such as corn, safflower, sunflower, sesame, soybean, and cottonseed.

Breakfast

Breakfast is the most important meal of the day. It's also a wonderful opportunity to eat fiber-rich foods. Plan to include a combination of fiber-rich and protein-rich foods, along with either a fruit or vegetable serving. Great sources of fiber for breakfast include hot or cold cereals and breads. Breakfast protein can come from nonfat or low-fat dairy products such as milk or soymilk. You can add fruits or vegetables either by drinking one glass of juice, or by mixing fruit with your cereal dish.

Another great breakfast option is a smoothie. These are easy to make in a blender, with either milk or soy milk, some fruits, and wheat germ or ground flaxseed. All of these options can help you start off your day on the right foot.

Lunch

Lunch is another great opportunity for a rich source of fiber and more fruits and vegetables. Try sandwiches on hearty whole-grain breads with fresh tomatoes, lettuce, and sprouts. For vegetable sources of protein, use bean dips such as hummus on the sandwich. Peanut butter is also a great sandwich filling, or you might try avocados.

If packing a lunch, include a vegetable and some fruit. For example, take some prewashed, prepackaged baby carrots or celery sticks. Or slice up a bell pepper into sticks. Easily portable fruits include apples, bananas, oranges, nectarines, grapes, and pears. Try to eat the fruits that are fresh and in season.

Salads are a great lunch that can be made more filling by adding beans, hard-boiled eggs, or starches such as whole-grain pastas. You can also add cubes of tofu or tempeh to your salads. Tofu can also be added to steamed vegetables, soup, and sauces. Soups are a fantastic source of multiple vegetables and beans. If you combine soups or salads with some hearty whole-grain breads or muffins, you can have a satisfying and nutrient-packed meal. For dessert, try some fresh fruit, or poached, baked, or frozen fruits, such as poached pears, baked apples, or fresh fruit sorbets.

FACT

Simple sugars are not "bad" in and of themselves, but when consumed in excess, they can have a harmful effect on cholesterol levels. Studies show that a diet high in simple sugars, which includes refined carbohydrates (enriched-flour breads and pastas) and hard candy, actually increases triglyceride levels and decreases levels of HDL or good cholesterol.

Dinner

For dinner, try to shift the emphasis to a vegetable- and grain-based main course with any meat dishes on the side. Or, in meals that call for sauces, use a combination of vegetables and meats to reduce the total amount of meat that you consume. For example, you can cut the amount of meat in stew in half and instead add in extra carrots, celery, and mushrooms. You can try chili with beans and no meat, or use ground turkey instead of beef and add more vegetables instead of meats. Try enjoying stir-fried vegetable dishes with only a small amount of skinless chicken, or simply use tofu instead of any meat product.

Keep in mind that when you eat beans, peas, or lentils together with a dairy product or with grains such as bread or rice, you can obtain the same amount of protein from your meal as if you had consumed a meat dish. Other benefits of eating more beans instead of meat is that they are much more affordable, they contain no saturated fats and no cholesterol, they are nutrient dense, and they are valuable sources of dietary fiber.

If you use canned beans in your foods, try to buy low-sodium varieties and use the liquid that they come packed in for cooking. That liquid is rich in soluble fiber—that's why it has that thick consistency.

ALERT!

It is not a good idea to transition immediately to a diet filled with fiber. Add more fiber-rich foods such as beans and whole grains gradually. This helps to prevent constipation and too much gas, neither of which are pleasant experiences. Be sure to drink plenty of fluids and also to follow bean preparation instructions carefully.

Heart-Healthy Dining for Winning Results

Dietary changes are very powerful. Blood cholesterol levels show signs of improvement in as few as three to four weeks. Here's a testimonial from fifty-four-year-old Joanne about the power of nutrition:

I was surprised and dismayed when my physician told me that I had high cholesterol at my annual checkup. I had always been health conscious, not at all overweight, and swam at least four times a week. My mom, prior to her death from cancer, suffered from high cholesterol for which she took medication. Since I was already dealing with symptoms of menopause, I did not want to take medication.

My doctor agreed that I could try to lower my total cholesterol without medication. I began a regimen of oatmeal or Cheerios for breakfast. I added almonds to my diet and took Metamucil occasionally. I increased my use of olive oil to replace vegetable oil. I stopped eating any packaged cookies, muffins, chips, or crackers. I added one extra day of walking a week and cut back swimming to three days.

When I returned to my physician two months later, I had lowered my cholesterol by 20 percent.

Keep in mind, however, that you must make a lifestyle change toward a healthier pattern of eating and not treat this as a short-term, fad diet for quick and easy weight loss. Eating healthy for life represents a commitment—to yourself and to those you love—to make a daily difference in supporting health through the foods that you eat. Treats are definitely a part of that picture. But for the most part, your daily diet will be one that is full of nutrient-dense, health-enhancing foods for a longer, healthier, and more enjoyable life.

Have fun reading the heart-healthy recipes in the following chapters for more ideas on how to plan tasty, enjoyable, and nutritious meals for your entire family's health and pleasure. These recipes, from the National Heart, Lung, and Blood Institute, were developed under the direction of leading medical and nutritional scientists during government-sponsored research and education projects devoted to keeping Americans healthy. These recipes have been specifically designed and tested to promote health. Now you can use the results of this important research to improve your personal health.

This collection includes a variety of ethnic dishes to find something to please every taste. Even children love these recipes. In addition, each recipe includes a nutrient breakdown so you know exactly what you're eating. Remember, heart-healthy cooking does not mean a sacrifice of flavor or pleasure.

Chapter 10

Heart-Healthy Soup, Appetizer, and Side-Dish Recipes

Bean and Macaroni Soup	Limas and Spinach
Corn Chowder	Smothered Greens
Gazpacho	Vegetable Stew
Mexican Pozole	Vegetables with a Touch of Lemon
Homemade Turkey Soup	Candied Yams
Minestrone Soup	Delicious Oven French Fries
Rockport Fish Chowder	Garlic Mashed Potatoes
Curtido (Cabbage) Salvadoreño	New Potato Salad
Pupusas Revueltas	Savory Potato Salad
Fresh Cabbage and Tomato Salad	Wonderful Stuffed Potatoes
Green Bean Sauté	Oriental Rice
Italian Vegetable Bake	

Source: *Keep the Beat: Heart Healthy Recipes,* NIH Publication No. 03-2921. (Visit the National Heart, Lung, and Blood Institute Web site, at *www.nhlbi.nih.gov,* for more information.)

Bean and Macaroni Soup

<table>
<tr><td colspan="2">

Yield: 16 servings
Serving size: 1 C

</td></tr>
<tr><td colspan="2">

Each serving provides:

</td></tr>
<tr><td>Calories: 158</td></tr>
<tr><td>Total fat: 1 g</td></tr>
<tr><td>Saturated fat: less than 1 g</td></tr>
<tr><td>Cholesterol: 0 mg</td></tr>
<tr><td>Sodium: 154 mg</td></tr>
<tr><td>Total fiber: 5 mg</td></tr>
<tr><td>Protein: 8 mg</td></tr>
<tr><td>Carbohydrates: 29 g</td></tr>
<tr><td>Potassium: 524 mg</td></tr>
</table>

2 cans (16 oz each) Great Northern beans
1 Tbsp olive oil
½ lb fresh mushrooms, sliced
1 C onion, coarsely chopped
2 C carrots, sliced
1 C celery, coarsely chopped
1 clove garlic, minced
3 C fresh tomatoes, peeled and cut up (or 1½ lb canned, cut up)*

1 tsp dried sage
1 tsp dried thyme
½ tsp dried oregano
Freshly ground black pepper, to taste
1 bay leaf
4 C elbow macaroni, cooked

*If using canned tomatoes, sodium content will be higher. Try no-salt-added canned tomatoes to keep sodium lower.

1. Drain beans and reserve liquid. Rinse beans.
2. Heat oil in 6-quart kettle. Add mushrooms, onion, carrots, celery, and garlic and sauté for 5 minutes.
3. Add tomatoes, sage, thyme, oregano, pepper, and bay leaf. Cover and cook over medium heat for 20 minutes.
4. Cook macaroni according to directions on package, using unsalted water. Drain when cooked. Do not overcook.
5. Combine reserved bean liquid with water to make 4 C.
6. Add liquid, beans, and cooked macaroni to vegetable mixture.
7. Bring to boil. Cover and simmer until soup is thoroughly heated. Stir occasionally.

This satisfying dish is virtually fat free—it uses just 1 tablespoon of oil for 16 servings.

Corn Chowder

1 Tbsp vegetable oil
2 Tbsp celery, finely diced
2 Tbsp onion, finely diced
2 Tbsp green pepper, finely diced
1 package (10 oz) frozen
*   whole-kernel corn*
1 C raw potatoes, peeled, diced
*   in ½-inch pieces*

2 Tbsp fresh parsley, chopped
1 C water
¼ tsp salt
Black pepper to taste
¼ tsp paprika
2 Tbsp flour
2 C low-fat or skim milk

Yield: 4 servings Serving size: 1 C
Each serving provides:
Calories: 186
Total fat: 5 g
Saturated fat: 1 g
Cholesterol: 5 mg
Sodium: 205 mg
Total fiber: 4 g
Protein: 7 g
Carbohydrates: 31 g
Potassium: 455 mg

1. Heat oil in medium saucepan. Add celery, onion, and green pepper, and sauté for 2 minutes.
2. Add corn, potatoes, water, salt, pepper, and paprika. Bring to boil, then reduce heat to medium. Cook covered for about 10 minutes or until potatoes are tender.
3. Place ½ C of milk in jar with tight-fitting lid. Add flour and shake vigorously.
4. Gradually add milk-flour mixture to cooked vegetables. Then add remaining milk.
5. Cook, stirring constantly, until mixture comes to boil and thickens.
6. Serve garnished with chopped, fresh parsley.

Here's a creamy chowder without the cream—or fat.

Gazpacho

| Yield: 4 servings |
| Serving size: 1¼ C |

Each serving provides:

Calories: 52

Total fat: less than 1 g

Saturated fat: less than 1 g

Cholesterol: 0 mg

Sodium: 41 mg

Total fiber: 2 g

Protein: 2 g

Carbohydrates: 12 g

Potassium: 514 mg

3 medium tomatoes, peeled, chopped
½ C cucumber, seeded, chopped
½ C green pepper, chopped
2 green onions, sliced

2 C low-sodium vegetable juice cocktail
1 Tbsp lemon juice
½ tsp basil, dried
¼ tsp hot pepper sauce
1 clove garlic, minced

1. In large mixing bowl, combine all ingredients.
2. Cover and chill in the refrigerator for several hours.

This chilled tomato soup is a classic—and chock full of healthy garden-fresh vegetables.

Mexican Pozole

| Yield: 10 servings |
| Serving size: 1 C |

Each serving provides:

Calories: 253

Total fat: 10 g

Saturated fat: 3 g

Cholesterol: 52 mg

Sodium: 425 mg

Total fiber: 4 g

Protein: 22 g

Carbohydrates: 19 g

Potassium: 485 mg

2 lb lean beef, cubed*
1 Tbsp olive oil
1 large onion, chopped
1 clove garlic, finely chopped
¼ tsp salt
⅛ tsp pepper

¼ C cilantro
1 can (15 oz) stewed tomatoes
2 oz tomato paste
1 can (1 lb, 13 oz) hominy

Skinless, boneless chicken breasts can be used instead of beef cubes.

1. In large pot, heat oil, then sauté beef.
2. Add onion, garlic, salt, pepper, cilantro, and enough water to cover meat. Cover pot and cook over low heat until meat is tender.
3. Add tomatoes and tomato paste. Continue cooking for about 20 minutes.
4. Add hominy and continue cooking over low heat for another 15 minutes, stirring occasionally. If too thick, add water for desired consistency.

Try a change of taste with this hearty Mexican soup.

Homemade Turkey Soup

6 lb turkey breast with bones
    (with at least 2 C meat)
2 medium onions
3 stalks celery
1 tsp dried thyme
½ tsp dried rosemary
½ tsp dried sage

1 tsp dried basil
½ tsp dried marjoram
½ tsp dried tarragon
½ tsp salt
black pepper, to taste
½ lb Italian pastina or pasta

Yield: 16 servings
(about 4 quarts of soup)
Serving size: 1 C

Each serving provides:
Calories: 201
Total fat: 2 g
Saturated fat: 1 g
Cholesterol: 101 mg
Sodium: 141 mg
Total fiber: 1 g
Protein: 33 g
Carbohydrates: 11 g
Potassium: 344 mg

1. Place turkey breast in large 6-quart pot. Cover with water until at least three-quarters full.
2. Peel onions, cut into large pieces, and add to pot. Wash celery stalks, slice, and add to pot.
3. Simmer covered for about 2½ hours.
4. Remove carcass from pot. Divide soup into smaller, shallower containers for quick cooling in refrigerator.
5. After cooling, skim off fat.
6. While soup cools, remove remaining meat from turkey carcass. Cut into pieces.
7. Add turkey meat to skimmed soup, along with herbs and spices.
8. Bring to boil and add pastina. Continue cooking on low boil for about 20 minutes, until pastina is done. Serve at once or refrigerate for later reheating.

*୧୭ This popular soup uses a "quick cool down"
method that lets you skim the fat right off the top—
making it even healthier.*

Minestrone Soup

Yield: 16 servings Serving size: 1 C
Each serving provides:
Calories: 112
Total fat: 4 g
Saturated fat: 0 g
Cholesterol: 0 mg
Sodium: 202 mg
Total fiber: 4 g
Protein: 4 g
Carbohydrates: 17 g
Potassium: 393 mg

¼ C olive oil
1 clove garlic, minced (or ⅛ tsp garlic powder)
1⅓ C onion, coarsely chopped
1½ C celery with leaves, coarsely chopped
1 can (6 oz) tomato paste
1 Tbsp fresh parsley, chopped
1 C carrots, sliced, fresh or frozen

4 ¾ C cabbage, shredded
1 can (1 lb) tomatoes, cut up
1 C canned red kidney beans, drained, rinsed
1½ C frozen peas
1½ C fresh green beans dash hot sauce
11 C water
2 C spaghetti, uncooked, broken

1. Heat oil in 4-quart saucepan. Add garlic, onion, and celery, and sauté for about 5 minutes.
2. Add all remaining ingredients except spaghetti. Stir until ingredients are well mixed.
3. Bring to boil and reduce heat; cover, and simmer for about 45 minutes or until vegetables are tender.
4. Add uncooked spaghetti and simmer for only 2–3 minutes.

🍲 *This cholesterol-free version of the classic Italian soup is brimming with fiber-rich beans, peas, and carrots.*

Rockport Fish Chowder

2 Tbsp vegetable oil
¼ C onion, coarsely chopped
½ C celery, coarsely chopped
1 C carrots, sliced
2 C potatoes, raw, peeled, cubed
¼ tsp thyme
½ tsp paprika
2 C bottled clam juice

8 whole peppercorns
1 bay leaf
1 lb fresh or frozen (and
    thawed) cod or haddock fil-
    lets, cut into ¾-inch cubes
¼ C flour
3 C low-fat milk
1 Tbsp fresh parsley, chopped

| Yield: 8 servings |
Serving size: 1 C
Each serving provides:
Calories: 186
Total fat: 6 g
Saturated fat: 1 g
Cholesterol: 34 mg
Sodium: 302 mg
Total fiber: 2 g
Protein: 15 g
Carbohydrates: 18 g
Potassium: 602 mg

1. Heat oil in large saucepan. Add onion and celery, and sauté for about 3 minutes.
2. Add carrots, potatoes, thyme, paprika, and clam broth. Wrap peppercorns and bay leaf in cheesecloth. Add to pot. Bring to boil, reduce heat, and simmer for 15 minutes, then add fish and simmer for an added 15 minutes, or until fish flakes easily and is opaque.
3. Remove fish and vegetables. Break fish into chunks. Bring broth to boil and continue boiling until volume is reduced to 1 C. Remove bay leaf and peppercorns.
4. Shake flour and ½ C low-fat milk in container with tight-fitting lid until smooth. Add to broth in saucepan, along with remaining milk. Cook over medium heat, stirring constantly, until mixture boils and is thickened.
5. Return vegetables and fish chunks to stock and heat thoroughly. Serve hot, sprinkled with chopped parsley.

ᏋᎯ Serve this chowder as an appetizer or meal in itself—
and eat like an admiral on a health cruise.

Curtido (Cabbage) Salvadoreño

Yield: 8 servings
Serving size: 1 C

Each serving provides:

Calories: 41	
Total fat: 1 g	
Saturated fat: less than 1 g	
Cholesterol: 0 mg	
Sodium: 293 mg	
Total fiber: 2 g	
Protein: 2 g	
Carbohydrates: 7 g	
Potassium: 325 mg	

1 medium head cabbage, chopped
2 small carrots, grated
1 small onion, sliced
½ tsp dried red pepper (optional)
½ tsp oregano
1 tsp olive oil
1 tsp salt
1 tsp brown sugar
½ C vinegar
½ C water

1. Blanch cabbage with boiling water for 1 minute. Discard water.
2. Place cabbage in large bowl. Add grated carrots, sliced onion, red pepper, oregano, olive oil, salt, brown sugar, vinegar, and water.
3. Place in refrigerator for at least 2 hours before serving.

Surprise your taste buds with this flavorful dish—esta terrifica!
Try this dish with Pupusas Revueltas (see recipe on the next page).

Pupusas Revueltas

1 lb chicken breast, ground
1 Tbsp vegetable oil
½ lb low-fat mozzarella cheese, grated
½ small onion, finely diced
1 clove garlic, minced

1 medium green pepper, seeded, minced
1 small tomato, finely chopped
½ tsp salt
5 C instant corn flour (masa harina)
6 C water

Yield: 12 servings Serving size: 2 pupusas
Each serving provides:
Calories: 290
Total fat: 7 g
Saturated fat: 3 g
Cholesterol: 33 mg
Sodium: 223 mg
Total fiber: 5 g
Protein: 14 g
Carbohydrates: 38 g
Potassium: 272 mg

1. In nonstick skillet, sauté chicken in oil over low heat until it turns white. Stir chicken constantly to keep it from sticking.
2. Add onion, garlic, green pepper, and tomato. Cook chicken mixture through. Remove skillet from stove and let mixture cool in refrigerator.
3. Meanwhile, place flour in large mixing bowl and stir in enough water to make stiff, tortilla-like dough.
4. When chicken mixture has cooled, mix in cheese.
5. Divide dough into 24 portions. With your hands, roll dough into balls and flatten each into ½-inch thick circle. Put spoonful of chicken mixture in middle of each circle of dough and bring edges to center. Flatten ball of dough again until it is ½-inch thick.
6. In very hot iron skillet, cook pupusas on each side until golden brown.
7. Serve hot.

Ground chicken and low-fat cheese help keep down the fat and calories in this tasty dish. Try this dish with Curtido Salvadoreño (see recipe on the previous page).

Fresh Cabbage and Tomato Salad

| Yield: 8 servings |
| Serving size: 1 C |

Each serving provides:

Calories: 43	
Total fat: 1 g	
Saturated fat: less than 1 g	
Cholesterol: 0 mg	
Sodium: 88 mg	
Total fiber: 3 g	
Protein: 2 g	
Carbohydrates: 7 g	
Potassium: 331 mg	

1 head small cabbage,
   sliced thinly
2 medium tomatoes, cut in cubes
1 C radishes, sliced
¼ tsp salt
2 tsp olive oil
2 Tbsp rice vinegar
   (or lemon juice)
½ tsp black pepper
½ tsp red pepper
2 Tbsp fresh cilantro, chopped

1. In large bowl, mix together cabbage, tomatoes, and radishes.
2. In another bowl, mix together the rest of the ingredients and pour over vegetables.

Tempt your children to eat more vegetables with this refreshing, tasty salad.

Green Bean Sauté

| Yield: 4 servings |
| Serving size: ¼ C |

Each serving provides:

Calories: 64	
Total fat: 4 g	
Saturated fat: less than 1 g	
Cholesterol: 0 mg	
Sodium: 282 mg	
Total fiber: 3 g	
Protein: 2 g	
Carbohydrates: 8 g	
Potassium: 161 mg	

1 lb fresh or frozen green beans,
   cut in 1-inch pieces
1 Tbsp vegetable oil
1 large yellow onion, halved
   lengthwise, thinly sliced
½ tsp salt
⅛ tsp black pepper
1 Tbsp fresh parsley, minced

1. If using fresh green beans, cook in boiling water for 10–12 minutes or steam for 2–3 minutes until barely fork tender. Drain well. If using frozen green beans, thaw first.
2. Heat oil in large skillet. Sauté onion until golden.
3. Stir in green beans, salt, and pepper. Heat through.
4. Before serving, toss with parsley.

In this dish, green beans and onions are lightly sautéed in just 1 tablespoon of oil.

Italian Vegetable Bake

1 can (28 oz) tomatoes, whole
1 medium onion, sliced
½ lb fresh green beans, sliced
½ lb fresh okra, cut into ½-inch pieces (or ½ of 10-oz package frozen, cut)
¾ C green pepper, finely chopped
2 Tbsp lemon juice

1 Tbsp fresh basil, chopped, or 1 tsp dried basil, crushed
1½ tsp fresh oregano leaves, chopped (or ½ tsp dried oregano, crushed)
3 medium (7-inch-long) zucchini, cut into 1-inch cubes
1 medium eggplant, pared, cut into 1-inch cubes
2 Tbsp Parmesan cheese, grated

Yield: 18 servings Serving size: ½ C
Each serving provides:
Calories: 27
Total fat: less than 1 g
Saturated fat: less than 1 g
Cholesterol: 1 mg
Sodium: 86 mg
Total fiber: 2 g
Protein: 2 g
Carbohydrates: 5 g
Potassium: 244 mg

1. Drain and coarsely chop tomatoes. Save liquid. Mix together tomatoes, reserved liquid, onion, green beans, okra, green pepper, lemon juice, and herbs. Cover and bake at 325°F for 15 minutes.
2. Mix in zucchini and eggplant. Continue baking, covered, 60–70 minutes more or until vegetables are tender. Stir occasionally.
3. Just before serving, sprinkle top with Parmesan cheese.

Try this colorful, low-sodium baked dish, prepared without added fat.

Limas and Spinach

Yield: 7 servings
Serving size: ½ C

Each serving provides:

Calories:	93
Total fat:	2 g
Saturated fat:	less than 1 g
Cholesterol:	0 mg
Sodium:	84 mg
Total fiber:	6 g
Protein:	5 g
Carbohydrates:	15 g
Potassium:	452 mg

2 C frozen lima beans
1 Tbsp vegetable oil
1 C fennel, cut in 4-oz strips
½ C onion, chopped
¼ C low-sodium chicken broth

4 C leaf spinach, washed
  thoroughly
1 Tbsp distilled vinegar
⅛ tsp black pepper
1 Tbsp raw chives

1. Steam or boil lima beans in unsalted water for about 10 minutes. Drain.
2. In skillet, sauté onions and fennel in oil.
3. Add beans and stock to onions and cover. Cook for 2 minutes.
4. Stir in spinach. Cover and cook until spinach has wilted, about 2 minutes.
5. Stir in vinegar and pepper. Cover and let stand for 30 seconds.
6. Sprinkle with chives and serve.

Your family will love vegetables cooked this way.

Smothered Greens

Yield: 5 servings
Serving size: 1 C

Each serving provides:

Calories:	80
Total fat:	2 g
Saturated fat:	less than 1 g
Cholesterol:	16 mg
Sodium:	378 mg
Total fiber:	4 g
Protein:	9 g
Carbohydrates:	9 g
Potassium:	472 mg

3 C water
¼ lb smoked turkey breast,
  skinless
1 Tbsp fresh hot pepper,
  chopped
¼ tsp cayenne pepper
¼ tsp cloves, ground

2 cloves garlic, crushed
½ tsp thyme
1 scallion, chopped
1 tsp ginger, ground
¼ C onion, chopped
2 lb greens (mustard, turnip,
  collard, kale, or mixture)

1. Place all ingredients except greens into large saucepan and bring to boil.
2. Prepare greens by washing thoroughly and removing stems.
3. Tear or slice leaves into bite-size pieces.
4. Add greens to turkey stock. Cook for 20–30 minutes until tender.

These healthy greens get their rich flavor from smoked turkey, instead of fatback.

Vegetable Stew

3 C water
1 cube vegetable bouillon,
   low sodium
2 C white potatoes, cut in
   2-inch strips
2 C carrots, sliced
4 C summer squash, cut in
   1-inch squares
1 C summer squash, cut in
   4 chunks

1 can (15 oz) sweet corn,
   rinsed, drained (or 2 ears
   fresh corn, 1½ C)
1 tsp thyme
2 cloves garlic, minced
1 scallion, chopped
½ small hot pepper, chopped
1 C onion, coarsely chopped
1 C tomatoes, diced (add other
   favorite vegetables, such as
   broccoli and cauliflower)

Yield: 8 servings Serving size: 1¼ C
Each serving provides:
Calories: 119
Total fat: 1 g
Saturated fat: less than 1 g
Cholesterol: 0 mg
Sodium: 196 mg
Total fiber: 4 g
Protein: 4 g
Carbohydrates: 27 g
Potassium: 524 mg

1. Put water and bouillon in large pot and bring to a boil.
2. Add potatoes and carrots, and simmer for 5 minutes.
3. Add remaining ingredients, except for tomatoes, and continue cooking for 15 minutes over medium heat.
4. Remove four chunks of squash and puree in blender.
5. Return pureed mixture to pot and let cook for 10 minutes more.
6. Add tomatoes and cook for another 5 minutes.
7. Remove from flame and let sit for 10 minutes to allow stew to thicken.

Here's a great new way to use summer vegetables.

Vegetables with a Touch of Lemon

½ small head cauliflower, cut
  into florets
2 C broccoli, cut into florets
2 Tbsp lemon juice

1 Tbsp olive oil
1 clove garlic, minced
2 tsp fresh parsley, chopped

1. Steam broccoli and cauliflower until tender (about 10 minutes).
2. In small saucepan, mix the lemon juice, oil, and garlic, and cook over low heat for 2 or 3 minutes.
3. Put vegetables in serving dish. Pour lemon sauce over them. Garnish with parsley.

This heart-healthy sauce uses lemon juice and herbs for a tangy taste.

Yield: 6 servings Serving size: ½ C
Each serving provides:
Calories: 22
Total fat: 2 g
Saturated fat: less than 1 g
Cholesterol: 0 mg
Sodium: 7 mg
Total fiber: 1 g
Protein: 1 g
Carbohydrates: 2 g
Potassium: 49 mg

Candied Yams

3 (1½ C) medium yams
¼ C brown sugar, packed
1 tsp flour, sifted
¼ tsp salt
¼ tsp ground cinnamon

¼ tsp ground nutmeg
¼ tsp orange peel
1 tsp soft tub margarine
½ C orange juice

1. Cut yams in half and boil until tender but firm (about 20 minutes). When cool enough to handle, peel and slice to ¼-inch thickness.
2. Combine sugar, flour, salt, cinnamon, nutmeg, and grated orange peel.
3. Place half of sliced yams in medium-size casserole dish. Sprinkle with spiced sugar mixture.
4. Dot with half the amount of margarine.
5. Add second layer of yams, using the rest of the ingredients in the same order as above. Add orange juice.
6. Bake uncovered for 20 minutes in oven that was preheated to 350°F.

A bit of margarine and some orange juice make this dish sweet.

Yield: 6 servings Serving size: ¼ C
Each serving provides:
Calories: 110
Total fat: less than 1 g
Saturated fat: less than 1 g
Cholesterol: 0 mg
Sodium: 115 mg
Total fiber: 2 g
Protein: 1 g
Carbohydrates: 25 g
Potassium: 344 mg

Delicious Oven French Fries

4 (2 lb) large potatoes
8 C ice water
1 tsp garlic powder
1 tsp onion powder
¼ tsp salt

1 tsp white pepper
¼ tsp allspice
1 tsp hot pepper flakes
1 Tbsp vegetable oil

Yield: 5 servings Serving size: 1 C		
Each serving provides:		
Calories: 238		
Total fat: 4 g		
Saturated fat: 1 g		
Cholesterol: 0 mg		
Sodium: 163 mg		
Total fiber: 5 g		
Protein: 5 g		
Carbohydrates: 48 g		
Potassium: 796 mg		

1. Scrub potatoes and cut into ½-inch strips.
2. Place potato strips into ice water, cover, and chill for 1 hour or longer.
3. Remove potatoes and dry strips thoroughly.
4. Place garlic powder, onion powder, salt, white pepper, allspice, and pepper flakes in plastic bag.
5. Toss potatoes in spice mixture.
6. Brush potatoes with oil.
7. Place potatoes in nonstick shallow baking pan.
8. Cover with aluminum foil and place in 475°F oven for 15 minutes.
9. Remove foil and continue baking uncovered for additional 15–20 minutes or until golden brown. Turn fries occasionally to brown on all sides.

Find french fries hard to resist? Here's a version to give in to.

Garlic Mashed Potatoes

*2 (1 lb) large potatoes, peeled,
quartered*
2 C skim milk

2 cloves garlic, large, chopped
½ tsp white pepper

Yield: 4 servings Serving size: ¾ C

Each serving provides:
Calories: 142
Total fat: less than 1 g
Saturated fat: less than 1 g
Cholesterol: 2 mg
Sodium: 69 mg
Total fiber: 2 g
Protein: 6 g
Carbohydrates: 29 g
Potassium: 577 mg

To use saucepan:

1. Cook potatoes, covered, in small amount of boiling water for 20–25 minutes or until tender. Remove from heat. Drain and re-cover.
2. Meanwhile, in small saucepan over low heat, cook garlic in milk until soft (about 30 minutes).
3. Add milk-garlic mixture and white pepper to potatoes. Beat with electric mixer on low speed, or mash with potato masher, until smooth.

To use microwave:

1. Scrub potatoes, pat dry, and prick with fork.
2. On plate, cook potatoes uncovered on 100 percent (high) power until tender (about 12 minutes), turning over once.
3. Let stand 5 minutes, then peel and quarter.
4. Meanwhile, in 4-C measuring glass, combine milk and garlic. Cook, uncovered, on 50 percent (medium) power until garlic is soft (about 4 minutes).
5. Continue as directed above.

*Whether with saucepan or microwave, you can make
this dish tasty without added fat or salt.*

New Potato Salad

16 (5 C) small new potatoes
2 Tbsp olive oil
¼ C green onions, chopped

¼ tsp black pepper
1 tsp dill weed, dried

1. Thoroughly clean potatoes with vegetable brush and water.
2. Boil potatoes for 20 minutes or until tender.
3. Drain and cool potatoes for 20 minutes.
4. Cut potatoes into fourths and mix with olive oil, onions, and spices.
5. Refrigerate and serve.

Onions and spices give this very low-sodium dish plenty of zip.

Yield: 5 servings Serving size: 1 C
Each serving provides:
Calories: 187
Total fat: 6 g
Saturated fat: 1 g
Cholesterol: 0 mg
Sodium: 12 mg
Total fiber: 3 g
Protein: 3 g
Carbohydrates: 32 g
Potassium: 547 mg

Savory Potato Salad

6 (about 2 lb) medium potatoes
2 stalks celery, finely chopped
2 scallions, finely chopped
¼ C red bell pepper, coarsely
    chopped
¼ C green bell pepper, coarsely
    chopped

1 Tbsp onion, finely chopped
1 egg, hard boiled, chopped
6 Tbsp light mayonnaise
1 tsp mustard
½ tsp salt
¼ tsp black pepper
¼ tsp dill weed, dried

1. Wash potatoes, cut in half, and place in saucepan in cold water.
2. Cook covered over medium heat for 25–30 minutes or until tender.
3. Drain and dice potatoes when cool.
4. Add vegetables and egg to potatoes, and toss.
5. Blend together mayonnaise, mustard, salt, pepper, and dill weed.
6. Pour dressing over potato mixture, and stir gently to coat evenly.
7. Chill for at least 1 hour before serving.

*Here's a potato salad that's both traditional and new—
with a high taste, low-fat twist.*

Yield: 10 servings Serving size: ½ C
Each serving provides:
Calories: 98
Total fat: 2 g
Saturated fat: less than 1 g
Cholesterol: 21 mg
Sodium: 212 mg
Total fiber: 2 g
Protein: 2 g
Carbohydrates: 18 g
Potassium: 291 mg

Wonderful Stuffed Potatoes

Yield: 8 servings
Serving size:
½ potato

Each serving provides:

Calories: 113	
Total fat: 3 g	
Saturated fat: 1 g	
Cholesterol: 1 mg	
Sodium: 151 mg	
Total fiber: 2 g	
Protein: 5 g	
Carbohydrates: 17 g	
Potassium: 293 mg	

4 medium baking potatoes
¾ C low-fat (1%) cottage cheese
¼ C low-fat (1%) milk
2 Tbsp soft margarine
1 tsp dill weed
¾ tsp herb seasoning
4–6 drops hot pepper sauce
2 tsp Parmesan cheese, grated

1. Prick potatoes with fork. Bake at 425°F for 60 minutes or until fork is easily inserted.
2. Cut potatoes in half lengthwise. Carefully scoop out potato, leaving about ½ inch of pulp inside shell. Mash pulp in large bowl.
3. By hand, mix in remaining ingredients, except Parmesan cheese. Spoon mixture into potato shells.
4. Sprinkle each top with ¼ teaspoon Parmesan cheese.
5. Place on baking sheet and return to oven. Bake for 15–20 minutes or until tops are golden brown.

Oriental Rice

Yield: 10 servings
Serving size: ½ C

Each serving provides:

Calories: 139	
Total fat: 5 g	
Saturated fat: less than 1 g	
Cholesterol: 0 mg	
Sodium: 86 mg	
Total fiber: 1 g	
Protein: 3 g	
Carbohydrates: 21 g	
Potassium: 124 mg	

1½ C water
1 C chicken stock or broth, fat skimmed from top
1⅓ C long-grain white rice, uncooked
2 tsp vegetable oil
2 Tbsp onion, finely chopped
1 C celery, finely chopped
2 Tbsp green pepper, finely chopped
½ C pecans, chopped
¼ tsp ground sage
½ C water chestnuts, sliced
¼ tsp nutmeg
Black pepper to taste

1. Bring water and stock to boil in medium-size saucepan.
2. Add rice and stir. Cover and simmer for 20 minutes.
3. Remove pan from heat. Let stand, covered, for 5 minutes or until all liquid is absorbed. Reserve.
4. Heat oil in large nonstick skillet.
5. Sauté onion and celery over moderate heat for 3 minutes. Stir in remaining ingredients, including reserved cooked rice. Fluff with fork before serving.

Chapter 11

Heart-Healthy Meat and Poultry Main-Dish Recipes

Bavarian Beef	Chicken Gumbo
Beef and Bean Chili	Chicken and Rice
Beef Stroganoff	Chicken Marsala
Black Skillet Beef with Greens and Red Potatoes	Chicken Orientale
	Chicken Ratatouille
Quick Beef Casserole	Crispy Oven-Fried Chicken
Scrumptious Meat Loaf	Finger-Licking Curried Chicken
Stir-Fried Beef and Potatoes	Grilled Chicken with Green Chili Sauce
Shish Kabob	
Stir-Fried Beef and Chinese Vegetables	Jamaican Jerk Chicken
	Very Lemony Chicken
Baked Pork Chops	Yosemite Chicken Stew and Dumplings
Spicy Veal Roast	
Barbecued Chicken	Turkey Meat Loaf
Chicken Stew	Autumn Turkey-Stuffed Cabbage

Source: *Keep the Beat: Heart Healthy Recipes,* NIH Publication No. 03-2921. (See the National Heart, Lung, and Blood Institute Web site, at *www.nhlbi.nih.gov,* for more information.)

Bavarian Beef

Yield: 5 servings
Serving size: 5 oz

Each serving provides:

Calories: 218	
Total fat: 7 g	
Saturated fat: 2 g	
Cholesterol: 60 mg	
Sodium: 323 mg	
Total fiber: 2 g	
Protein: 24 g	
Carbohydrates: 14 g	
Potassium: 509 mg	

1¼ lb lean beef stew meat, trimmed of fat, cut in 1-inch pieces
1 Tbsp vegetable oil
1 large onion, thinly sliced
1½ C water
¾ tsp caraway seeds
½ tsp salt

⅛ tsp black pepper
1 bay leaf
¼ C white vinegar
1 Tbsp sugar
½ small head red cabbage, cut into 4 wedges
¼ C gingersnaps, crushed

1. Brown meat in oil in heavy skillet. Remove meat and sauté onion in remaining oil until golden. Return meat to skillet. Add water, caraway seeds, salt, pepper, and bay leaf. Bring to boil. Reduce heat, cover, and simmer for 1¼ hours.
2. Add vinegar and sugar, and stir. Place cabbage on top of meat. Cover and simmer for an added 45 minutes.
3. Remove meat and cabbage, arrange on platter, and keep warm.
4. Strain drippings from skillet and skim off fat. Add enough water to drippings to yield 1 C of liquid.
5. Return to skillet with crushed gingersnaps. Cook and stir until thickened and mixture boils. Pour over meat and vegetables, and serve.

໒ *This classic German stew is made with lean, trimmed beef stew meat and cabbage.*

Beef and Bean Chili

2 lb lean beef stew meat,
 trimmed of fat, cut in 1-inch
 cubes
3 Tbsp vegetable oil
2 C water
2 tsp garlic, minced
1 large onion, finely chopped
1 Tbsp flour
2 tsp chili powder
1 green pepper, chopped

2 lb (or 3 C) tomatoes, chopped
1 Tbsp oregano
1 tsp cumin
2 C canned kidney beans*

*To cut back on sodium,
 try using "no salt added"
 canned kidney beans or
 beans prepared at home
 without salt.

Yield: 9 servings Serving size: 8 oz
Each serving provides:
Calories: 284
Total fat: 10 g
Saturated fat: 2 g
Cholesterol: 76 mg
Sodium: 162 mg
Total fiber: 4 g
Protein: 33 g
Carbohydrates: 16 g
Potassium: 769 mg

1. Brown meat in large skillet with half of vegetable oil. Add water. Simmer covered for 1 hour until meat is tender.
2. Heat remaining vegetable oil in second skillet. Add garlic and onion, and cook over low heat until onion is softened. Add flour and cook for 2 minutes.
3. Add garlic-onion-flour mixture to cooked meat. Then add remaining ingredients to meat mixture. Simmer for ½ hour.

ॐ Here's a lower-fat chili that's lost none of its heat.

Beef Stroganoff

Yield: 5 servings
Serving size: 6 oz

Each serving provides:

Calories: 499	
Total fat: 10 g	
Saturated fat: 3 g	
Cholesterol: 80 mg	
Sodium: 200 mg	
Total fiber: 4 g	
Protein: 41 g	
Carbohydrates: 58 g	
Potassium: 891 mg	

1 lb lean beef (top round),
   cubed
2 tsp vegetable oil
¾ Tbsp onion, finely chopped
1 lb mushrooms, sliced
¼ tsp salt
Pepper to taste

¼ tsp nutmeg
½ tsp dried basil
¼ C white wine
1 C plain low-fat yogurt
6 C macaroni, cooked in
   unsalted water

1. Cut beef into 1-inch cubes.
2. Heat 1 teaspoon oil in nonstick skillet. Sauté onion for 2 minutes.
3. Add beef and sauté for 5 minutes more. Turn to brown evenly. Remove from pan and keep hot.
4. Add remaining oil to pan and sauté mushrooms.
5. Add beef and onions to pan with seasonings.
6. Add wine and yogurt, and gently stir in. Heat, but do not boil.*
7. Serve with macaroni.

If thickening is desired, use 2 teaspoons of cornstarch. Calories are same as flour, but cornstarch has double the thickening power. The calories for cornstarch are not included in the nutrients per serving given above. To add cornstarch, take small amount of wine and yogurt broth and put aside to cool. Stir in cornstarch. Add some of warm broth to cornstarch paste and stir. Then, add cornstarch mixture to pan.

❧ Lean top round beef and plain low-fat yogurt transform
this rich dish into a heart-healthy meal.

Black Skillet Beef with Greens and Red Potatoes

1 lb top round beef
1 Tbsp paprika
1½ tsp oregano
½ tsp chili powder
¼ tsp garlic powder
¼ tsp black pepper
⅛ tsp red pepper
⅛ tsp dry mustard
8 red-skinned potatoes, halved
3 C onion, finely chopped

2 C beef broth
2 cloves large garlic, minced
2 large carrots, peeled, cut into
   very thin, 2½-inch strips
2 bunches (½ lb) mustard
   greens, kale, or turnip
   greens, stems removed,
   coarsely torn as needed
Nonstick cooking spray

| Yield: 6 servings |
| Serving size: 7 oz |

Each serving provides:

Each serving provides:
Calories: 340
Total fat: 5 g
Saturated fat: 2 g
Cholesterol: 64 mg
Sodium: 109 mg
Total fiber: 8 g
Protein: 30 g
Carbohydrates: 45 g
Potassium: 1,278 mg

1. Partially freeze beef. Thinly slice across grain into long strips ⅛-inch thick and 3 inches wide.
2. Combine paprika, oregano, chili powder, garlic powder, black pepper, red pepper, and dry mustard. Coat strips of meat with spice mixture.
3. Spray large, heavy skillet with nonstick coating. Preheat pan over high heat. Add meat and cook, stirring, for 5 minutes. Then add potatoes, onion, broth, and garlic, and cook, covered, over medium heat for 20 minutes. Stir in carrots, lay greens over top, and cook covered until carrots are tender, about 15 minutes.
4. Serve in large serving bowl with crusty bread for dunking.

&❧ *Here's a one-dish meal that tastes even better than it sounds.*

Quick Beef Casserole

½ lb lean ground beef	½ tsp black pepper
1 C onion, chopped	¼ tsp paprika
1 C celery, chopped	1 C frozen peas
1 C green pepper, cubed	2 small carrots, diced
3½ C tomatoes, diced	1 C uncooked rice
¼ tsp salt	1½ C water

1. In skillet, brown ground beef and drain off fat.
2. Add rest of ingredients. Mix well. Cover and cook over medium heat until boiling. Reduce to low heat and simmer for 35 minutes. Serve hot.

Tired? Busy? You don't need hours to make healthy dishes. Try this one-skillet wonder.

Yield: 8 servings
Serving size: 1⅓ C

Each serving provides:

Calories: 201

Total fat: 5 g

Saturated fat: 2 g

Cholesterol: 16 mg

Sodium: 164 mg

Total fiber: 3 g

Protein: 9 g

Carbohydrates: 31 g

Potassium: 449 mg

Scrumptious Meat Loaf

1 lb ground beef, extra lean	½ tsp hot pepper, chopped
½ C (4 oz) tomato paste	2 cloves garlic, chopped
¼ C onion, chopped	2 scallions, chopped
¼ C green peppers, chopped	½ tsp ground ginger
¼ C red peppers, chopped	⅛ tsp ground nutmeg
1 C fresh tomatoes, blanched and chopped	1 tsp orange rind, grated
½ tsp mustard, low sodium	½ tsp thyme, crushed
¼ tsp ground black pepper	¼ C bread crumbs, finely grated

1. Mix all ingredients together.
2. Place in 1-pound loaf pan (preferably with drip rack) and bake covered at 350°F for 50 minutes.
3. Uncover pan and continue baking for 12 minutes.

Got the meat loaf blahs? This recipe transforms the ordinary into the extraordinary. For a different take on meat loaf, try the turkey version on page 173.

Yield: 6 servings
Serving size: 6 1¼-inch-thick slices

Each serving provides:

Calories: 193

Total fat: 9 g

Saturated fat: 3 g

Cholesterol: 45 mg

Sodium: 91 mg

Total fiber: 2 g

Protein: 17 g

Carbohydrates: 11 g

Potassium: 513 mg

Stir-Fried Beef and Potatoes

1½ lb sirloin steak
2 tsp vegetable oil
1 clove garlic, minced
1 tsp vinegar
⅛ tsp salt

⅛ tsp pepper
2 large onions, sliced
1 large tomato, sliced
3 C boiled potatoes, diced

1. Trim fat from steak and cut into small, thin pieces.
2. In large skillet, heat oil and sauté garlic until golden.
3. Add steak, vinegar, salt, and pepper. Cook for 6 minutes, stirring beef until brown.
4. Add onion and tomato. Cook until onion is transparent. Serve with boiled potatoes.

🥄 *Vinegar and garlic give this easy-to-fix dish its tasty zip.*

Yield: 6 servings Serving size: 1¼ C
Each serving provides:
Calories: 274
Total fat: 5 g
Saturated fat: 1 g
Cholesterol: 56 mg
Sodium: 96 mg
Total fiber: 3 g
Protein: 24 g
Carbohydrates: 33 g
Potassium: 878 mg

Shish Kabob

2 Tbsp olive oil
½ C chicken broth
¼ C red wine
1 lemon, juice only
1 tsp chopped garlic
¼ tsp salt
½ tsp rosemary

⅛ tsp black pepper
2 lb lean lamb, cut into 1-inch cubes
24 cherry tomatoes
24 mushrooms
24 small onions

1. Combine oil, broth, wine, lemon juice, garlic, salt, rosemary, and pepper. Pour over lamb, tomatoes, mushrooms, and onions. Marinate in refrigerator for several hours or overnight.
2. Put together skewers of lamb, onions, mushrooms, and tomatoes. Broil 3 inches from heat for 15 minutes, turning every 5 minutes.

🥄 *The delicious taste of these kabobs comes from the lively marinade of wine, lemon juice, rosemary, and garlic.*

Yield: 8 servings Serving size: 1 kabob, with 3 oz of meat
Each serving provides:
Calories: 274
Total fat: 12 g
Saturated fat: 3 g
Cholesterol: 75 mg
Sodium: 207 mg
Total fiber: 3 g
Protein: 26 g
Carbohydrates: 16 g
Potassium: 728 mg

Stir-Fried Beef and Chinese Vegetables

Yield: 6 servings
Serving size: 6 oz

Each serving provides:

Calories: 200	
Total fat: 9 g	
Saturated fat: 2 g	
Cholesterol: 40 mg	
Sodium: 201 mg	
Total fiber: 3 g	
Protein: 17 g	
Carbohydrates: 12 g	
Potassium: 552 mg	

2 Tbsp dry red wine
1 Tbsp soy sauce
½ tsp sugar
1½ tsp gingerroot, peeled, grated
1 lb boneless round steak, fat trimmed, cut across grain into 1½-inch strips
2 Tbsp vegetable oil
2 medium onions, each cut into 8 wedges

½ lb fresh mushrooms, rinsed, trimmed, sliced
2 stalks (½ C) celery, bias cut into ¼-inch slices
2 small green peppers, cut into thin lengthwise strips
1 C water chestnuts, drained, sliced
2 Tbsp cornstarch
¼ C water

1. Prepare marinade by mixing together wine, soy sauce, sugar, and ginger.
2. Marinate meat in mixture while preparing vegetables.
3. Heat 1 tablespoon oil in large skillet or wok. Stir-fry onions and mushrooms for 3 minutes over medium-high heat.
4. Add celery and cook for 1 minute. Add remaining vegetables and cook for 2 minutes or until green pepper is tender but crisp. Transfer vegetables to warm bowl.
5. Add remaining 1 tablespoon oil to skillet. Stir-fry meat in oil for about 2 minutes, or until meat loses its pink color.
6. Blend cornstarch and water. Stir into meat. Cook and stir until thickened. Then return vegetables to skillet. Stir gently and serve.

Stir-frying uses very little oil, as this dish shows.

Baked Pork Chops

6 lean center-cut pork chops,
    ½-inch thick*
1 egg white
1 C evaporated skim milk
¾ C cornflake crumbs
¼ C fine dry bread crumbs
4 tsp paprika
2 tsp oregano
¾ tsp chili powder
½ tsp garlic powder

½ tsp black pepper
⅛ tsp cayenne pepper
⅛ tsp dry mustard
½ tsp salt
Nonstick cooking spray as
    needed

*Try the recipe with skinless,
    boneless chicken or turkey
    parts, or fish—bake for just
    20 minutes.

Yield: 6 servings Serving size: 1 chop	
Each serving provides:	
Calories: 216	
Total fat: 8 g	
Saturated fat: 3 g	
Cholesterol: 62 mg	
Sodium: 346 mg	
Total fiber: 1 g	
Protein: 25 g	
Carbohydrates: 10 g	
Potassium: 414 mg	

1. Preheat oven to 375°F.
2. Trim fat from pork chops.
3. Beat egg white with evaporated skim milk. Place chops in milk mixture and let stand for 5 minutes, turning once.
4. Meanwhile, mix cornflake crumbs, bread crumbs, spices, and salt.
5. Use nonstick cooking spray on 13" × 9" baking pan.
6. Remove chops from milk mixture and coat thoroughly with crumb mixture.
7. Place chops in pan and bake at 375°F for 20 minutes.
8. Turn chops and bake for additional 15 minutes or until no pink remains.

⁀ You can really sink your chops into these—they're made spicy and moist with egg whites, evaporated milk, and a lively blend of herbs.

Spicy Veal Roast

| Yield: 12 servings |
| Serving size: 3 oz |

Each serving provides:

| Calories: 206 |
| Total fat: 8 g |
| Saturated fat: 3 g |
| Cholesterol: 124 mg |
| Sodium: 149 mg |
| Total fiber: 1 g |
| Protein: 30 g |
| Carbohydrates: 2 g |
| Potassium: 459 mg |

¼ tsp salt
½ tsp black pepper
½ tsp cinnamon
1½ tsp cumin
3 lb boned lean veal shoulder,
     trimmed, rolled, tied
4 tsp olive oil

½ lb onions, peeled
½ clove garlic, peeled
2 tsp dried tarragon
4 sprigs fresh parsley
1 tsp thyme
1 bay leaf

1.   Mix together salt, pepper, cinnamon, and cumin. Rub over roast.
2.   Heat 2 teaspoons of oil in large skillet. Add onions, garlic, and tarragon. Cover and cook over low heat for 10 minutes. Set aside.
3.   Heat remaining 2 teaspoons of oil in ovenproof pan large enough to hold all ingredients. Brown meat on all sides.
4.   Add garlic-onion mixture. Add parsley, thyme, and bay leaf. Cover.
5.   Bake in 325°F oven for 1½ hours, or until meat is tender.
6.   Remove meat to serving platter. Skim fat from cooking juices. Remove bay leaf and parsley. Cut roast in ¼- to ½-inch slices. Pour a little cooking juice over roast and serve rest on side.

🥄 *Skimming the fat from the cooking juices in this dish helps lower the fat content.*

Barbecued Chicken

3 lb chicken parts (breast, drumstick, and thigh), skin and fat removed
1 large onion, thinly sliced
3 Tbsp vinegar
3 Tbsp Worcestershire sauce
2 Tbsp brown sugar
Black pepper to taste
1 Tbsp hot pepper flakes
1 Tbsp chili powder
1 C chicken stock or broth, fat skimmed from top

1. Place chicken in 13" × 9" × 2" pan. Arrange onions over top.
2. Mix together vinegar, Worcestershire sauce, brown sugar, pepper, hot pepper flakes, chili powder, and stock.
3. Pour mixture over chicken and bake at 350°F for 1 hour or until done. While cooking, baste occasionally.

🐋 *Don't forget to remove the skin and fat to keep this zesty dish heart healthy.*

Yield: 8 servings Serving size: 1 chicken part with sauce
Each serving provides:
Calories: 176
Total fat: 6 g
Saturated fat: 2 g
Cholesterol: 68 mg
Sodium: 240 mg
Total fiber: 1 g
Protein: 24 g
Carbohydrates: 7 g
Potassium: 360 mg

Chicken Stew

8 pieces chicken (breasts or legs)
1 C water
2 cloves small garlic, minced
1 small onion, chopped
1½ tsp salt
½ tsp pepper
3 medium tomatoes, chopped
1 tsp parsley, chopped
¼ C celery, finely chopped
2 medium potatoes, peeled, chopped
2 small carrots, chopped
2 bay leaves

1. Remove skin from chicken, along with any extra fat. In large skillet, combine chicken, water, garlic, onion, salt, pepper, tomatoes, and parsley. Tightly cover and cook over low heat for 25 minutes.
2. Add celery, potatoes, carrots, and bay leaves and continue to cook for 15 more minutes or until chicken and vegetables are tender. Remove bay leaves before serving.

🐋 *This stew is as hearty as any, but healthier than most.*

Yield: 8 servings Serving size: 1 piece of chicken
Each serving provides:
Calories: 206
Total fat: 6 g
Saturated fat: 2 g
Cholesterol: 75 mg
Sodium: 489 mg
Total fiber: 2 g
Protein: 28 g
Carbohydrates: 10 g
Potassium: 493 mg

Chicken Gumbo

Yield: 8 servings
Serving size: ¾ C

Each serving provides:
Calories: 165
Total fat: 4 g
Saturated fat: 1 g
Cholesterol: 51 mg
Sodium: 81 mg
Total fiber: 2 g
Protein: 21 g
Carbohydrates: 11 g
Potassium: 349 mg

1 tsp vegetable oil
¼ C flour
3 C low-sodium chicken broth
1½ lb chicken breast, skinless, boneless, cut into 1-inch strips
1 C (½ lb) white potatoes, cubed
1 C onions, chopped
1 C (½ lb) carrots, coarsely chopped

½ medium carrot, grated
¼ C celery, chopped
4 cloves garlic, finely minced
2 stalks scallion, chopped
1 whole bay leaf
½ tsp thyme
½ tsp black pepper, ground
2 tsp hot (or jalapeño) pepper
1 C (½ lb) okra, sliced into ½-inch pieces

1. Add oil to large pot and heat over medium flame.
2. Stir in flour. Cook, stirring constantly, until flour begins to turn golden brown.
3. Slowly stir in all broth using wire whisk. Cook for 2 minutes. Broth mixture should not be lumpy.
4. Add rest of ingredients except okra. Bring to boil, then reduce heat and let simmer for 20–30 minutes.
5. Add okra and let cook for 15–20 more minutes.
6. Remove bay leaf and serve hot in bowl or over rice.

Simple but filling—this dish feeds the need.

Chicken and Rice

6 chicken pieces (legs and
  breasts), skinless
2 tsp vegetable oil
4 C water
2 tomatoes, chopped
½ C green pepper, chopped
¼ C red pepper, chopped
¼ C celery, diced
1 medium carrot, grated
¼ C corn, frozen

½ C onion, chopped
¼ C fresh cilantro, chopped
2 cloves garlic, chopped fine
⅛ tsp salt
⅛ tsp pepper
2 C rice
½ C frozen peas
2 oz Spanish olives
¼ C raisins

Yield: 6 servings Serving size: 1 C of rice and 1 piece of chicken
Each serving provides:
Calories: 448
Total fat: 7 g
Saturated fat: 2 g
Cholesterol: 49 mg
Sodium: 352 mg
Total fiber: 4 g
Protein: 24 g
Carbohydrates: 70 g
Potassium: 551 mg

1. In large pot, brown chicken pieces in oil.
2. Add water, tomatoes, green and red peppers, celery, carrots, corn, onion, cilantro, garlic, salt, and pepper. Cover and cook over medium heat for 20–30 minutes or until chicken is done.
3. Remove chicken from pot and place in refrigerator. Add rice, peas, and olives to pot. Cover pot and cook over low heat for about 20 minutes until rice is done.
4. Add chicken and raisins, and cook for another 8 minutes.

Let this Latino-inspired dish—full of heart-healthy ingredients—inspire you.

Chicken Marsala

Yield: 4 servings
Serving size: 1
chicken breast with
⅓ C of sauce

Each serving provides:
Calories: 285
Total fat: 8 g
Saturated fat: 2 g
Cholesterol: 85 mg
Sodium: 236 mg
Total fiber: 1 g
Protein: 33 g
Carbohydrates: 11 g
Potassium: 348 mg

⅛ tsp black pepper
¼ tsp salt
¼ C flour
4 (5 oz total) chicken breasts,
    boned, skinless
1 Tbsp olive oil

½ C Marsala wine
½ C chicken stock, fat skimmed
    from top
½ lemon, juice only
½ C mushrooms, sliced
1 Tbsp fresh parsley, chopped

1. Mix together pepper, salt, and flour. Coat chicken with seasoned flour.
2. In heavy-bottomed skillet, heat oil. Place chicken breasts in skillet and brown on both sides, then remove and set aside.
3. To skillet, add wine and stir until heated. Add juice, stock, and mushrooms. Stir, reduce heat, and cook for about 10 minutes, until sauce is partially reduced.
4. Return browned chicken breasts to skillet. Spoon sauce over chicken.
5. Cover and cook for about 5–10 minutes or until chicken is done.
6. Serve sauce over chicken. Garnish with chopped parsley.

Want flavor without lots of salt and fat? Try this dish, which combines wine, lemon juice, and mushrooms into a delicious sauce.

Chicken Orientale

8 boneless, skinless chicken breasts, cut into chunks
8 fresh mushrooms
Black pepper to taste
8 whole white onions, parboiled
2 oranges, quartered
8 canned pineapple chunks, unsweetened

8 cherry tomatoes
1 can (6 oz) frozen, concentrated apple juice, thawed
1 C dry white wine
2 Tbsp soy sauce, low-sodium
Dash ground ginger
2 Tbsp vinegar
¼ C vegetable oil

1. Sprinkle chicken breasts with pepper.
2. Thread 8 skewers as follows: chicken, mushroom, chicken, onion, chicken, orange quarter, chicken, pineapple chunk, cherry tomato. Place kabobs in shallow pan.
3. Combine remaining ingredients and spoon over kabobs. Marinate in refrigerator for at least 1 hour, then drain.
4. Broil kabobs 6 inches from heat for 15 minutes for each side. Brush with marinade every 5 minutes. After done, discard leftover marinade and serve kabobs.

ê❧ *Kabobs look as great as they taste, and these are made with no added salt and very little oil, in order to keep them heart healthy.*

Yield: 8 servings Serving size: ½ kabob
Each serving provides:
Calories: 359
Total fat: 11 g
Saturated fat: 2 g
Cholesterol: 66 mg
Sodium: 226 mg
Total fiber: 3 g
Protein: 28 g
Carbohydrates: 34 g
Potassium: 756 mg

Chicken Ratatouille

Yield: 4 servings
Serving size: 1½ C

Each serving provides:

Calories: 266	
Total fat: 8 g	
Saturated fat: 2 g	
Cholesterol: 66 mg	
Sodium: 253 mg	
Total fiber: 6 g	
Protein: 30 g	
Carbohydrates: 21 g	
Potassium: 1,148 mg	

1 Tbsp vegetable oil
4 medium chicken breast halves, skinned, fat removed, boned, and cut into 1-inch pieces
2 zucchini, about 7 inches long, unpeeled, thinly sliced
1 small eggplant, peeled, cut into 1-inch cubes
1 medium onion, thinly sliced
1 medium green pepper, cut into 1-inch pieces
½ lb fresh mushrooms, sliced
1 can (16 oz) whole tomatoes, cut up
1 clove garlic, minced
1½ tsp dried basil, crushed
1 Tbsp fresh parsley, minced to taste black pepper

1. Heat oil in large nonstick skillet. Add chicken and sauté for about 3 minutes or until lightly browned.
2. Add zucchini, eggplant, onion, green pepper, and mushrooms. Cook for about 15 minutes, stirring occasionally.
3. Add tomatoes, garlic, basil, parsley, and pepper. Stir and continue to cook for about 5 minutes or until chicken is tender.

It may be hard to say "ratatouille," but this one-dish recipe will show you that it's very easy to eat.

Crispy Oven-Fried Chicken

½ C skim milk or buttermilk
1 tsp poultry seasoning
1 C cornflakes, crumbled
1½ Tbsp onion powder
1½ Tbsp garlic powder
2 tsp black pepper

2 tsp dried hot pepper, crushed
1 tsp ginger, ground
8 pieces chicken, skinless
   (4 breasts, 4 drumsticks)
Pinch of paprika
1 tsp vegetable oil

Yield: 6 servings Serving size: ½ breast or 2 small drumsticks
Each serving provides:
Calories: 256
Total fat: 5 g
Saturated fat: 1 g
Cholesterol: 82 mg
Sodium: 286 mg
Total fiber: 1 g
Protein: 30 g
Carbohydrates: 22 g
Potassium: 339 mg

1. Preheat oven to 350°F.
2. Add ½ teaspoon of poultry seasoning to milk.
3. Combine all other spices with cornflake crumbs and place in plastic bag.
4. Wash chicken and pat dry. Dip chicken into milk, shake to remove excess, then quickly shake in bag with seasoning and crumbs.
5. Refrigerate for 1 hour.
6. Remove from refrigerator and sprinkle lightly with paprika for color.
7. Evenly space chicken on greased baking pan.
8. Cover with aluminum foil and bake for 40 minutes. Remove foil and continue baking for an added 30–40 minutes or until meat can be easily pulled away from bone with fork. Drumsticks may require less baking time than breasts. (Do not turn chicken during baking.)

🐝 *Crumbs will form crispy "skin." Kids will love this chicken—it tastes batter-dipped and fried, but is actually good for the heart.*

Finger-Licking Curried Chicken

Yield: 6 servings Serving size: ½ breast or 2 small drumsticks
Each serving provides:
Calories: 213
Total fat: 6 g
Saturated fat: 2 g
Cholesterol: 81 mg
Sodium: 363 mg
Total fiber: 1 g
Protein: 28 g
Carbohydrates: 10 g
Potassium: 384 mg

1½ tsp curry powder
1 tsp thyme, crushed
1 scallion, chopped
1 Tbsp hot pepper, chopped
1 tsp black pepper, ground
8 cloves garlic, crushed
1 Tbsp ginger, grated

¾ tsp salt
8 pieces chicken, skinless
  (breast and drumstick)
1 Tbsp olive oil
1 C water
1 medium white potato, diced
1 large onion, chopped

1. Mix together curry powder, thyme, scallion, hot pepper, cayenne pepper, black pepper, garlic, ginger, onion, and salt.
2. Sprinkle seasoning mixture on chicken.
3. Marinate for at least 2 hours in refrigerator.
4. Heat oil in skillet over medium flame. Add chicken and sauté.
5. Add water and allow chicken to cook over medium flame for 30 minutes.
6. Add diced potatoes and cook for an additional 30 minutes.
7. Add onions and cook for 15 minutes more or until meat is tender.

🐂 *The name tells all—ginger and curry powder make this dish irresistible.*

Grilled Chicken with Green Chili Sauce

4 chicken breasts (boneless,
  skinless)
¼ C olive oil
Juice from 2 limes
¼ tsp oregano
½ tsp black pepper
¼ C water

10–12 tomatillos, husks
  removed, cut in half
½ medium onion, quartered
2 cloves garlic, finely chopped
2 jalapeño peppers
2 Tbsp cilantro, chopped
¼ tsp salt
¼ C low-fat sour cream

Yield: 4 servings
Serving size: 1 breast

Each serving provides:

Calories: 210
Total fat: 5 g
Saturated fat: 1 g
Cholesterol: 73 mg
Sodium: 91 mg
Total fiber: 3 g
Protein: 29 g
Carbohydrates: 14 g
Potassium: 780 mg

1. Combine oil, juice from one lime, oregano, and black pepper in shallow, glass baking dish. Stir.
2. Place chicken breasts in baking dish and turn to coat each side. Cover dish and refrigerate overnight. Turn chicken periodically to marinate it on both sides.
3. Put water, tomatillos, and onion into saucepan. Bring to gentle boil and cook uncovered for 10 minutes or until tomatillos are tender.
4. In blender, place cooked onion, tomatillos, and any remaining water. Add garlic, jalapeño peppers, cilantro, salt, and juice of second lime. Blend until all ingredients are smooth. Place sauce in bowl and refrigerate.
5. Place chicken breasts on hot grill and cook until done. Place chicken on serving platter. Spoon tablespoon of low-fat sour cream over each chicken breast. Pour sauce over sour cream.

In this recipe, the chicken is marinated to make it tender without using a lot of fat.

Jamaican Jerk Chicken

Yields: 6 servings
Serving size: ½ breast or 2 small drumsticks

Each serving provides:

Calories: 199	
Total fat: 4 g	
Saturated fat: 1 g	
Cholesterol: 81 mg	
Sodium: 267 mg	
Total fiber: 1 g	
Protein: 28 g	
Carbohydrates: 12 g	
Potassium: 338 mg	

½ tsp cinnamon, ground
1½ tsp allspice, ground
1½ tsp black pepper, ground
1 Tbsp hot pepper, chopped
1 tsp hot pepper, crushed, dried
2 tsp oregano, crushed
2 tsp thyme, crushed
½ tsp salt

6 cloves garlic, finely chopped
1 C onion, pureed or finely chopped
¼ C vinegar
3 Tbsp brown sugar
8 pieces chicken, skinless (4 breasts, 4 drumsticks)

1. Preheat oven to 350°F.
2. Combine all ingredients except chicken in large bowl. Rub seasoning over chicken and marinate in refrigerator for 6 hours or longer.
3. Evenly space chicken on nonstick or lightly greased baking pan.
4. Cover with aluminum foil and bake for 40 minutes. Remove foil and continue baking for an additional 30–40 minutes or until the meat can be easily pulled away from the bone with a fork.

The spices and peppers in this dish will transport you to a whole new taste.

Very Lemony Chicken

1½ lb chicken breast, skinned, fat removed
½ C fresh lemon juice
2 Tbsp white wine vinegar
½ C fresh lemon peel, sliced

3 tsp fresh oregano, chopped (or 1 tsp dried oregano, crushed)
1 medium onion, sliced
¼ tsp salt
Black pepper to taste
½ tsp paprika

Yield: 4 servings Serving size: 1 breast with sauce
Each serving provides:
Calories: 179
Total fat: 4 g
Saturated fat: 1 g
Cholesterol: 73 mg
Sodium: 222 mg
Total fiber: 2 g
Protein: 28 g
Carbohydrates: 8 g
Potassium: 350 mg

1. Place chicken in 13" × 9" × 2" glass baking dish.
2. Mix lemon juice, vinegar, lemon peel, oregano, and onions.
3. Pour over chicken, cover, and marinate in refrigerator several hours, turning occasionally, or overnight.
4. Sprinkle with salt, pepper, and paprika.
5. Cover and bake at 300°F for 30 minutes. Uncover and bake for additional 30 minutes or until done.

This tangy chicken scores high on taste, while being lower in calories, saturated fat, and cholesterol.

Yosemite Chicken Stew and Dumplings

Yield: 6 servings
Serving size: 1¼ C
stew with 2 dumplings

Each serving provides:
Calories: 301
Total fat: 6 g
Saturated fat: 1 g
Cholesterol: 43 mg
Sodium: 471 mg
Total fiber: 5 g
Protein: 24 g
Carbohydrates: 37 g
Potassium: 409 mg

For Stew:

1 lb chicken, skinless, boneless,
    cut into 1-inch cubes
½ C onion, coarsely chopped
1 medium carrot, peeled, thinly
    sliced
1 stalk celery, thinly sliced
¼ tsp salt
Black pepper to taste
1 pinch ground cloves
1 bay leaf
3 C water

1 tsp cornstarch
1 tsp dried basil
1 package (10 oz) frozen peas

For Cornmeal Dumplings:

1 C yellow cornmeal
¾ C sifted all-purpose flour
2 tsp baking powder
½ tsp salt
1 C low-fat milk
1 Tbsp vegetable oil

To prepare stew:

1. Place chicken, onion, carrot, celery, salt, pepper, cloves, bay leaf, and water in large saucepan. Heat to boiling. Cover and reduce heat to simmer. Cook for about 30 minutes or until chicken is tender.
2. Remove chicken and vegetables from broth. Strain broth.
3. Skim fat from broth. Measure and, if necessary, add water to make 3 C of liquid.
4. Add cornstarch to 1 C of cooled broth and mix by shaking vigorously in jar with tight-fitting lid.
5. Pour mix into saucepan with remaining broth. Cook, stirring constantly, until liquid comes to boil and is thickened.
6. Add basil, peas, and reserved vegetables to sauce. Stir to combine.
7. Add chicken and heat slowly to boiling while preparing cornmeal dumplings.

To prepare dumplings:

1. Put cornmeal, flour, baking powder, and salt into large mixing bowl.
2. Mix milk and oil. Add milk mixture all at once to dry ingredients. Stir just enough to moisten flour and evenly distribute liquid. Dough will be soft.
3. Drop by full tablespoons on top of stew. Cover saucepan tightly. Heat to boiling. Reduce heat to simmering, and steam for about 20 minutes. Do not lift cover.

ₑ◗ This satisfying dish keeps the fat down so you can enjoy its dumplings without turning into one.

Turkey Meat Loaf

1 lb lean turkey, ground
½ C regular oats, dry
1 large egg

1 Tbsp onion, dehydrated
¼ C catsup

1. Combine all ingredients and mix well.
2. Bake in loaf pan at 350°F or to internal temperature of 165°F for 25 minutes.
3. Cut into five slices and serve.

ₑ◗ Here's a healthier version of an old diner favorite.

Yield: 5 servings Serving size: 1 slice (3 oz)
Each serving yields:
Calories: 192
Total fat: 7 g
Saturated fat: 2 g
Cholesterol: 103 mg
Sodium: 214 mg
Total fiber: 1 g
Protein: 21 g
Carbohydrates: 23 g
Potassium: 292 mg

Autumn Turkey-Stuffed Cabbage

Yield: 5 servings
Serving size: 2 rolls

Each serving provides:

Calories: 235	
Total fat: 9 g	
Saturated fat: 3 g	
Cholesterol: 56 mg	
Sodium: 235 mg	
Total fiber: 3 g	
Protein: 20 g	
Carbohydrates: 18 g	
Potassium: 545 mg	

1 head cabbage
½ lb lean ground beef
½ lb ground turkey
2 small onions, one minced,
   one sliced
1 slice stale whole-wheat bread,
   crumbled
¼ C water

⅛ tsp black pepper
1 can (16 oz) diced tomatoes
1 C water
1 medium carrot, sliced
1 Tbsp lemon juice
2 Tbsp brown sugar
1 Tbsp cornstarch

1. Rinse and core cabbage. Carefully remove 10 outer leaves and place in saucepan. Cover with boiling water and simmer for 5 minutes. Remove cooked cabbage leaves and drain on paper towel.
2. Shred ½ C of raw cabbage and set aside.
3. Brown ground beef and turkey, and minced onion in skillet. Drain fat.
4. Place cooked and drained meat mixture, bread crumbs, water, and pepper in mixing bowl.
5. Drain tomatoes, reserving liquid, and add ½ C tomato juice from can to meat mixture. Mix well. Place ¼ C of filling on each parboiled, drained cabbage leaf. Fold. Place folded side down in skillet.
6. Add tomatoes, sliced onion, water, shredded cabbage, and carrot. Cover and simmer for about 1 hour or until cabbage is tender, basting occasionally.
7. Remove cabbage rolls to serving platter, keep warm.
8. Mix lemon juice, brown sugar, and cornstarch together in small bowl. Add to vegetables and liquid in skillet and cook, stirring occasionally, until thickened and clear. Serve over cabbage rolls.

🍜 This dish cuts the fat by mixing turkey and lean beef.

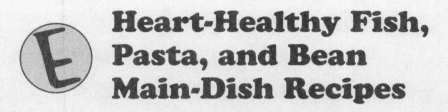

Chapter 12

Heart-Healthy Fish, Pasta, and Bean Main-Dish Recipes

Source: *Keep the Beat: Heart Healthy Recipes,* NIH Publication No. 03-2921. (Visit the National Heart, Lung, and Blood Institute Web site, at *www.nhlbi.nih.gov,* for more information.)

Baked Salmon Dijon

Yield: 6 servings
Serving size: 1 piece
(4 oz)

Each serving provides:
Calories: 196
Total fat: 7 g
Saturated fat: 2 g
Cholesterol: 76 mg
Sodium: 229 mg
Total fiber: less than 1 g
Protein: 27 g
Carbohydrates: 5 g
Potassium: 703 mg

1 C fat-free sour cream
2 tsp dried dill
3 Tbsp scallions, finely chopped
2 Tbsp Dijon mustard
2 Tbsp lemon juice

1½ lb salmon fillet with skin, cut in center
½ tsp garlic powder
½ tsp black pepper
Fat-free cooking spray, as needed

1. Whisk sour cream, dill, onion, mustard, and lemon juice in small bowl to blend.
2. Preheat oven to 400°F. Lightly oil baking sheet with cooking spray.
3. Place salmon, skin side down, on prepared sheet. Sprinkle with garlic powder and pepper, then spread with the sauce.
4. Bake salmon until just opaque in center, about 20 minutes.

This salmon entrée is easy to make and will be enjoyed by the whole family!

Baked Trout

Yield: 6 servings
Serving size: 1 piece

Each serving provides:
Calories: 236
Total fat: 9 g
Saturated fat: 3 g
Cholesterol: 104 mg
Sodium: 197 mg
Total fiber: less than 1 g
Protein: 34 g
Carbohydrates: 2 g
Potassium: 865 mg

2 lb trout fillet, cut into 6 pieces*
3 Tbsp lime juice (about 2 limes)
1 medium tomato, chopped
½ medium onion, chopped
3 Tbsp cilantro, chopped

½ tsp olive oil
¼ tsp black pepper
¼ tsp salt
¼ tsp red pepper (optional)

*Any kind of fish can be used.

1. Preheat oven to 350°F.
2. Rinse fish and pat dry. Place in baking dish.
3. In separate dish, mix remaining ingredients together and pour over fish.
4. Bake for 15–20 minutes or until fork-tender.

You'll reel them in with this nutritious delicious dish.

Catfish Stew and Rice

2 medium potatoes
1 can (14½ oz) tomatoes,
   cut up*
1 C onion, chopped
1 C (8-oz bottle) clam juice
   or water
1 C water
2 cloves garlic, minced
½ head cabbage, coarsely
   chopped

1 lb catfish fillets
Green onion, sliced (optional)
1½ Tbsp Chili and Spice
   Seasoning (see page 201)
2 C cooked rice (white or brown)

*Reduce the sodium by using
   low- or no-added-sodium
   canned tomatoes.

Yield: 4 servings Serving size: 1 C of stew with ½ C of rice
Each serving provides:
Calories: 363
Total fat: 8 g
Saturated fat: 2 g
Cholesterol: 87 mg
Sodium: 355 mg
Total fiber: 4 g
Protein: 28 g
Carbohydrates: 44 g
Potassium: 1,079 mg

1. Peel potatoes and cut into quarters.
2. In large pot, combine potatoes, tomatoes and their juice, onion, clam juice, water, and garlic. Bring to boil and reduce heat. Cook covered over medium-low heat for 10 minutes.
3. Add cabbage and return to boil. Reduce heat. Cook covered over medium-low heat for 5 minutes, stirring occasionally.
4. Meanwhile, cut fillets into 2-inch lengths. Coat with Chili and Spice Seasoning.
5. Add fish to vegetables. Reduce heat and simmer covered for 5 minutes or until fish flakes easily with fork.
6. Serve in soup plates. Garnish with sliced green onion, if desired. Serve with scoop of hot cooked rice.

¿🍽 *Catfish isn't just a Southern treat anymore. Everyone can go "down home" with this dish.*

Fish Veronique

Yield: 4 servings Serving size: 1 fillet with sauce
Each serving provides:
Calories: 166
Total fat: 2 g
Saturated fat: 1 g
Cholesterol: 61 mg
Sodium: 343 mg
Total fiber: less than 1 g
Protein: 24 g
Carbohydrates: 9 g
Potassium: 453 mg

1 lb white fish (such as cod, sole, or turbot)
¼ tsp salt
⅛ tsp black pepper
¼ C dry white wine
¼ C chicken stock or broth, skim fat from top
1 Tbsp lemon juice
1 Tbsp soft margarine
2 Tbsp flour
¾ C low-fat or skim milk
½ C seedless grapes
Nonstick cooking spray, as needed

1. Spray 10" × 6" baking dish with nonstick spray. Place fish in pan and sprinkle with salt and pepper.
2. Mix wine, stock, and lemon juice in small bowl and pour over fish.
3. Cover and bake at 350°F for 15 minutes.
4. Melt margarine in small saucepan. Remove from heat and blend in flour. Gradually add milk and cook over moderately low heat, stirring constantly, until thickened.
5. Remove fish from oven, and pour liquid from baking dish into "cream" sauce, stirring until blended. Pour sauce over fish and sprinkle with grapes.
6. Broil about 4 inches from heat for 5 minutes or until sauce starts to brown.

Here's a trick to treat the taste buds: Remove the fat from the chicken broth and add low-fat milk to get a healthy sauce that tastes rich and looks creamy.

Mediterranean Baked Fish

*1 lb fish fillets (sole, flounder, or
    sea perch)*
2 tsp olive oil
1 large onion, sliced
*1 can (16 oz) whole tomatoes,
    drained (juice reserved),
    coarsely chopped*
*½ C tomato juice (reserved from
    canned tomatoes)*
1 bay leaf

1 clove garlic, minced
1 C dry white wine
¼ C lemon juice
¼ C orange juice
1 Tbsp fresh orange peel, grated
1 tsp fennel seeds, crushed
½ tsp dried oregano, crushed
½ tsp dried thyme, crushed
½ tsp dried basil, crushed
Black pepper to taste

Yield: 4 servings Serving size: 4-oz fillet with sauce
Each serving provides:
Calories: 178
Total fat: 4 g
Saturated fat: 1 g
Cholesterol: 56 mg
Sodium: 260 mg
Total fiber: 3 g
Protein: 22 g
Carbohydrates: 12 g
Potassium: 678 mg

1. Heat oil in large nonstick skillet. Add onion and sauté over moderate heat for 5 minutes or until soft.
2. Add all remaining ingredients except fish. Stir well and simmer uncovered for 30 minutes.
3. Arrange fish in 10" × 6" baking dish. Cover with sauce. Bake uncovered at 375°F for about 15 minutes or until fish flakes easily.

&⬩ *Taste the Mediterranean in this dish's tomato,
onion, and garlic sauce.*

Mouth-Watering Oven-Fried Fish

2 lb fish fillets
1 Tbsp lemon juice, fresh
¼ C skim milk or 1% buttermilk
2 drops hot pepper sauce
1 tsp fresh garlic, minced
¼ tsp white pepper, ground

¼ tsp salt
¼ tsp onion powder
½ C cornflakes, crumbled,
   or regular bread crumbs
1 Tbsp vegetable oil
1 fresh lemon, cut in wedges

Yield: 6 servings Serving size: 1 cut piece
Each serving provides:
Calories: 183
Total fat: 2 g
Saturated fat: less than 1 g
Cholesterol: 80 mg
Sodium: 325 mg
Total fiber: 1 g
Protein: 30 g
Carbohydrates: 10 g
Potassium: 453 mg

1. Preheat oven to 475°F.
2. Wipe fillets with lemon juice and pat dry.
3. Combine milk, hot pepper sauce, and garlic.
4. Combine pepper, salt, and onion powder with cornflake crumbs and place on plate.
5. Let fillets sit briefly in milk. Remove and coat fillets on both sides with seasoned crumbs. Let stand briefly until coating sticks to each side of fish.
6. Arrange on lightly oiled shallow baking dish.
7. Bake for 20 minutes on middle rack without turning.
8. Cut into 6 pieces. Serve with fresh lemon.

🥄 *This heart-healthy dish can be made with many kinds of fish—to be enjoyed over and over.*

Scallop Kabobs

3 medium green peppers, cut
   into 1½-inch squares
1½ lb fresh bay scallops
1 pt cherry tomatoes
¼ C dry white wine

¼ C vegetable oil
3 Tbsp lemon juice
Dash garlic powder
Black pepper to taste
4 skewers

1. Parboil green peppers for 2 minutes.
2. Alternately thread first three ingredients on skewers.
3. Combine next five ingredients.
4. Brush kabobs with wine/oil/lemon mixture, then place on grill (or under broiler).
5. Grill for 15 minutes, turning and basting frequently.

🐟 *These colorful kabobs use scallops, which are naturally low in saturated fat.*

Yield: 4 servings Serving size: 1 kabob (6 oz)
Each serving provides:
Calories: 224
Total fat: 6 g
Saturated fat: 1 g
Cholesterol: 43 mg
Sodium: 355 mg
Total fiber: 3 g
Protein: 30 g
Carbohydrates: 13 g
Potassium: 993 mg

Chillin' Out Pasta Salad

2½ C (8 oz) medium shell pasta
1 C (8 oz) plain nonfat yogurt
2 Tbsp spicy brown mustard
2 Tbsp salt-free herb seasoning
1½ C celery, chopped

1 C green onion, sliced
1 lb small shrimp, cooked
3 C (about 3 large) tomatoes,
   coarsely chopped

1. Cook pasta according to directions—but do not add salt to water. Drain and cool.
2. In large bowl, stir together yogurt, mustard, and herb seasoning.
3. Add pasta, celery, and green onion, and mix well. Chill for at least 2 hours.
4. Just before serving, carefully stir in shrimp and tomatoes.

🐟 *Cook up this taste feast and set the table for a new family favorite.*

Yield: 12 servings Serving size: ½ C
Each serving provides:
Calories: 140
Total fat: 1 g
Saturated fat: less than 1 g
Cholesterol: 60 mg
Sodium: 135 mg
Total fiber: 1 g
Protein: 14 g
Carbohydrates: 19 g
Potassium: 295 mg

Spinach-Stuffed Sole

Yield: 4 servings
Serving size: 1 fillet roll

Each serving provides:
Calories: 273
Total fat: 9 g
Saturated fat: 4 g
Cholesterol: 95 mg
Sodium: 163 mg
Total fiber: 2 g
Protein: 39 g
Carbohydrates: 6 g
Potassium: 880 mg

1 tsp olive oil
½ lb fresh mushrooms, sliced
½ lb fresh spinach, chopped
¼ tsp oregano leaves, crushed
1 clove garlic, minced
1½ lb sole fillets or other
    white fish

2 Tbsp sherry
4 oz (1 C) part-skim mozzarella
    cheese, grated
Nonstick cooking spray, as
    needed

1. Preheat oven to 400°F.
2. Coat 10" × 6" baking dish with nonstick cooking spray.
3. Heat oil in skillet and sauté mushrooms for about 3 minutes or until tender.
4. Add spinach and continue cooking for about 1 minute or until spinach is barely wilted. Remove from heat and drain liquid into prepared baking dish.
5. Add oregano and garlic to drained sautéed vegetables. Stir to mix ingredients.
6. Divide vegetable mixture evenly among fillets and place in center of each.
7. Roll each fillet around mixture and place seam-side down in prepared baking dish.
8. Sprinkle with sherry, then grated mozzarella cheese. Bake for 15–20 minutes or until fish flakes easily. Lift out with slotted spoon.

*Heart healthy doesn't have to mean plain cooking,
as this special dish shows.*

Classic Macaroni and Cheese

2 C macaroni
½ C onions, chopped
½ C evaporated skim milk
1 medium egg, beaten
¼ tsp black pepper

1¼ C (4 oz) low-fat sharp
cheddar cheese, finely
shredded
Nonstick cooking spray, as
needed

Yield: 8 servings Serving size: ½ C	
Each serving provides:	
Calories: 200	
Total fat: 4 g	
Saturated fat: 2 g	
Cholesterol: 34 mg	
Sodium: 120 mg	
Total fiber: 1 g	
Protein: 11 g	
Carbohydrates: 29 g	
Potassium: 119 mg	

1. Cook macaroni according to directions—but do not add salt to the cooking water. Drain and set aside.
2. Spray casserole dish with nonstick cooking spray.
3. Preheat oven to 350°F.
4. Lightly spray saucepan with nonstick cooking spray. Add onions to saucepan and sauté for about 3 minutes.
5. In another bowl, combine macaroni, onions, and rest of the ingredients, and mix thoroughly.
6. Transfer mixture into casserole dish.
7. Bake for 25 minutes or until bubbly. Let stand for 10 minutes before serving.

🍴 *This recipe proves you don't have to give up your favorite dishes to eat heart-healthy meals. Here's a lower-fat version of a true classic.*

Sweet-and-Sour Seashells

Yield: 18 servings
Serving size: ½ C

Each serving provides:

Calories: 158	
Total fat: 2 g	
Saturated fat: less than 1 g	
Cholesterol: 0 mg	
Sodium: 35 mg	
Total fiber: 2 g	
Protein: 4 g	
Carbohydrates: 31 g	
Potassium: 150 mg	

1 lb uncooked small seashell pasta (9 C cooked)
2 Tbsp vegetable oil
¾ C sugar
½ C cider vinegar
½ C wine vinegar
½ C water
3 Tbsp prepared mustard
Black pepper to taste
1 jar (2 oz) sliced pimentos
2 small cucumbers
2 small onions, thinly sliced
18 leaves lettuce

1. Cook pasta in unsalted water, drain, rinse with cold water, and drain again. Stir in oil.
2. Transfer to 4-quart bowl. In blender, place sugar, vinegars, water, prepared mustard, salt, pepper, and pimento. Process at low speed for 15–20 seconds, or just enough so flecks of pimento can be seen. Pour over pasta.
3. Score cucumber peel with fork tines. Cut cucumber in half lengthwise, then slice thinly. Add to pasta with onion slices. Toss well.
4. Marinate, covered, in refrigerator for 24 hours. Stir occasionally.
5. Drain, and serve on lettuce.

🍃 Drain the marinade before serving this dish in order to lower the fat and sodium—but keep all the great taste.

Black Beans with Rice

1 lb black beans, dry
7 C water
1 medium green pepper,
* coarsely chopped*
1½ C onion, chopped
1 Tbsp vegetable oil
2 bay leaves
1 clove garlic, minced

½ tsp salt
1 Tbsp vinegar (or lemon juice)
6 C rice, cooked in unsalted
* water*
1 jar (4 oz) sliced pimento,
* drained*
1 lemon, cut into wedges

Yield: 6 servings Serving size: 8 oz	
Each serving provides:	
Calories: 508	
Total fat: 4 g	
Saturated fat: 1 g	
Cholesterol: 0 mg	
Sodium: 206 mg	
Total fiber: 14 g	
Protein: 21 g	
Carbohydrates: 98 g	
Potassium: 852 mg	

1. Pick through beans to remove bad ones. Soak beans overnight in cold water. Drain and rinse.
2. In large soup pot or Dutch oven, stir together beans, water, green pepper, onion, oil, bay leaves, garlic, and salt. Cover and boil for 1 hour.
3. Reduce heat and simmer, covered, for 3–4 hours or until beans are very tender. Stir occasionally, and add water if needed.
4. Remove and mash about a third of beans. Return to pot. Stir and heat through.
5. When ready to serve, remove bay leaves and stir in vinegar or lemon juice.
6. Serve over rice. Garnish with sliced pimento and lemon wedges.

❧ A delicious Caribbean favorite that's
made with very little added fat.

Caribbean Pink Beans

Yield: 16 servings
Serving size: ½ C

Each serving provides:

Calories: 133	
Total fat: less than 1 g	
Saturated fat: less than 1 g	
Cholesterol: 0 mg	
Sodium: 205 mg	
Total fiber: 5 g	
Protein: 6 g	
Carbohydrates: 28 g	
Potassium: 495 mg	

1 lb pink beans
10 C water
2 medium plantains, finely chopped
1 large tomato, finely chopped
1 small red pepper, finely chopped
1 medium white onion, finely chopped
3 cloves garlic, finely chopped
1½ tsp salt

1. Rinse and pick through beans. Put beans in large pot and add 10 C of water. Place pot in refrigerator and allow beans to soak overnight.
2. Cook beans until soft. Add more water, as needed, while beans are cooking.
3. Add plantains, tomato, pepper, onion, garlic, and salt. Continue cooking at low heat until plantains are soft.

This dish stays healthy by using beans prepared without lard or other fat. Try it with rice.

Vegetarian Spaghetti Sauce

Yield: 6 servings
Serving size: ¾ C

Each serving provides:

Calories: 102	
Total fat: 5 g	
Saturated fat: 1 g	
Cholesterol: 0 mg	
Sodium: 459 mg	
Total fiber: 5 g	
Protein: 3 g	
Carbohydrates: 14 g	
Potassium: 623 mg	

2 Tbsp olive oil
2 small onions, chopped
3 cloves garlic, chopped
1¼ C zucchini, sliced
1 Tbsp oregano, dried
1 Tbsp basil, dried
1 can (8 oz) tomato sauce
1 can (6 oz) tomato paste*
2 medium tomatoes, chopped
1 C water

*Reduce sodium by using 6-oz can of no-salt-added tomato paste. New sodium content for each serving is 260 mg.

1. In medium skillet, heat oil. Sauté onions, garlic, and zucchini in oil for 5 minutes on medium heat.
2. Add remaining ingredients and simmer, covered, for 45 minutes.
3. Serve over spaghetti.

Simple and simply delicious—here's a healthy sauce to serve with spaghetti or other pasta.

New Orleans Red Beans

1 lb dry red beans
2 qt water
1½ C onion, chopped
1 C celery, chopped
4 bay leaves
1 C green peppers, chopped

3 Tbsp garlic, chopped
3 Tbsp parsley, chopped
2 tsp dried thyme, crushed
1 tsp salt
1 tsp black pepper

Yield: 8 servings Serving size: 1¼ C
Each serving provides:
Calories: 171
Total fat: less than 1 g
Saturated fat: less than 1 g
Cholesterol: 0 mg
Sodium: 285 mg
Total fiber: 7 g
Protein: 10 g
Carbohydrates: 32 g
Potassium: 665 mg

1. Pick through beans to remove bad ones. Rinse beans rinse thoroughly.
2. In large pot, combine beans, water, onion, celery, and bay leaves. Bring to boil. Reduce heat, cover, and cook over low heat for about 1½ hours or until beans are tender. Stir. Mash beans against side of pan.
3. Add green pepper, garlic, parsley, thyme, salt, and black pepper. Cook uncovered over low heat until creamy, about 30 minutes. Remove bay leaves.
4. Serve with hot cooked brown rice, if desired.

This vegetarian dish is virtually fat-free and entirely delicious.

Summer Vegetable Spaghetti

Yield: 9 servings Serving size: 1 C of spaghetti and ¾ C of sauce with vegetables

Each serving provides:
Calories: 271
Total fat: 3 g
Saturated fat: 1 g
Cholesterol: 4 mg
Sodium: 328 mg
Total fiber: 5 g
Protein: 11 g
Carbohydrates: 51 g
Potassium: 436 mg

2 C small yellow onions, cut in eighths
2 C (about 1 lb) ripe tomatoes, peeled, chopped
2 C (about 1 lb) yellow and green squash, thinly sliced
½ C (about ½ lb) fresh green beans, cut
⅔ C water
2 Tbsp fresh parsley, minced
1 clove garlic, minced
½ tsp chili powder
¼ tsp salt
Black pepper to taste
1 can (6 oz) tomato paste
1 lb spaghetti, uncooked
½ C Parmesan cheese, grated

1. Combine first 10 ingredients in large saucepan. Cook for 10 minutes, then stir in tomato paste. Cover and cook gently for 15 minutes, stirring occasionally, until vegetables are tender.
2. Cook spaghetti in unsalted water according to package directions.
3. Spoon sauce over drained hot spaghetti. Sprinkle Parmesan cheese on top.

This lively vegetarian pasta dish is delicious hot or cold.

Zucchini Lasagna

½ lb lasagna noodles, cooked
    in unsalted water
¾ C part-skim mozzarella
    cheese, grated
1½ C fat-free cottage cheese*
¼ C Parmesan cheese, grated
1½ C raw zucchini, sliced
2½ C no-salt-added tomato
    sauce

2 tsp basil, dried
2 tsp oregano, dried
¼ C onion, chopped
1 clove garlic
⅛ tsp black pepper

*Use unsalted cottage cheese to
    reduce the sodium content.
    New sodium content for each
    serving is 196 mg.

Yield: 6 servings
Serving size: 1 piece

Each serving provides:
Calories: 276
Total fat: 5 g
Saturated fat: 2 g
Cholesterol: 11 mg
Sodium: 380 mg
Total fiber: 5 g
Protein: 19 g
Carbohydrates: 41 g
Potassium: 561 mg

1. Preheat oven to 350°F. Lightly spray 9" × 13" baking dish with vegetable oil spray.
2. In small bowl, combine ⅛ C mozzarella and 1 tablespoon Parmesan cheese. Set aside.
3. In medium bowl, combine remaining mozzarella and Parmesan cheese with all of the cottage cheese. Mix well and set aside.
4. Combine tomato sauce with remaining ingredients. Spread thin layer of tomato sauce in bottom of baking dish. Add a third of noodles in single layer. Spread half of cottage cheese mixture on top. Add layer of zucchini.
5. Repeat layering. Add thin coating of sauce. Top with noodles, sauce, and reserved cheese mixture. Cover with aluminum foil.
6. Bake for 30–40 minutes. Cool for 10–15 minutes. Cut into 6 portions.

*Say "Cheese!" This healthy version of a favorite
comfort food will leave you smiling.*

Chapter 13

Heart-Healthy Bread, Dessert, and Dressing Recipes

Apricot-Orange Bread	1-2-3 Peach Cobbler
Banana-Nut Bread	Rice Pudding
Good-for-You Cornbread	Chili and Spice Seasoning
Homestyle Biscuits	Fresh Salsa
Apple Coffee Cake	Hot 'N Spicy Seasoning
Frosted Cake	Vinaigrette Salad Dressing
Rainbow Fruit Salad	Yogurt Salad Dressing
Banana Mousse	Mango Shake
Tropical Fruit Compote	Summer Breezes Smoothie
Crunchy Pumpkin Pie	

Source: *Keep the Beat: Heart Healthy Recipes,* NIH Publication No. 03-2921. (Visit the National Heart, Lung, and Blood Institute Web site, at *www.nhlbi.nih.gov,* for more information.)

Apricot-Orange Bread

Yield: 2 loaves Serving size: ½-inch slice

Each serving provides:
Calories: 97
Total fat: 2 g
Saturated fat: less than 1 g
Cholesterol: 6 mg
Sodium: 113 mg
Total fiber: 1 g
Protein: 2 g
Carbohydrates: 18 g
Potassium: 110 mg

1 package (6 oz) dried apricots, cut into small pieces
2 C water
2 Tbsp margarine (trans-fat free)
1 C sugar
1 egg, slightly beaten
1 Tbsp orange peel, freshly grated

3½ C all-purpose whole-grain flour, sifted
½ C fat-free dry milk powder
2 tsp baking powder
1 tsp baking soda
1 tsp salt
½ C orange juice
½ C pecans, chopped

1. Preheat oven to 350°F. Lightly oil two, 9" × 5" loaf pans.
2. Cook apricots in water in covered medium-size saucepan for 10–15 minutes or until tender but not mushy. Drain and reserve ¾ C liquid. Set apricots aside to cool.
3. Cream together margarine and sugar. By hand, beat in egg and orange peel.
4. Sift together flour, dry milk, baking powder, soda, and salt. Add to creamed mixture alternately with reserved apricot liquid and orange juice.
5. Stir apricot pieces and pecans into batter.
6. Turn batter into prepared pans.
7. Bake for 40–45 minutes or until bread springs back when lightly touched in center.
8. Cool for 5 minutes in pans. Remove from pans and completely cool on wire rack before slicing.

ॐ *This bread is low in all the right places—saturated fat, cholesterol, and sodium—without losing any taste and texture.*

Banana-Nut Bread

1 C ripe bananas, mashed
⅓ C low-fat buttermilk
½ C brown sugar, packed
¼ C margarine
1 egg

2 C all-purpose whole-grain
* flour, sifted*
1 tsp baking powder
½ tsp baking soda
½ tsp salt
½ C pecans, chopped

Yield: 2 loaves Serving size: ½-inch slice
Each serving provides:
Calories: 133
Total fat: 5 g
Saturated fat: 1 g
Cholesterol: 12 mg
Sodium: 138 mg
Total fiber: 1 g
Protein: 2 g
Carbohydrates: 20 g
Potassium: 114 mg

1. Preheat oven to 350°F. Lightly oil two, 9" × 5" loaf pans.
2. Stir together mashed bananas and buttermilk. Set aside.
3. Cream brown sugar and margarine together until light. Beat in egg. Add banana mixture and beat well.
4. Sift together flour, baking powder, baking soda, and salt. Add all at once to liquid ingredients. Stir until well blended.
5. Stir in nuts, and turn into prepared pans.
6. Bake for 50–55 minutes or until toothpick inserted in center comes out clean. Cool for 5 minutes in pans.
7. Remove from pans and complete cooling on a wire rack before slicing.

Bananas and low-fat buttermilk lower the fat for this old favorite, while keeping all the moistness.

Good-for-You Cornbread

Yield: 10 servings Serving size: 1 square

Each serving provides:

Calories: 178	
Total fat: 6 g	
Saturated fat: 1 g	
Cholesterol: 22 mg	
Sodium: 94 mg	
Total fiber: 1 g	
Protein: 4 g	
Carbohydrates: 27 g	
Potassium: 132 mg	

1 C cornmeal
1 C flour
¼ C white sugar
1 tsp baking powder
1 C 1% fat buttermilk

1 egg, whole
¼ C tub margarine
   (trans-fat free)
1 tsp vegetable oil (to grease
   baking pan)

1. Preheat oven to 350°F.
2. Mix together cornmeal, flour, sugar, and baking powder.
3. In another bowl, combine buttermilk and egg. Beat lightly.
4. Slowly add buttermilk and egg mixture to dry ingredients.
5. Add margarine, and mix by hand or with mixer for 1 minute.
6. Bake for 20–25 minutes in an 8" × 8", greased baking dish. Cool. Cut into 10 squares.

Homestyle Biscuits

Yield: 15 servings Serving size: One 2-inch biscuit

Each serving provides:

Calories: 99	
Total fat: 3 g	
Saturated fat: less than 1 g	
Cholesterol: less than 1 mg	
Sodium: 72 mg	
Total fiber: 1 g	
Protein: 2 g	
Carbohydrates: 15 g	
Potassium: 102 mg	

2 C flour
2 tsp baking powder
¼ tsp baking soda
¼ tsp salt

2 Tbsp sugar
⅔ C 1% fat buttermilk
3⅓ Tbsp vegetable oil

1. Preheat oven to 450°F.
2. In medium bowl, combine flour, baking powder, baking soda, salt, and sugar.
3. In small bowl, stir together buttermilk and all of the oil. Pour over flour mixture and stir until well mixed.
4. On lightly floured surface, knead dough gently for 10–12 strokes. Roll or pat dough to ¾-inch thickness. Cut with 2-inch biscuit or cookie cutter, dipping cutter in flour between cuts. Transfer biscuits to an ungreased baking sheet.
5. Bake for 12 minutes or until golden brown. Serve warm.

Apple Coffee Cake

5 C tart apples, cored, peeled,
    chopped
1 C sugar
1 C dark raisins
½ C pecans, chopped
¼ C vegetable oil

2 tsp vanilla
1 egg, beaten
2 C all-purpose whole-grain
    flour, sifted
1 tsp baking soda
2 tsp ground cinnamon

1. Preheat oven to 350°F.
2. Lightly oil a 13" × 9" × 2" pan.
3. In large mixing bowl, combine apples with sugar, raisins, and pecans. Mix well and let stand for 30 minutes.
4. Stir in oil, vanilla, and egg. Sift together flour, soda, and cinnamon, and stir into apple mixture about a third at a time—just enough to moisten dry ingredients.
5. Turn batter into pan. Bake for 35–40 minutes. Cool cake slightly before serving.

Apples and raisins keep this cake moist— which means less oil and more health.

Yield: 20 servings Serving size: One 3½-inch by 2½-inch piece
Each serving provides:
Calories: 196
Total fat: 8 g
Saturated fat: 1 g
Cholesterol: 11 mg
Sodium: 67 mg
Total fiber: 2 g
Protein: 3 g
Carbohydrates: 31 g
Potassium: 136 mg

Frosted Cake

Yield: 16 servings
Serving size: 1 slice

Each serving provides:
Calories: 241
Total fat: 5 g
Saturated fat: 2 g
Cholesterol: 57 mg
Sodium: 273 mg
Total fiber: 1 g
Protein: 4 g
Carbohydrates: 45 g
Potassium: 95 mg

For Cake:

2¼ C cake flour
2¼ tsp baking powder
4 Tbsp margarine (trans-fat free)
1¼ C sugar
4 eggs
1 tsp vanilla
1 Tbsp orange peel
¾ C skim milk

For Icing:

3 oz low-fat cream cheese
2 Tbsp skim milk
6 Tbsp cocoa
2 C confectioners' sugar, sifted
½ tsp vanilla extract

To prepare cake:

1. Preheat oven to 325°F.
2. Grease 10-inch round pan (at least 2½ inches high) with small amount of cooking oil or use nonstick cooking oil spray. Powder pan with flour. Tap out excess flour.
3. Sift together flour and baking powder.
4. In separate bowl, beat together margarine and sugar until soft and creamy.
5. Beat in eggs, vanilla, and orange peel.
6. Gradually add flour mixture, alternating with milk, beginning and ending with flour.
7. Pour mixture into pan. Bake for 40–45 minutes or until done. Let cake cool for 5–10 minutes before removing from pan. Let cool completely before icing.

To prepare icing:

1. Cream together cream cheese and milk until smooth. Add cocoa. Blend well.
2. Slowly add sugar until icing is smooth. Mix in vanilla.
3. Smooth icing over top and sides of cooled cake.

Rainbow Fruit Salad

For Fruit Salad:

1 large mango, peeled, diced
2 C fresh blueberries
2 bananas, sliced
2 C fresh strawberries, halved
2 C seedless grapes
2 nectarines, unpeeled, sliced
1 kiwi fruit, peeled, sliced

For Honey-Orange Sauce:

⅓ C unsweetened orange juice
2 Tbsp lemon juice
1½ Tbsp honey
¼ tsp ground ginger
Dash nutmeg

1. Prepare the fruit.
2. Combine all ingredients for sauce and mix.
3. Just before serving, pour honey-orange sauce over fruit.

🐦 *You can't go wrong with this salad—it's juicy, fresh, naturally low in fat and sodium, and cholesterol free. Enjoy it as a salad or as a dessert.*

Yield: 12 servings Serving size: 4-oz cup
Each serving provides:
Calories: 96
Total fat: 1 g
Saturated fat: less than 1 g
Cholesterol: 0 mg
Sodium: 4 mg
Total fiber: 3 g
Protein: 1 g
Carbohydrates: 24 g
Potassium: 302 mg

Banana Mousse

2 Tbsp low-fat milk
4 tsp sugar
1 tsp vanilla

1 medium banana, cut in quarters
1 C plain low-fat yogurt
8 slices (¼ inch each) banana

1. Place milk, sugar, vanilla, and banana in blender. Process for 15 seconds at high speed until smooth.
2. Pour mixture into small bowl and fold in yogurt. Chill.
3. Spoon into four dessert dishes and garnish each with two banana slices just before serving.

🐦 *This creamy dessert is a dream—yet low in saturated fat, cholesterol, and sodium.*

Yield: 4 servings Serving size: ½ C
Each serving provides:
Calories: 94
Total fat: 1 g
Saturated fat: 1 g
Cholesterol: 4 mg
Sodium: 47 mg
Total fiber: 1 g
Protein: 1 g
Carbohydrates: 18 g
Potassium: 297 mg

Tropical Fruit Compote

Yield: 8 servings Serving size: 1 C	
Each serving provides:	
Calories: 148	
Total fat: less than 1 g	
Saturated fat: less than 1 g	
Cholesterol: 0 mg	
Sodium: 3 mg	
Total fiber: 3 g	
Protein: 1 g	
Carbohydrates: 38 g	
Potassium: 310 mg	

¾ C water
½ C sugar
2 tsp fresh lemon juice
1 piece lemon peel
½ tsp rum or vanilla extract (optional)
1 pineapple, cored, peeled, cut into 8 slices

2 mangos, peeled, pitted, cut into 8 pieces
3 bananas, peeled, cut into 8 diagonal pieces
Fresh mint leaves to taste (optional)

1. In saucepan, combine ¾ C of water with sugar, lemon juice, and lemon peel (and rum or vanilla extract, if desired). Bring to boil, then reduce heat and add fruit. Cook at very low heat for 5 minutes.
2. Pour off syrup into cup.
3. Remove lemon rind from saucepan, and cool cooked fruit for 2 hours.
4. To serve, arrange fruit in serving dish and pour a few teaspoons of syrup over fruit.

Fresh or cooked, fruits are a great low-calorie dessert. Top with low-fat or fat-free sour cream.

Crunchy Pumpkin Pie

For Crust:

1 C oats
¼ C whole-wheat flour
¼ C ground almonds
2 Tbsp brown sugar
¼ tsp salt
3 Tbsp vegetable oil
1 Tbsp water

For Filling:

¼ C brown sugar, packed
½ tsp ground cinnamon
¼ tsp ground nutmeg
¼ tsp salt
1 egg, beaten
4 tsp vanilla
1 C canned pumpkin
⅔ C evaporated skim milk

Yield: 9 servings Serving size: ¹/₉ of 9-inch pie
Each serving provides:
Calories: 169
Total fat: 7 g
Saturated fat: 1 g
Cholesterol: 24 mg
Sodium: 207 mg
Total fiber: 3 g
Protein: 5 g
Carbohydrates: 22 g
Potassium: 223 mg

To prepare crust:

1. Preheat oven to 425°F.
2. Mix oats, flour, almonds, sugar, and salt in small mixing bowl.
3. Blend oil and water in measuring cup with fork or small wire whisk until emulsified.
4. Add oil mixture to dry ingredients and mix well. If needed, add small amount of water to hold mixture together.
5. Press into 9-inch pie pan, and bake for 8–10 minutes, or until light brown.
6. Turn down oven to 350°F.

To prepare filling:

7. Mix sugar, cinnamon, nutmeg, and salt in bowl.
8. Add egg and vanilla, and mix to blend ingredients.
9. Add pumpkin and milk, and stir to combine.

Putting it together:

10. Pour filling into prepared pie shell.
11. Bake for 45 minutes at 350°F or until knife inserted near center comes out clean.

1-2-3 Peach Cobbler

Yield: 8 servings
Serving size: 1 piece

Each serving provides:

Calories: 271

Total fat: 4 g

Saturated fat: less than 1 g

Cholesterol: less than 1 mg

Sodium: 263 mg

Total fiber: 2 g

Protein: 4 g

Carbohydrates: 54 g

Potassium: 284 mg

½ tsp ground cinnamon
1 Tbsp vanilla extract
2 Tbsp cornstarch
1 C peach nectar
¼ C pineapple juice or peach juice (if desired, use juice reserved from canned peaches)
2 cans (16 oz each) peaches, packed in juice and drained, or 1¾ lb fresh sliced

1 Tbsp margarine (trans-fat free)
1 C dry pancake mix
⅔ C whole-grain flour
½ C sugar
⅔ C evaporated skim milk
Nonstick cooking spray, as needed
½ tsp nutmeg
1 Tbsp brown sugar

1. Combine cinnamon, vanilla, cornstarch, peach nectar, and pineapple or peach juice in saucepan over medium heat. Stir constantly until mixture thickens and bubbles.
2. Add sliced peaches to mixture.
3. Reduce heat and simmer for 5–10 minutes.
4. In another saucepan, melt margarine and set aside.
5. Lightly spray 8-inch-square glass dish with cooking spray. Pour hot peach mixture into dish.
6. In another bowl, combine pancake mix, flour, sugar, and melted margarine. Stir in milk. Quickly spoon this over peach mixture.
7. Combine nutmeg and brown sugar. Sprinkle on top of batter.
8. Bake at 400°F for 15–20 minutes or until golden brown.
9. Cool and cut into 8 pieces.

¿❧ *What could be better than peach cobbler straight from the oven?*
Try this healthier version of the classic favorite.

Rice Pudding

6 C water
2 sticks cinnamon
1 C rice

3 C skim milk
⅔ C sugar
½ tsp salt

1. Put water and cinnamon sticks into medium saucepan. Bring to boil.
2. Stir in rice. Cook on low heat for 30 minutes until rice is soft and water has evaporated.
3. Add skim milk, sugar, and salt. Cook for another 15 minutes until mixture thickens.

🍃 *Skim milk gives a whole lot of flavor without whole milk's fat and calories.*

Yield: 5 servings Serving size: ½ C
Each serving provides:
Calories: 372
Total fat: 1 g
Saturated fat: less than 1 g
Cholesterol: 3 mg
Sodium: 366 mg
Total fiber: 1 g
Protein: 10 g
Carbohydrates: 81 g
Potassium: 363 mg

Chili and Spice Seasoning

¼ C paprika
2 Tbsp dried oregano, crushed
2 tsp chili powder
1 tsp garlic powder

1 tsp black pepper
½ tsp red (cayenne) pepper
½ tsp dry mustard

Mix together all ingredients. Store in airtight container.

🍃 *This spicy seasoning will heat up your catfish stew—and other dishes too.*

Yield: ⅓ C Serving size: 1 table-spoon
Each serving provides:
Calories: 26
Total fat: 1 g
Saturated fat: 0 g
Cholesterol: 0 mg
Sodium: 13 mg
Total fiber: 2 g
Protein: 1 g
Carbohydrates: 5 g
Potassium: 180 mg

Fresh Salsa

Yield: 8 servings Serving size: ½ C
Each serving provides:
Calories: 42
Total fat: 2 g
Saturated fat: less than 1 g
Cholesterol: 0 mg
Sodium: 44 mg
Total fiber: 2 g
Protein: 1 g
Carbohydrates: 7 g
Potassium: 337 mg

6 tomatoes, preferably Roma
   (or 3 large tomatoes)
½ medium onion, finely
   chopped
1 clove garlic, finely minced
2 jalapeño peppers, finely
   chopped

3 Tbsp cilantro, chopped
Fresh lime juice to taste
⅛ tsp oregano, finely crushed
⅛ tsp salt
⅛ tsp pepper
½ avocado, diced (black skin)

1. Combine all ingredients in glass bowl.
2. Serve immediately or refrigerate and serve within 4–5 hours.

Fresh herbs add plenty of flavor to this salsa—so you use less salt.

Hot 'N Spicy Seasoning

Yield: ⅓ C Serving size: ½ teaspoon
Each serving provides:
Calories: 1
Total fat: 1 g
Saturated fat: 0 g
Cholesterol: 0 mg
Sodium: 0 mg
Total fiber: 0 g
Protein: 0 g
Carbohydrates: less than 1 g
Potassium: 4 mg

1½ tsp white pepper
½ tsp cayenne pepper
½ tsp black pepper
1 tsp onion powder

1¼ tsp garlic powder
1 Tbsp basil, dried
1½ tsp thyme, dried

Mix all ingredients together. Store in an airtight container.

*Spices can make the ordinary extraordinary. Here's a great all purpose
spice mix. Try this mix with meat, poultry, fish, or vegetable dishes.
Use it instead of salt—even in the salt shaker.*

Vinaigrette Salad Dressing

1 bulb garlic, separated into
   cloves, peeled
½ C water
1 Tbsp red-wine vinegar

¼ tsp honey
1 Tbsp virgin olive oil
½ tsp black pepper

1. Place garlic cloves into small saucepan and pour in enough water (about ½ C) to cover them.
2. Bring water to boil, then reduce heat and simmer until garlic is tender (about 15 minutes).
3. Reduce liquid to 2 tablespoons and increase heat for 3 minutes.
4. Pour contents into small sieve over bowl. With wooden spoon, mash garlic through sieve.
5. Whisk vinegar into garlic mixture, then mix in oil and seasoning.

Try this recipe to dress up a salad for a special meal.

Yield: 4 servings Serving size: 2 tablespoons
Each serving provides:
Calories: 33
Total fat: 3 g
Saturated fat: 1 g
Cholesterol: 0 mg
Sodium: 0 mg
Total fiber: 0 g
Protein: 0 g
Carbohydrates: 1 g
Potassium: 9 mg

Yogurt Salad Dressing

8 oz fat-free plain yogurt
¼ C fat-free mayonnaise
2 Tbsp chives, dried

2 Tbsp dill, dried
2 Tbsp lemon juice

Mix all ingredients in bowl and refrigerate.

So easy—so healthy—so good. Try it!

Yield: 8 servings Serving size: 2 tablespoons
Each serving provides:
Calories: 23
Total fat: 0 g
Saturated fat: 0 g
Cholesterol: 1 mg
Total fiber: 0 g
Sodium: 84 mg
Protein: 2 g
Carbohydrates: 4 g
Potassium: 104 mg

Mango Shake

Yield: 4 servings
Serving size: ¾ C

Each serving provides (with mango and banana):

Calories: 106
Total fat: 2 g
Saturated fat: 1 g
Cholesterol: 5 mg
Sodium: 63 mg
Total fiber: 2 g
Protein: 5 g
Carbohydrates: 20 g
Potassium: 361 mg

2 C low-fat milk
4 Tbsp frozen mango juice
　(or 1 fresh mango, peeled
　and pitted)*
1 small banana

2 ice cubes

*Variation: Instead of mango
　juice, try orange, papaya,
　or strawberry juice.

Put all ingredients into blender. Blend until foamy.
Serve immediately.

🍃 *Kids love this drink's creamy, sweet taste.*

Summer Breezes Smoothie

Yield: 3 servings
Serving size: 1 C

Each serving provides:

Calories: 121
Total fat: less than 1 g
Saturated fat: less than 1 g
Cholesterol: 1 mg
Sodium: 64 mg
Total fiber: 2 g
Protein: 6 g
Carbohydrates: 24 g
Potassium: 483 mg

1 C fat-free, plain yogurt
6 medium strawberries
1 C pineapple, crushed, canned
　in juice

1 medium banana
1 tsp vanilla extract
4 ice cubes

1. Place all ingredients in blender and puree until smooth.
2. Serve in frosted glass.

🍃 *Here's a perfect low-fat thirst quencher.*

Chapter 14

Successful Weight Management

Healthy weight management is an important part of a healthy lifestyle. Maintaining a healthy weight requires an understanding of the factors that contribute to weight gain and the key strategies to prevent it, as you will learn in this chapter. Ideally, this achievement reflects a combination of good nutrition, consistent physical activity, and effective stress management, topics described in following chapters. When you keep your weight at a healthy level, you reduce your odds of disease, disability, and early death.

What Is a Healthy Weight?

A healthy weight is one that minimizes your risk of illness and disease and falls within the range of weight appropriate for your height . A person may suffer from poor health if overly heavy. Similarly, a person can experience poor health if overly thin. Therefore, a reasonable weight goal is in between those two extremes. Among individuals this can fall within a broad range, as people come in a variety of sizes and shapes due to strong genetic factors. Each person should find his or her own healthy weight for his or her own body type.

Understanding Body Composition

It's not the size of the package that is important, it's what is inside that counts. Your body is composed of fat mass and lean body mass. Together, this is referred to as your body composition. Ideally, you want to keep the percentage of fat quite a bit lower than the percentage of non-fat mass. (Your nonfat mass includes your bones, organs, and muscle.) And, if you decide to lose weight, you want to lose fat, not valuable muscle tissue that gives you strength and support.

FACT

The good news for those who are overweight is that even a small reduction in weight, as little as 10 percent of total body weight, leads to remarkable improvements in health. For example, research subjects who lost 10 percent of total body weight have experienced reductions in high blood pressure, blood glucose, and total cholesterol levels, as well as improvements in body composition.

Just because a person appears to be thin does not make him or her healthy. Some people who are thin in appearance are actually unhealthy when it comes to body composition. Typically, they are weak, sedentary, and may be smokers. They may eat very little food and have an unbalanced diet. Oftentimes, people with this type of profile believe that they are healthy as long as they are thin. They could not be more mistaken.

Being significantly underweight poses serious threats to good health. For premenopausal women, being too underweight can lead to infertility or osteoporosis. People who suffer from disorders such as anorexia or bulimia also experience poor health. In particular, people who are ano-rectic will consume muscle tissue from their body's stores to survive when fat stores are depleted, including tissue from the heart muscle. It is not uncommon for people who are recovering from anorexia to have a heart attack when the weight they begin to gain creates excess stress on an already weakened heart.

At the same time, a person who may be more stocky and robust in appearance, but who exercises regularly, eats a balanced diet of nutrient-rich fresh foods, and who does not smoke, is much healthier. In fact, a study by Steven N. Blair, P.E.D., Director of Research and President of the Cooper Institute in Dallas, Texas, showed that men who exercised regu-larly but who were a little bit heavier had a lower risk of death than those men who were thin but completely inactive.

The message, therefore, is not that thin is in or that every person must have the same body. Rather, the message is that you should aim to main-tain a weight that is healthy for you and your body type.

All Body Fat Is Not Equal

To make matters even more complex, researchers have found that the amount of body fat is not the only factor that is important. What is equally, if not more significant, is where the fat is deposited on your body. Studies show that people whose bodies store fat around the abdominal area, also referred to as an "apple shaped" body, are at higher risk of heart disease, stroke, high blood pressure, and Type 2 diabetes than those people who are more "pear shaped" and carry their excess fat around their legs and thighs.

QUESTION?

Why does abdominal fat create a higher risk of heart disease than fat elsewhere?
The exact reasons why abdominal fat poses greater risks are not known, but one factor that may contribute is the fact that abdominal fat puts greater stress on internal organs that become surrounded with fat.

To determine whether or not you have abdominal obesity, you need to measure your waist circumference. For purposes of this measurement, your waist is considered to be halfway between the lowest rib and the top of your hipbone, measured when you are upright and your trunk is perpendicular to the floor. A waist circumference of greater than forty inches for men, or greater than thirty-five inches for women, may indicate a higher risk of heart disease. Abdominal obesity is also considered one of the risk factors of the metabolic syndrome (see Chapter 19).

The Body Mass Index

Another method to assess whether your weight may put you at risk is to calculate your body mass index (BMI). The BMI expresses weight relative to height. It provides a general guideline to check whether you are in a healthy weight range. A high BMI score may indicate increased risks for heart disease, high blood pressure, diabetes, and high cholesterol. BMI guidelines are not accurate for estimating risks for people who are healthy at higher weight levels, such as muscular competitive athletes or pregnant women. These guidelines also do not apply to growing children or frail and sedentary older adults.

Instructions for calculating your BMI are included in Appendix B. If your BMI is greater than 25, you fall into the category of overweight. A BMI between 18.5 and 24.9 is considered a healthy weight. If your BMI score is less than 18.5, you are considered to be underweight.

ALERT!

According to the American Heart Association, the age-adjusted prevalence of overweight and obesity among American adults, as determined by a BMI score of 25 or higher, increased from 56 percent in 1988–1994 to 65 percent in 1999–2000.

Benefits of Losing Excess Fat

Losing excess fat is not only an important factor in reducing the risk of heart disease, but also in reducing the risk of many diseases, including gallbladder disease and several types of cancer.

In addition to the reduced risk for numerous diseases, losing weight provides multiple physical, mental, and emotional benefits. People who lose excess fat weight feel better, have more energy, have fewer aches and pains, and can enjoy a higher quality of life. People may also experience an improved sense of self-esteem and a feeling of greater control over their life that leads to a greater sense of self-confidence.

Excess weight strains your heart and your circulatory system. Your heart must work harder to pump more blood through your body. Extra weight also strains your musculoskeletal system and puts greater stress on your joints.

People who carry excess weight are more likely to have certain risk factors for heart disease, including high LDL cholesterol, low HDL cholesterol, high triglycerides, Type 2 diabetes, or high blood pressure. At the same time, when people who are overweight lose excess body fat, even as few as five to ten pounds, they can typically expect reductions in their total cholesterol, LDL cholesterol, and triglycerides, accompanied by increases in HDL cholesterol. All of these benefits add up to a reduced risk of heart disease.

FACT

More than 60 percent of adults in the United States are overweight or obese. Being overweight can contribute to high LDL cholesterol, low HDL cholesterol, high VLDL cholesterol, and high triglycerides.

Causes of Weight Gain

In simplistic terms, one can say that the cause of weight gain is taking in excess calories. But this does not take into full consideration the complex social factors that make it difficult to live an active lifestyle, to enjoy wholesome fresh foods, and to separate emotional factors from the need to eat. Furthermore, as researchers learn more and more about the differences among people's metabolic profiles, it seems that depending on what types of foods are consumed, some people are more prone to gain weight easily and to have a more difficult time of losing it. The overall picture is complex, but a few simple factors play key roles.

Super-Sizing of Foods

In our day and age, it is easy for people to overeat. The super-sizing of food portions by food manufacturers adds to this tendency. Since most of the cost of food production is in the labor and not in the raw materials, food producers have financial incentives to increase the size of food products in order to attract more customers. The increased amount of cost involved in providing a larger serving size is outweighed by the greater number of customers who purchase their product, since it is perceived as a better value or more food for the money. This perception of value by the consumer, however, fails to take into consideration that they are actually purchasing more food than they need. And all that excess consumption leads to excess weight.

In fact, this issue is so prevalent that in December 2003, the U.S. Federal Trade Commission (FTC) recommended that the U.S. Food and Drug Administration (FDA) re-examine the portion sizes on food labels. The FTC made this recommendation based on the fact that "they [food labels] may significantly understate the amount of particular foods and calories that people typically consume."

Officials at the FTC believe that current food labeling practices confuse consumers over serving sizes so that consumers "may underestimate the number of calories and other nutrients that they eat." For example, a typical three-ounce bag of chips is labeled as "two servings," but packaged as a single serving. Twenty-ounce soft drinks are also packaged as a single serving but described as two servings on the food label. The FTC recommends that the FDA look at whether serving-size listings are "sufficiently clear and prominent."

Until government officials clear up current labeling practices, however, it is up to you to make judgments about serving sizes on your own. Take time to read food labels carefully, and compare the weight of the package with what is noted as the weight of a serving on the label. Also, read the serving-size guidelines at the end of this chapter carefully.

Emotional Overeating

While emotional overeating may not rise to the level of a clinical eating disorder, many people overeat in response to cues that are completely unrelated to hunger. Stress can play a role, as can environmental factors in the home. For example, if your parents rewarded you with a food treat when you accomplished tasks, you may continue to give yourself this type of treat when you finish something as an adult. Similarly, if food was used to cope with emotions rather than discussing, facing, or experiencing emotions, it can continue to play that role in adult life.

Researchers suggest that if you eat the foods you really like in measured amounts with meals and avoid them when you are hungry, you can reduce your cravings. The reason is that by giving in to your body's desire to certain foods, you can train your body to want that treat even more. For example, if you only eat chocolate when you're ravenous, you can increase the strength of your cravings.

Keeping a journal can be helpful for people who find that they eat in response to these types of emotional cues, rather than to true feelings of hunger. In the journal, you can record what triggered an eating episode, what you were thinking and feeling at the time, and what feelings you were avoiding by eating. This process may be very revealing as you start to unravel some of your more unconscious eating behaviors that lead to overconsumption of food.

Eating Highly Refined, Processed Foods

Another factor that can contribute to overeating is choosing foods that are highly refined and processed. In this case, the overeating often occurs in response to genuine hunger cues. For example, breads and pastas that are made with enriched flour rather than with whole grains lack fiber that provides important feelings of fullness and satiety. Drinking juices instead of eating fruits is also another missed opportunity to eat fiber-rich foods.

Fiber, both soluble and insoluble, is critically important to health. Not only does it provide roughage that is good for digestion, but it also lowers cholesterol levels and makes you feel full. It truly is hard to over-eat when your meals are filled with wholesome fresh fruits, vegetables, and whole grains.

Lack of Physical Activity

Living an active lifestyle in today's technology-driven world is a challenge. It is actually much easier to live a sedentary life today than it is to live an active life. Many of us start our day by traveling to work or to school via cars or buses. We spend much of our day seated in chairs with few breaks from our sitting lifestyle. When we return home at the end of the day, we are tired and hungry and the last thing we feel like doing is "exercising."

FACT

All day long, we use devices that remove movement from our day. We drive cars, take escalators and elevators, use automatic door and garage openers, and have remote controls for every form of device. We shop, perform research, play games, and communicate with others via our computers. We order food to be delivered to our homes.

Without a conscious effort to move, it's actually quite easy to be completely inactive all day long. When this lack of movement is combined with overconsumption of foods, it's easy to see how the combination can quickly add to increased weight gain.

Loss of Lean Body Mass

An aspect of the picture that affects metabolism and activity levels is the natural decline in lean body mass that occurs with aging. After the age of thirty-five, both men and women lose approximately one-third to one-half pound of muscle each year. If your total weight is not changing, this means that this loss of lean body mass has been replaced by an equivalent gain of fat mass. Although your weight may not have changed, the difference between these two types of tissues is extremely significant from the point of view of weight management.

The loss of lean body mass means your body is composed of less of the metabolically more active tissue as well as a decrease in the muscle that provides strength to move and accomplish physical tasks. So not only is the body burning fewer calories even at rest, but it also becomes more tired and less capable of doing things such as walking up the stairs, running after children, and lifting and carrying grocery bags.

This is the beginning of a cycle of reduced daily physical activity that leads to even more fat gain. Over time, the ratio of fat becomes high and the amount of lean is low. The older adult may no longer have the strength to even climb a flight of stairs or get up and move around at all, and the pounds can easily add up.

Health benefits can be gained from even a modest weight loss. You do not need to become a size two or look like a cover model. You just need to be sure that you lose the weight in a healthy way.

Yo-Yo or Starvation Dieting

Diets that involve simply avoiding food altogether, known as starvation diets, don't work. You need to eat nutritious foods to lose weight and keep it down. According to nutritionist Dawn James, M.S., R.D., Executive Director of Wenmat fitness facilities in Sacramento, California, trying this strategy will actually do more harm than good. She says:

> Starvation dieting convinces your body that you're living in a famine. Your metabolism slows down. Your fat cells become more efficient at storing fat to get you through the famine and you burn lean body mass—muscle protein—for fuel. This means you have a smaller engine to burn calories and fat. You burn fewer calories for the same amount of effort.

Also, when you starve yourself you are more likely to get so hungry, you might binge. In fact, according to James, starvation diets have a 95-percent failure rate.

When people go on starvation diets and do not include exercise, they lose both fat and hard-earned muscle tissue. This loss of lean body mass from dieting results in a decreased resting metabolic rate, similar to when people lose lean body mass as they age. The lower metabolic rate makes it even harder to keep weight off after you end the starvation diet. Therefore, to maintain the lower weight, you must keep eating less food;

otherwise, weight is usually regained, mostly as body fat. This cycle of weight loss and gain is called the yo-yo effect.

ALERT!

If you're out of shape, a new regular exercise program can build up your muscles. It may seem discouraging at first because you may see a weight gain. (Remember, muscle weighs more than fat.) But for every pound of muscle you gain, you also burn about thirty to fifty more calories a day, for the same amount of effort. Over time, the added muscle will help you lose and manage your weight.

"Yo-yo" dieting is the tendency for people to lose and regain the same weight over and over again, rather than make any permanent changes in weight management. Some researchers believe that this can even be more detrimental to health than not dieting at all.

Healthy weight loss should occur at the rate of no more than one to two pounds per week. At this healthy rate, you are losing body fat rather than muscle tissue. You are also more likely to keep it off and avoid the yo-yo syndrome.

Strategies for Successful Weight Management

The bottom line when it comes to healthy weight management is that healthy lifestyle changes will help to bring your weight to a healthy level. Depending on how much excess fat you have, this process may take a longer time. However, any lifestyle changes you are able to make will improve your health and your feelings of well-being.

Do Your Best to Be Your Best

Managing your weight is part of a healthy lifestyle. To achieve success, it's best to make changes gradually and to have realistic expectations. The following tips can help you get started:

- Examine your eating habits. Are you meeting the necessary requirements?

- Portion size matters. Learn what healthy single servings of food should be, and adjust your portion sizes.
- Get active each and every day. Every movement counts.
- Incorporate strength or weight training to increase your lean body mass.

As you improve your daily habits, instead of focusing on changes in your scale weight, notice changes in how you feel. Do you have more energy? Are you feeling stronger? Are you sleeping better at night?

If you're the type who needs a goal in the form of a number, such as weight, to keep you motivated, think about measuring your progress in other ways. Get your cholesterol and blood sugar levels tested. Check whether your resting heart rate and blood pressure levels are going down. Most importantly, know you're doing the best that you can for your long-term well-being.

The best approach for weight management is one that is grounded in the following basics: healthy nutrition, regular physical activity that includes lifestyle activity, and stress management. For details on how to incorporate these healthy lifestyle habits into your life, see the chapter that treats the specific topic (Chapters 8, 15, and 16, respectively).

Avoid Overeating

While it is important to eat a diet full of foods that enhance health and to avoid eating those foods that can be harmful to health, keep in mind that overeating any foods can lead to excess weight that is harmful to health. One of the ways to avoid overeating is to learn what a reasonable serving size should look like. Here are some helpful visual cues:

One serving of fresh fruit or vegetables is about the size of a tennis ball.

One serving of canned fruit or cooked vegetables is about the size of a computer mouse.

One serving of dried fruit is about the size of a golf ball.

One serving of fruit as juice measures ¾ C.*

One serving of vegetable juice measures 1 C.*

One serving of sliced bread is about the size of a CD case.

One serving of cold cereal is about the size of a baseball.

One serving of hot cereal is about the size of an English muffin.

One serving of rice or pasta is about the size of a regular scoop of ice cream.

*It's recommended that no more than one each of your fruit and vegetable servings be from juice since juice does not provide the same amount of dietary fiber as the fruit itself.

There are several strategies you can use to avoid overeating when you are eating out. For instance, you can share a main course with a friend, order a meal of various side dishes, or simply take half of the order home to eat later. Another way to avoid overeating is to be sure to eat the recommended amounts of grains, fruits, and vegetables. The high fiber content of these foods help you to feel satiated, and when you are feeling so full, you are much less likely to overeat.

Keep in mind that lifestyle habits are not easy to change. Be gentle with yourself and appreciate your small successes on a daily basis. Over time, you will find that your life has transformed in so many more ways than simply managing your weight. The weight that you lose, whatever the amount, represents your body's quest to find its best balance in the midst of a lifestyle dedicated to creating health.

Chapter 15

Getting Active to Improve Your Numbers

A long with eating a balanced diet of minimally processed whole foods, being active on most days of the week is critical to creating healthy cholesterol levels. Getting active for health does not mean spending hours at the gym. In fact, you never even have to go to the gym to get the amount of exercise that is proven to improve your health. This chapter will give you the knowledge of why physical activity is beneficial and how you can get moving to enjoy those results.

Physical Activity Benefits Heart Health

People are designed to be active creatures. Not so long ago, we had to perform physical work to feed, clothe, and shelter ourselves. Modern living has changed all of that, but it cannot change the fundamental need of people to move and use their bodies in order to maintain optimum functioning. As average levels of physical activity have declined, medical professionals have observed an accompanying decline in the body's physical functioning. Researchers are also studying the relationship of physical inactivity with decline in mental functioning.

Numerous studies now substantiate the fact that a minimal amount of physical movement is not only beneficial, but essential. Many aspects of aging, such as the loss of strength, balance, and the ability to move and care for oneself, were formerly thought to be the natural result of the aging process. Research today tells us that many of these consequences are not actually the result of aging. Rather, they are the result of disuse of the body and a failure to take advantage of its physical capabilities. To retain our vitality and energy, we need to keep ourselves physically active.

How Does Activity Affect the Heart?

Physical inactivity is a major risk factor for heart disease. The heart is a muscle that benefits from regular use to keep it and the circulatory system healthy. When a person is inactive, the heart muscle is weaker. With each beat, an unfit heart muscle pumps a lower volume of blood than a stronger, more fit heart.

Because less blood is pumped, the heart has to beat more frequently in order to ensure adequate circulation of blood around the body. This more rapid heart rate can also result in an increase in blood pressure over time, causing stiffness and hardening of the arteries and impacting the health of the circulatory system. In contrast, when the heart is strong and healthy, stroke volume is strong. The heart rate is slower, and a more healthy tone is maintained in the arterial walls.

Increasing physical activity leads to an increase in the levels of HDL, or good cholesterol. This change is independent of any weight loss that may also occur as increased activity burns up more calories. Physical activity also lowers LDL and triglyceride levels.

Studies show that regular physical activity not only lowers bad cholesterol and triglycerides and increases good cholesterol, but that it also reduces risk of death from all causes, reduces feelings of depression and anxiety, and helps build and maintain healthy bones, muscles, and joints.

FACT

Only moderate amounts of physical activity are required to reverse the downward spiral toward ill health. A moderate amount of activity can mean as little as thirty minutes of brisk walking on most days of the week.

Here's the testimony of Laurie, a fifty-two-year-old woman who discovered the importance of active, healthy living.

> I have struggled with my weight and appearance all my life. I was overweight through high school. In college I lost about thirty pounds but did it the wrong way—poor diet and no exercise. I never felt good about myself. I did start exercising, but still did not eat well, always afraid of gaining weight.
>
> About nine years ago I found myself divorced, kids grown, and on my own. I made a decision that I can and would learn how to take care of myself emotionally and physically. I determined that my diet and exercise plan would be about making me a strong, healthy woman. I started seeing a personal trainer who has helped me tremendously with nutrition and strength training. I was blessed with meeting a partner who shared my newly found zest for life. He and I meal plan and shop together. We ride bikes and often work out together . . . I stopped paying so much attention to what I weigh, but more to how I look and feel. I am in perimenopause and have not had to take any drugs. My total cholesterol level is 150.
>
> I have also learned to balance my life . . . I have learned that there is no magic formula. You have to figure out what works for you because if it doesn't, you won't do it.

It's clear that physical activity provides countless benefits. If you are particularly concerned about the health of your heart and your cholesterol levels, being active on a regular basis is among the best things that you can do for yourself.

Studies also show that people who are physically active after a first heart attack have a significantly lower risk of having a second heart attack when compared to people who remained inactive. According to Lyn Steffen-Batey, Ph.D., assistant professor of epidemiology at the University of Texas School of Public Health, during a study that compared risk levels, "Patients who kept physically active after a first heart attack had a 60-percent lower risk of fatal heart attack or a second nonfatal heart attack than those who did not." What was significant about this study was that it measured all types of physical activity, such as gardening and housework, instead of only looking at gym-based types of exercise.

ALERT!

According to surveys, only 45 percent of adults in 2001 met the minimum activity recommendation to provide health benefits of thirty minutes on most days of the week. The good news is that this represents an improvement from previous years, in which only 26 percent of adults met these recommendations. Let's hope we can continue to keep up the good work.

How Much Activity Is Necessary?

According to guidelines issued by the U.S. Surgeon General, the U.S. Department of Health and Human Services, and the National Heart, Lung, and Blood Institute, the minimum amount of activity for health includes the following factors:

- Should continue for at least 30 minutes total
- Can be accumulated in bouts as short as 8 to 10 minutes
- Should be of moderate intensity, such as brisk walking
- Should occur on most, preferably all, days of the week
- Should include some resistance exercise and stretching during the week

The guidelines also note that more activity and a higher intensity will provide greater health and fitness benefits. The general guidelines listed above set forth minimum amounts of activity necessary to enjoy health benefits. Clearly, this level of exercise will not prepare you to run a marathon or to climb Mount Everest, but such events may not be among your immediate goals. You may simply want to feel better and know you are doing something good for your health. The message for you is loud and clear—with moderate amounts of physical activity on a regular basis, you can achieve this goal.

What Is Moderate Activity?

Research shows that activity can come in a variety of ways and still provide health benefits. The good news is that with so many activities to choose from, you are likely to find something that you enjoy and are able to incorporate into your life on a regular basis. The following are examples of moderate amounts of physical activity:

Examples of Moderate Amounts of Activities	
Types of Activity	**Length of Time**
Washing and waxing a car	45–60 minutes
Washing windows or floors	45–60 minutes
Playing volleyball	45 minutes
Playing touch football	30–45 minutes
Gardening	30–45 minutes
Walking 1¾ miles	35 minutes (20-minute mile, or pace of 3 miles/hour)
Basketball (shooting baskets)	30 minutes
Bicycling 5 miles	30 minutes
Dancing fast (social)	30 minutes
Pushing a stroller 1½ miles	30 minutes
Raking leaves	30 minutes
Walking 2 miles	30 minutes (15-minute mile, or pace of 4 miles/hour)
Water aerobics	30 minutes
Swimming laps	20 minutes
Wheelchair basketball	20 minutes

You can also perform some activities that are performed at a higher intensity, such as bicycling, jumping rope, running, shoveling snow, or climbing stairs for a shorter amount of time (fifteen minutes or so) to get similar results. However, it is not necessary to do high-intensity exercises to achieve health benefits, particularly those associated with improvements in cholesterol levels. Moderate intensity exercise can improve heart health.

The most important thing is that you find something that you can and will do regularly, and that you do it for at least thirty minutes on most days of the week. Remember that you can break up those thirty minutes. For example, you can take a ten-minute morning walk, run a quick errand on a bicycle at noon for ten minutes, and then take another ten-minute walk at the end of the day. That adds up to a total of thirty minutes in one day.

Lifestyle Activity Is Important

Many of us are so conditioned into thinking that exercise means going to the gym that we forget that everyday life presents us with numerous opportunities to get active during the day. If you have time to go to the gym, that's fantastic. But if you don't, do not despair. You can create more movement opportunities during your day that make a difference. Look for every opportunity to be active.

If you can make time for regular workouts in a gym, that's great. Keep in mind, however, that studies show that people who live an otherwise sedentary life and work out for one hour per day are not burning as many calories as people who do not go to the gym but who take part in lifestyle activities throughout the day.

Here are some examples of lifestyle activity:

- Walk to run an errand in the neighborhood, rather than taking a car.
- Play outdoor games with children instead of watching television together.
- Park farther away from the shop.

- Get off the train or bus one stop early and walk the rest of the way.
- Carry your groceries to your car or load them into your car yourself.
- Wash your car instead of taking it to the car wash.
- Rake leaves instead of using a leaf blower.
- Get up to switch appliances on or off instead of always using remote control.
- Ride a bicycle for transportation instead of driving a car.
- Do some vigorous house cleaning, such as vacuuming, sweeping, or mopping.

Be creative. Find more and more ways that you can move during your day. These activities all add up and make a difference. For example, according to estimates for a 150-pound person, standing up for three ten-minute phone calls will burn twenty calories. In contrast, sitting for thirty minutes during those three phone calls burns only four calories. Simply by standing for those brief intervals, you have created a sixteen-calorie deficit. While sixteen calories may not seem like much, when it is repeated hour after hour, day after day, it and other small actions start to mean the difference between unwanted pounds and maintaining your ideal weight. If you added walking or pacing to your phone calls, it would even provide greater benefits.

You may recall that after you eat during the day, your blood is filled with sugars and fats, blood glucose and triglycerides. These are sources of fuel that you can use immediately. However, if you are not active and do not use up this energy, it ends up ultimately stored as fat. One of the keys to keeping all systems healthy is to use up this fuel for its intended purpose and stimulate your heart, lungs, muscles, skeletal, and nervous systems.

Walk Your Way to a Healthy Heart

One of the best forms of exercise that provides a healthful challenge for the human body is walking. It is economical, easy to fit into your day, bears a low risk of injury, and it is effective in improving health. Numerous studies show that people who walk regularly have less risk of death or disability from disease.

Studies have shown that people who participate in regular walking programs have higher levels of HDL cholesterol, lower levels of total and LDL cholesterol, and lower levels of triglycerides or blood fats. In addition to reducing these risks of heart disease, walking helps you to enjoy many other benefits, including maintaining a healthy weight, improving the condition of bones and muscles, and reducing stress and tension.

FACT

A study showed that older men who started walking about two miles a day had a 50-percent lower risk of heart attack than men who only walked a quarter mile. In addition, the study found that the risk of a heart attack dropped an additional 15 percent for every additional half mile walked per day.

Your Walking Program: The First Steps

You're ready to get going with your daily walking, but you're not quite sure how to begin. That's natural. Even though you learned to walk as an infant and have been doing it ever since, a regular walking program does include a few details that you need to address. The following information provides you with everything you need to know to get moving.

Check with Your Health-Care Provider

Before you get started with any exercise program, it is a good idea to check with your health-care provider. If you are apparently healthy and under the age of sixty-five, then you are likely to be fine with a moderate exercise program. If, however, you are older or have any known chronic conditions such as arthritis, diabetes, or heart disease, you need to check with your health-care provider. A walking program is likely to have multiple benefits for you, but it is always better to be safe than sorry. Check with your doctor in case there are any specific limitations that you need to be aware of.

Find the Right Shoes

Walking is fortunately an economical activity. Your most important and significant investment is in the shoes that you will wear. Take the time to find a comfortable, sturdy shoe that fits the needs of your foot and provides good arch support. Shoe technology these days is actually quite sophisticated. Go to a reputable athletic footwear store that allows returns if the shoe is not a good fit for you.

If you plan to walk both at home and at the office, consider investing in two pairs of shoes. This way you can always leave a pair at work. Otherwise, you will have to carry your shoes daily. It's important to make getting active as easy as possible. Again, while this represents a bigger investment in the beginning, it will pay multiple dividends over time in your improved health and quality of life.

Buy shoe inserts. Today's shoes do not come with insoles that last as long as the outer part of the shoe. Yet, the cushioning that provides you with support is essential to keep you comfortable and to prevent injury. When you purchase your shoes, ask the salesperson to also help you to find an appropriate insole. This will make a tremendous difference in your long-term comfort.

Choose the Right Clothing and Accessories

As far as sportswear for walking, you want to wear fabrics that breathe, such as cotton or polyester blends. Many modern fabrics also feature wicking qualities that actually draw your perspiration away from your skin. This can definitely enhance your walking comfort. Women who need the extra support should wear an athletic sports bra. Comfort is your primary objective.

Sun protection is also important. Be sure to wear sunscreen. A hat is also a good idea to protect your face. Depending on how sensitive you are to sun exposure, you may want to purchase a hat that also shields the back of your neck. Sunglasses provide coverage for your eyes. Choose a pair that is lightweight and comfortable. More than anything, you want your time during your walks to be as enjoyable as possible. Find the accessories that work best for you.

FACT

Consider wearing bright colors. Not only will they cheer you up, but they will also help to make sure that you are visible to any traffic. You can purchase reflector vests as well to make you more visible.

Stay Hydrated

Staying properly hydrated is essential for good health. If you are taking short walks, it's not necessary to carry a water bottle with you. However, if you are going for walks that are longer than an hour, it's a good idea to either bring your own water supply or choose a route that goes by water fountains. Some companies market fanny packs that serve as water bottle carriers that are handy for longer walks. Most importantly, remember to drink plenty of fluids, before and after your walk, and during your walk if possible. For moderate levels of walking, plan on about five to seven ounces of water every fifteen to twenty minutes.

Consider a Pedometer

A pedometer may not be a necessary purchase, but it is a great tool to measure your progress and keep you motivated. Studies show that if you take 10,000 steps on most days of the week, you will realize many health benefits. (This equates to about five miles a day.) Furthermore, if you take 12,000 to 15,000 steps per day, it can help you accomplish your weight loss goals.

The steps the pedometer measures do not have to be performed at a particular intensity level or for a specific duration. What they represent is that you have maintained a level of daily activity that contributes to your health.

The motivational aspect of the pedometer is that it helps you realize exactly how much you move around during the day. If you've had a busy, active, day you can supplement that with a short walk to reach your daily goal. If your day has been fairly inactive, then you can save time for a longer walk. This can help you to become a more active person on a daily basis, which can make a significant difference in your overall caloric expenditure as well as your health and well-being.

Your Walking Program: Get Moving!

You can walk indoors at a shopping mall or on a treadmill. You can walk outdoors through your neighborhood or at local parks or schools. You can walk alone or use the exercise as a time to catch up with friends or even to conduct business. You can use it to enhance your recreational pursuits, such as golfing or hiking, or you can simply do it as a way to stay in shape. Regardless of where and when you walk, you need to warm up your body to prepare it for getting active.

If you want to learn some stretching and toning exercises to add to your walking program, or if you want to incorporate more activity as your energy level improves, check out *The Everything® Weight Training Book* (Adams Media, 2002). Weight training is not just for bodybuilders anymore; all people can achieve great health benefits with appropriate use of weights.

Walking Warm-Up

When you begin, start out at a comfortable pace. Let your arms hang naturally at your sides so they swing rhythmically with each step. Be sure to stand tall and maintain good posture. After about five minutes of walking, if you enjoy performing some stretches to make your walk more comfortable, you can. Research shows, however, that pre-exercise stretching does not prevent injury. At the same time, it does not do any harm, so if you find it comfortable, go ahead and incorporate a few stretches. Do not hold the stretches for more than ten to twenty seconds, however, as you do not want to cool down and lose the benefits of your warm-up. After you complete your stretches, you can continue with your walk.

Walking Technique

Posture is the most important aspect of walking technique. Stand tall with your ears above your shoulders, arms at your sides, shoulders above hips, and abdominal muscles slightly pulled in to actively support your lower back. If you want to increase the intensity of your walk, bend your elbows and swing your arms more vigorously. Take more steps, rather than longer strides. Keep your focus ahead to maintain good posture. Let your heel strike first and push forward through the ball of your foot. Keep your elbows in and avoid swinging your arms across your body.

Walking Cool Down

After you finish the more brisk portion of your walk, take time to slowly bring your body back to the way it felt when you began. Gradually slow back down to the comfortable pace you started out with. By the time you stop walking, your breathing should be relaxed and your heart rate should be calm. You only need to spend a few minutes on your walking cool down, but be sure to take this time.

After your walk is a great time to include some final stretches. Unlike the beginning of your walk, your muscles are warm and ready to enjoy a long stretch. Good stretches to perform include shoulder rolls for the neck and shoulders, a standing calf stretch for the back of the lower leg, hamstring stretch for the back of the upper leg, standing side stretch for the side of the torso, and standing cat stretch to release the lower back. Breathe deeply, and hold each stretch anywhere from twenty to thirty seconds. Enjoy your stretches and your feeling of accomplishment. You have just made a great positive effort to enhance your health. You deserve to enjoy it and feel good about yourself.

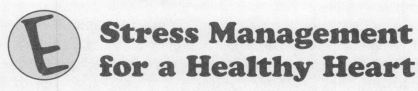

Chapter 16

Stress Management for a Healthy Heart

S tress. Even the sound of the word evokes feelings of tension. Stress is a daily aspect of modern living. Stress can keep you motivated and even save your life. If unmanaged, however, stress can kill you. Excess stress weakens the immune system. Furthermore, stress can make any disease condition worse. In this chapter, we will discover what stress is, how stress contributes to heart disease, how you can identify stress, and what steps you can take to reduce stress and restore balance to your life.

What Is Stress?

Stress is actually a natural physiological response to something that triggers a feeling of fear or threat. This response, called "fight or flight," is designed to help us to survive life-threatening situations. The natural chemical response that affects your mind and body is like a miracle drug that can help save your life in the face of a dangerous emergency. For example, if your house catches on fire in the middle of the night, stress can help you to think fast and effectively the minute you wake up. As soon as you realize you are in danger, stress gives you energy to jump out of bed and run for your life. You have extra strength to save loved ones that may be in danger. In an instant, your mind is alert, your heart is pounding, your muscles are strong, and you have super-human energy.

The Stress Response

The body's response to stress is stimulated by stress hormones, like adrenalin and cortisol, released by your body to prepare you for action. Among other things, these stress hormones do the following:

- Increase your heart rate and blood pressure to pump an extra burst of oxygen-rich blood around your body so you can get moving.
- Stop the flow of blood to your digestive system and skin by constricting arteries.
- Increase blood flow to the brain and muscles by relaxing arteries.
- Increase perspiration to cool the body.
- Speed up breathing rate and open bronchial tubes to draw more oxygen-rich air into the lungs.

When you look at all of these changes, it's easy to see how this chemically induced state of emergency preparedness is extremely useful in life-threatening situations.

The modern challenge, however, is to manage the stress response, which may be triggered when you're not in any physical danger at all. In fact, most contemporary stresses are mental and emotional. You find yourself stuck in traffic, missing deadlines at work, getting ready to make a presentation, or worrying that your child won't make the soccer team. For some people, these stress levels stay high throughout the day. Both body and mind feel the strain, and the body gets no opportunity to physically release any of this tension energy.

The stress response protects the body in a number of ways. It triggers the body to release blood sugar into the bloodstream to provide immediately available energy for fuel. It beefs up the blood-clotting mechanism in the event of any potential injury. In addition, your body becomes extremely alert to enable you to spot immediately any signs of danger.

How Stress Harms Health

Stress can be harmful to health if it mounts to levels at which you feel that you can no longer cope. This usually occurs after stress levels have remained high over a prolonged period of time.

Physical and mental symptoms of excessive stress include high blood pressure, rapid pulse, chronic muscle tension, headaches, digestive problems, irritability, depression, anxiety, loss of ability to concentrate, altered sleeping or eating habits, and increased use of drugs or alcohol. High stress can even increase the risk of a heart attack. Understanding stress and having skills to manage stress effectively, therefore, is important to your overall health and wellness.

Stress and Heart Disease

The American Heart Association does not include stress as one of the leading risk factors for heart disease. However, this may have more to do with the difficulty of teasing out stress from other risk factors than with the fact that stress does not contribute to risk of heart disease. In other words, it is difficult to prove that stress is an independent risk factor given that it also contributes to other behaviors, such as smoking, physical inactivity, and overeating, that all undermine health. The American Heart Association, however, does note that individual responses to stress may be a contributing factor to heart disease risk.

Stress and Heart Function

After studying the long-term effects of stress, some researchers believe that prolonged stress can cause damage to blood vessels. A 2002 study reported that mental stress causes the inner lining of the blood vessels (the endothelial lining) to constrict, which can increase the risk of sudden cardiac death. This constriction leads to endothelial dysfunction, a precursor to the development of atherosclerosis.

Over time, the blood vessels lose their ability to dilate effectively until the blood vessels cannot respond appropriately to changes in blood demands. For example, constricted arteries would be unable to provide an increased blood flow to meet the needs of working muscles in the legs or to meet the increased demands of blood flow to a heart that is pumping more vigorously to support physical activity.

ALERT!

For people with diabetes, stress can have a detrimental effect on management of blood glucose levels. While individual responses vary, people with Type 2 diabetes find that stress often increases blood glucose levels. Since high levels of blood glucose can also damage the health of blood vessels, it is particularly important for people with diabetes to effectively manage stress.

Stress and Blood Cholesterol Levels

Studies show that long-term stress is associated with elevated blood cholesterol levels. In these studies, however, it is difficult to isolate the exact cause. Some scientists theorize that stress indirectly causes high cholesterol by providing a fertile ground for bad health habits. For example, people who feel highly stressed are likely to overeat high-fat foods, smoke, and drink excess amounts of alcohol. Other researchers believe that the chemical changes that are part of the stress response may play a role in affecting blood fats and blood sugars, vessel health, and heart function.

Identifying Stress in Your Life

Most contemporary stress-inducing situations are not dangerous in and of themselves. What makes them stressful is the way you react to them. Some people thrive in situations that make others miserably tense and anxious. For example, you may hate meeting deadlines, while a friend works productively under that type of pressure. If you are frequently rushed or competitive and feel overwhelmed by this, or you let small frustrations get to you, or you find it hard to forget your worries and relax, tackling your stress levels will most likely improve your health. At the same time, you can certainly make your life more enjoyable.

Other types of stress are not caused by your attitude, but are rather the product of a busy life. For example, if you are driving in heavy traffic and someone quickly cuts in front of you, that is a stressful situation. You have a legitimate fear for your safety as a car accident could result. Your reaction, however, does not require you to burn off any physical energy. Rather, you remain seated in your car. You are likely to tighten your muscles and experience feelings of tension and anxiety as your body undergoes the physiological and biochemical changes associated with the "fight or flight" response.

Often, when you feel "stressed out," it is a generalized feeling of stress. If you take a moment to examine your situation, however, you will find that your feelings are actually the cumulative result of numerous individual pressures that have finally reached the boiling point. One of the first steps to learn how to manage stress effectively is to identify these individual pressures—the types of things in your life that cause you stress. Your awareness is the first step.

The next time you start to feel overwhelmed and stressed out, explore these feelings in greater depth. Ask yourself the following questions to determine what is causing these emotions:

- Am I overcommitted?
- Am I taking care of others and neglecting my own self-care?
- Am I trying to accomplish everything on my own without asking for any support from anyone else?

- Are my expectations unrealistic?
- What is going on in my life right now that gives me a sense of struggle?

If you are the type of person who finds it helpful to keep a journal, try to record things that trigger your stress. Write down what happened, what you were thinking or feeling, and how you reacted physically. This can give you valuable insight into the cumulative triggers you face throughout the day.

When you start to identify the causes for your feelings and you also note how you react to these stressors, you bring more awareness and understanding to your personal situation. Once you realize what triggers your stress, then you are ready to consider taking realistic steps to cope with your personal matters.

Strategies for Dealing with Stress

It's important for your health and mental wellness that you feel a sense of control over your life. Stress management and relaxation are learned skills, and they require strategies for success. The strategies discussed in this section can help you manage stress successfully.

It's important to make time to learn stress management skills and relaxation techniques. Learning how to manage stress or how to eliminate some of the stressors in your life is important when it comes to keeping your immune system strong, to reducing your risk of illness, and to improving your feelings of well-being.

Identify Priorities and Manage Time Effectively

Time management is a critical skill to develop in order to successfully manage stress. Everyone has the same number of hours in the day. Some people, however, are more effective managers of their time and priorities. To get organized, first identify your priorities. Next, make a realistic plan for how long it will take to get things done. Do the best that you can, and remember to also leave time for yourself.

If you feel that you need help in this area, consider taking a course in time or stress management. Consult your health-care provider about available resources. You may want to enroll in a group course or work one-on-one with a counselor.

Rely on Social Support

Social support is a very important factor in effective stress management. Friends and family can help you to talk over troublesome topics and help you keep your perspective. Take time to make friends and to maintain relationships. Even a cherished pet can provide you with companionship and dispel feelings of loneliness and isolation.

If you feel that you need more support, go ahead and ask for help from others in your home, workplace, or community. Your employer may have an employee assistance program that can provide you with confidential counseling. Your church or community center may also have helpful resources. Make it a priority to develop relationships with people who influence your life positively.

FACT

Studies indicate that pet ownership can contribute to heart health. In a study that compared heart rate and blood pressure responses to different stressors of people who owned pets with those who didn't, researchers found that pet owners consistently had reduced stress reactions as measured by lower heart rates and blood pressures. The pet owners were most relaxed when their pets were present.

Forgiveness is important to coping with difficult emotions. Negative feelings and stressful situations can adversely affect your health. When you forgive others for actions that you feel were unfair or inappropriate, you can release or heal strong negative emotions. It's important to learn coping skills that include how to let go of negative feelings and restore your peace of mind.

Express Yourself Without Anger

Remember that people who get angry easily are much more likely to die from a heart attack. If you find that you are often irritated or annoyed, learn constructive methods to deal with disagreeable situations. Learn more effective communication skills to defuse conflicts. Make sure that you are not allowing resentment to build up inside you. Over time, denial of anger can lead to unhealthy blow-ups or chronic negative feelings. The healthiest approach is to learn how to effectively express your feelings in positive and constructive ways.

It may help to remember some simple alternatives to becoming angry or frustrated in stressful situations. If possible, leave the scene of a stressful situation before it gets to you. Talk to someone you trust about how you feel, or take some time on your own to brainstorm nonstressful ways to respond to a stressful issue. Most importantly, remember to breathe deeply, and ask yourself, "In the scheme of things, does this really matter?"

ALERT!

Numerous studies demonstrate that people who are more likely to become angry have about a three times greater risk of having a heart attack or sudden cardiac death than those who are less prone to become angry. Other studies show that as people experience anger, they are more likely to have an arrhythmia, or irregular heartbeat.

Nature Outings

Studies show that spending time in nature promotes feelings of calm and relaxation. When you look at a beautiful sunset, enjoy the sounds of the pounding surf, or enjoy a beautiful view from the side of a mountain, it helps to put all the small frustrations back in the proper perspective. Find something active outside that you enjoy, and take time to put it in your schedule.

Regular physical activity is an important health behavior that can return multiple dividends. Not only will you feel better, look great, and manage your weight effectively, but you also will manage stress better by being active on a regular basis. Something as simple as a short walk can be a powerful positive outlet for tension.

Make Time for Self-Care

One of the biggest contributors to feelings of stress is the sense that life is out of control. To avoid this, make time for yourself. You deserve time for your own self-care. For one thing, it supports your health, which in turn helps you to better support all the people around you that you care about. Take a moment to identify things that you enjoy, that bring you pleasure, and that are fun and restorative. Make it a point to incorporate these activities into your schedule.

It is never easy to change a habit. Unless stress is managed and the reasons for maintaining the behavioral change are foremost in your mind, old habits prevail. A calm, clear, and focused mind and a healthy, realistic attitude are important for achieving any goal. This holds equally true for the incorporation of healthy lifestyle habits.

Restoring Health Through Relaxation

Research suggests that relaxation techniques can be used to counteract the stress response, with significant health benefits. Regular relaxation can reduce blood cortisol levels, blood pressure, cholesterol, and blood glucose.

FACT

Clinical trials show that relaxation can reduce headaches, pain, anxiety, and menopausal symptoms. At the same time, it can enhance healing, immune cell response, concentration, and feelings of well-being. It has even been shown to improve fertility rates in infertile women.

Research done in the 1970s by Dr. Herbert Benson of Harvard University began to explore the relationship between mental techniques and physiological effects. Benson studied people who participated in transcendental meditation. He coined the term "the relaxation response," which is defined as "a calm state brought about by sitting quietly and repeating a sound, words, or muscular activity over and over. When everyday thoughts intrude, the person passively disregards them and returns to the repetition." The relaxation response reflects a physiological state brought about by reducing stress and calming the mind.

The following effects are the result of the relaxation response:

- Reduced blood pressure
- Reduced heart rate
- Slower breathing rate
- Restoration of blood flow to the extremities
- Reduction in perspiration
- Release of muscular tension

When you look at the results of the relaxation response and compare them to the list at the beginning of the chapter, it's easy to see how relaxation counteracts the stress response and restores the body to a state of balance.

As a result of numerous studies in this area, relaxation techniques are used to help people with problems such as hypertension and cardiac arrhythmias, among others. While these skills are useful for people who are managing chronic disease, they are also valuable for promoting health and preventing stress-related illnesses. Make time to explore and learn techniques that help you to relax. Some people use prayer, while others meditate or engage in practices like yoga or tai chi. Find the methods that work for you.

Researchers have observed that people who learn effective stress management techniques are much more successful at achieving long-lasting behavioral change in the areas of improved nutrition, smoking cessation, increased physical activity, and weight management. This simply makes good common sense.

Relaxation and Deep Breathing

One of the easiest ways to achieve relaxation is to engage in deep, mindful breathing exercises. This can help to trigger the relaxation response. This type of exercise is easy to learn, quick to perform, and requires no equipment. As you continue to explore other methods of relaxation, use the following breathing exercise to help you ease tensions and restore your sense of balance and calm. It will do the health of your body, mind, and spirit a world of good. As you emerge from your restorative relaxation time, remind yourself that you have the power to create your own health and to enjoy all that life has to offer to you.

A Simple Breathing Exercise

This exercise is an excellent introduction to relaxation and to meditation techniques. It increases self and body awareness. A two- to three-minute "breathing break" during the day is very restorative. To perform this simple exercise, sit or lie comfortably with your hands resting in your lap. Relax your muscles and close your eyes.

Make no effort to control your breath, simply breathe naturally. As you breathe in and out, focus your attention on the breath and how the body moves with each inhalation and exhalation.

Take a few moments to focus inward. Notice the movement of your body as you breathe. Observe your inhalation and exhalation. Pay particular attention to how the breath moves your body. Observe your chest, shoulders, rib cage, and belly. Notice subtleties such as whether the chest or belly rises with inhalation and how your body responds to exhalation. Don't try to control your breath, simply focus your attention on it. This singular focus brings you into the present moment and into the immediate experience of your body. It often results in slower, deeper breaths that further relax your body. Continue for two to three minutes and then gently open your eyes. Over time, you can lengthen the period of relaxation, if you prefer.

Chapter 17

Smoke-Free for Heart Health

Smoking cigarettes greatly increases your risk of having a heart attack or stroke. Chemicals such as nicotine in cigarettes damage the lining of blood vessels and reduce HDL, or good cholesterol. In spite of the fact that nicotine is highly addictive, you can apply any of several strategies to successfully kick your smoking habit. The good news is that within minutes of your last cigarette, your body starts to change for the better.

The Harmful Effects of Smoking

You've probably already been told that smoking is bad for you. But do you really know what it can do? Consider the following facts. Smokers have a higher risk of lung diseases such as cancer, emphysema, bronchitis, and pulmonary fibrosis; a higher risk of throat, bladder, and pancreatic cancer; and twice the risk of having rheumatoid arthritis.

Additional negative consequences of cigarette smoking for women include that it increases birth defects and reduces birth weight in infants born to smoking mothers, reduces fertility in women trying to get pregnant, and raises the risk of having a miscarriage or stillborn baby. Men who smoke have a higher incidence of erectile dysfunction. Exposure to cigarette smoke heightens the likelihood of children catching colds, infections, asthma, and respiratory ailments such as bronchitis and pneumonia.

Smoking also creates bad breath, impairs your sense of taste and smell, inflames gums, yellows teeth, and causes facial wrinkling and a more aged appearance. Smoking low-tar, low-nicotine, or menthol cigarettes does not reduce the risk of heart disease or negate any of the above consequences.

FACT

Smoking cigarettes is not only harmful to your lungs, but it is also very damaging to the health of your heart and circulatory system. In fact, more smokers die from heart attacks and strokes than from lung cancer or respiratory disease. Smoking is the cause of more than 440,000 deaths per year, according to the American Heart Association.

Effects of Smoking on the Heart

When compared to nonsmokers, smokers have twice the risk of having a heart attack or stroke. Furthermore, smokers who have a heart attack are much more likely to die. Smoking increases the risk of sudden cardiac death.

Cigarette smoking specifically harms the heart and circulatory system in a number of ways, including the following:

- Damaging the lining of the arteries
- Decreasing HDL cholesterol
- Accelerating plaque formation by increasing oxidation of LDL cholesterol
- Escalating heart rate and blood pressure by narrowing of the arteries
- Reducing the amount of available oxygen in the bloodstream by increasing levels of carbon monoxide
- Raising the likelihood of blood clot formation

According to David J. Bouchier-Hayes, M.D., professor of surgery at the Royal College of Surgeons in Ireland, Beaumont Hospital in Dublin, "When blood vessels are exposed to cigarette smoke it causes the vessels to behave like a rigid pipe rather than a flexible tube, thus the vessels can't dilate in response to increased blood flow." This condition is called endothelial dysfunction and is a precursor to atherosclerosis.

Risks of Secondhand Smoke

Studies confirm that secondhand smoke is also injurious. For the nonsmoker, secondhand smoke poses the same risks as inhaled smoke pose to the smoker because the lethal chemicals are in the smoke itself. Therefore, passive smoking or simply breathing smoke-filled air draws those same chemicals into the lungs and bloodstream.

In women, smoking increases the risk of ischemic strokes, intracerebral and subarachnoid hemorrhage, and problems with dangerous blood clots and burst blood vessels, according to the American Heart Association.

According to research studies, nonsmokers exposed to environmental tobacco smoke were at a 25-percent higher relative risk of developing heart disease than nonsmokers not exposed to environmental tobacco smoke. According to the American Heart Association, approximately 37,000 to 40,000 nonsmokers die each year from cardiovascular disease resulting from exposure to passive tobacco smoke. Accordingly, the 2002 American Heart Association Guidelines for Primary Prevention of

Cardiovascular Disease and Stroke recommend no exposure to tobacco smoke to prevent heart attack and stroke. While it may be impossible to completely prevent exposure to secondhand smoke, you will benefit from avoiding it as much as you can.

The Benefits of Quitting

By quitting smoking, you reduce your risk of heart disease. At the same time, your odds of developing disease will continue to improve over the years. The benefits of quitting include less risk for numerous diseases, improved cholesterol and other lipid levels, and increased self-esteem and feelings of well being. Quitting also benefits those people around you who may suffer from consequences of secondhand smoke.

Quitting Improves Your Health

The health benefits of kicking the smoking habit truly start right away. Within twenty minutes of your last cigarette, nicotine is no longer causing constriction of blood vessels. As a result, your blood pressure decreases, your heart rate slows, and the temperature of your hands and feet rises as circulation improves. Within eight hours of your last cigarette, carbon monoxide levels drop in the bloodstream, and oxygen levels increase. Within twenty-four hours, the chances of having a heart attack are reduced. Within forty-eight hours, nerve endings begin to regenerate, and your sense of smell and taste start to return.

ALERT!

Quitting the cigarette habit can improve your sex life. According to evidence from research, men who smoke fewer than ten cigarettes a day had a 16-percent higher risk of erectile dysfunction in comparison to men who had never smoked. Men who smoked more than one pack of cigarettes daily had a whopping 60-percent higher risk of erectile dysfunction when compared to nonsmokers.

During the first year of not smoking, your body continues to heal itself from the stress of absorbing all the cigarette toxins. Coughing, sinus congestion, fatigue, and shortness of breath start to fade as the strength of the lungs is restored. After a smoke-free year, the increased risk from smoking is cut in half. With each passing year, the risk continues to diminish.

Quitting Saves Time and Money

Another great benefit of quitting is that you will save quite a bit of money by giving up the cigarette habit. Your savings come mostly from the fact that you no longer need to buy cigarettes. Since smoking increases your risk for so many diseases, you also save money by staying healthy and not creating huge medical bills. In addition, you no longer need to spend time and effort looking for or buying cigarettes, lighters, and matches or in searching for places to light up.

Getting Ready to Give Up Cigarettes

Seventy percent of adult smokers want to quit. Quitting, however, is not easy. Many smokers try multiple times before they eventually succeed. Thorough preparation can increase your odds of achieving a smoke-free future. The federal government provides resources to assist people. In a program set forth on the Web site ✑*www.smokefree.gov*, the preparatory phase consists of five steps that can be remembered by the acronym "START."

The five steps include the following:

S = Set a quit date.
T = Tell family, friends, and coworkers that you plan to quit.
A = Anticipate and plan for the challenges that you will face.
R = Remove cigarettes and other tobacco products from your home, car, and work.
T = Talk to your health-care provider.

The following sections examine each of these steps in detail.

Set a Quit Date

Once you have your mind made up that the benefits of not smoking far outweigh the risks of smoking, then you are ready to set a quit date. Be sure that you are genuinely ready to make this commitment before you decide upon your quit date. Choose a specific day at least two weeks in advance. This gives you plenty of time to prepare, without losing your motivation to quit.

If you smoke at work, it may make things easier on you if you select either a weekend or vacation day to get started. Or, to make the occasion more memorable, select a special occasion such as your birthday, anniversary, or a national holiday.

Tell Others Your Plan

Social support is the single most important factor in determining whether you are successful in changing poor habits into good ones. The help of your family and friends makes changing any behavioral pattern much easier. Share your quitting plans with those who are close to you to solicit their support.

The National Cancer Institute offers a smoking cessation guide with several helpful tips for developing your support system. First of all, the institute advises you to be sure to remind friends that your moods may change. Let them know that the longer you go without cigarettes, the sooner you will return to your old self. Also, if you have a friend or family close to you who also smokes, see if he or she is interested in quitting with you. If not, ask him or her not to smoke around you. Seek out an ex-smoker to give you encouragement and advice during your tough moments.

Anticipate Challenges and Plan Ahead

Most people tend to form habitual patterns of smoking, such as immediately after a meal or when enjoying an alcoholic drink. These are the times that will present you with the strongest cravings. In addition to emotional cravings, most smokers also experience withdrawal symptoms including mood swings, feelings of irritability and depression, anxiety or restlessness, insomnia, headaches, difficulty concentrating, and increased hunger.

These symptoms are worst the first few weeks, and they are extremely powerful during the first week of quitting. To help manage the cravings, use the time before you quit to concentrate on the moments you observe that you want a cigarette most. Note when you have a cigarette and how you are feeling at the time. Then consider alternative ways to cope with those feelings and alternative activities during those times. For example, instead of having a cigarette after a meal, chew gum, drink water, squirt your mouth with breath spray, or brush your teeth. Be proactive in planning these alternatives, and buy the gum, breath spray, or whatever else you will need before you get to your scheduled quitting day.

FACT

Consider joining a support group, either in person, on the phone, or in an Internet chat room. You can check with the American Cancer, Heart, or Lung Association for leads on groups that you can join. Social support can be a great way to help you quit.

If it is helpful to you to keep a journal, write down your observations. An even easier way to create this record of your smoking pattern is to wrap a piece of paper around your pack of cigarettes and secure it with a rubber band. Every time that you have a cigarette, write down the time of day, place, and your reason for having the cigarette. Later, take the list that you have created and write down alternative strategies for each of those instances.

Remove Cigarettes and Other Tobacco Products

Stop purchasing cartons of cigarettes. Don't save any packs as souvenirs of your willpower to quit. Those extra packs of cigarettes only make it all too easy to start smoking again.

Take a look around you. Take note of all the visual cues that support your smoking so you can start eliminating them from your environment. For example, throw out ashtrays, lighters, and matches. Remove the lighter in your car. Clean your home, office, and car by using air freshener and ridding all remnants of cigarette smoke. Make an appointment with your dentist to have your teeth cleaned and polished.

Talk to Your Health-Care Provider

Be sure to discuss your quitting plan with your health-care provider. If you are taking any prescription medications, find out how your drug therapy may be affected by changing your smoking habits.

Nicotine is powerfully addictive. There are medications that can help you avoid withdrawal symptoms. Enlist the support of your health-care provider, and discuss your options together.

Aids to Stop Smoking

Many products exist today to aid the transition to a smoke-free life. Studies show that people who use nicotine replacement therapy are almost twice as successful as those who do not. Some smoking cessation aids are available over the counter; others require a prescription.

ALERT!

Consult with your health-care provider before you start using any nicotine replacement therapy methods as they can cause certain side effects. Pregnant women should be particularly cautious and work closely with their physician.

Nicotine Gum, Lozenges, and Patches

Nicotine gum, lozenges, and patches are available over the counter at your local pharmacy or grocery store. These products provide a low level of nicotine, without the accompanying toxins that come from smoking, to help you overcome the withdrawal symptoms.

The most common mistake people make with these products is not using enough. Do not skimp or underestimate the amount that you think that you will need. Follow the directions on the package, and do not forget to continue to use your product. Over time, you can reduce the amount that you use. Always keep some of the medication around to help you avoid cravings.

Nicotine Inhalers and Nasal Sprays

Nicotine inhalers and nasal sprays both require a prescription from your doctor. Nasal sprays can provide immediate relief. Furthermore, sprays come in different concentrations so that you can reduce the amount of nicotine that you put into your system over time.

Nicotine inhalers deliver nicotine into your system in much the same manner as cigarettes. For example, when you use a nicotine inhaler, you breathe the medication in through a mouthpiece. The nicotine is absorbed through the mouth's lining.

When using an inhaler, gum, or lozenges, avoid eating or drinking acidic foods such as tomatoes, oranges, coffee, or soda within the first half hour of using the product—the acidic foods can neutralize the helpful effects of the product.

Bupropion Pills

In contrast to the nicotine replacement therapies, bupropion pills do not contain nicotine. Bupropion pills are an antidepressant that help to reduce withdrawal symptoms and cigarette cravings. If you and your physician think this would be a good approach for you, you can even start taking the pill before your quit date.

This medication does require a prescription, however, and as it does have side effects, it is not appropriate for everyone. Medical experts recommend that pregnant women, people with eating disorders or who experience seizures, and people who drink heavily not use this medication.

Nicotine Poisoning

Be especially careful to not smoke when you are using one of the nicotine replacement therapies. Keep in mind that these products are providing nicotine to your body and that it is possible to overdose. Be aware of the signs of nicotine poisoning, which can include severe headaches, weakness, dizziness, nausea, vomiting, diarrhea, cold sweats, blurred vision, hearing difficulties, or mental confusion.

QUESTION?

What should I do if I think I have nicotine poisoning?
Contact your health-care provider if you experience any of the symptoms of nicotine poisoning when you are using a nicotine replacement product and you smoke. If you have any of these symptoms from merely wearing the patch, remove it immediately. Wash the surface of your skin with water, and contact your physician.

After You Quit—Avoiding Relapse

Quitting the cigarette habit is among the most challenging tasks that you will face. Be prepared, particularly in the first few days and weeks, to have alternate plans to keep you busy and to help you avoid dwelling on your urges to have a cigarette. Be especially prepared for those times of day when you are accustomed to sitting back and lighting up. Here are some suggestions for other ways to use this time:

- Take a walk.
- Allow yourself time for a nap.
- Have some healthy snacks around to chew on.
- Drink lots of water.
- Chew gum or suck on candy.
- Use breath spray.
- Perform breathing exercises.
- Hold something in your hand, like a pencil.
- Pick up a craft like knitting or crocheting to keep your hands busy.
- Enjoy a hot bath.
- Listen to music.
- Spend time with or call supportive friends.
- Buy yourself some fun magazines or a good book that you want to read.
- Visit public places where smoking is not allowed so that you cannot light up.

Certain pastimes should also be avoided in these first few critical weeks. To help you stay away from these triggers:

- Keep away from drinking alcoholic beverages.
- Limit caffeinated beverages, as too many can make you feel tense.
- Pass up invitations to spend time with people who smoke.
- If you must spend time with smokers, immediately inform them that you have quit.
- Practice refusing the offer of a cigarette so you will be prepared with your reply.
- Steer clear of places where other people are smoking.
- Eat regularly, and include snacks to avoid extreme feelings of hunger.
- Surround yourself with supportive friends and family, and stay away from circumstances that inflame strong emotions such as anger, resentment, or loneliness.
- Avoid high stress situations as much as possible.
- Try not to push yourself into feeling overly tired.
- Pamper and spoil yourself, and indulge in other pleasures.

FACT

Nicotine is a poison. If infants, children, or pets come into contact with or eat a nicotine patch, even if a used one, it can cause serious harm. This is a medical emergency. If this occurs, contact your health-care provider or poison control center immediately. Consider this to be another powerful reason to quit your habit as soon as possible.

When a strong smoking urge strikes, immediately engage in one of your alternate activities. If you find yourself daydreaming about smoking, turn your thoughts to another subject. Continue to remind yourself of all the great benefits that you will experience once you have quit your habit. Post visual reminders—photos of loved ones, or whatever motivates you—to keep you on track with your goal.

If you do slip up, stop and forgive yourself. Get right back on your program. Remember that one cigarette is less harmful than an entire pack. Remind yourself that you can succeed and that you have strong reasons to quit.

Smoke-Free for Life

Nicotine can be as addicting as heroin, so give yourself plenty of pats on the back for quitting and staying quit. It is quite an accomplishment, and you deserve a reward. One tangible way that you can reward yourself is to set aside a quit jar, where you put all the money you would normally have spent on your smoking habit. As often as you used to go out and buy a pack of cigarettes, put the money you would have used into your jar. After one month, take all the funds and indulge yourself by buying something purely for fun. Keep up this reward practice as long as you need that type of incentive and reminder to stay quit.

Another critical factor is to follow the instructions of your nicotine replacement medication, if you are using one to assist you with quitting. A common mistake is for people to discontinue using the patch or gum a little sooner than recommended because they feel that they have successfully overcome the urge to smoke. This can often lead to a relapse. Avoid this temptation. The first few months may continue to be challenging, so give yourself the extra support.

Another behavior that often leads to a relapse is the thought, "I'll just have one more. What can it hurt?" Studies show that even one more cigarette can often lead to a relapse and the need to repeat the difficult process of quitting. Remind yourself that the toughest time is those first few weeks. If it helps, write down the reasons you want to quit and post them in a visible place.

Starting a new exercise program can often help to stay smoke-free. A walking program is not only easy, but it also can improve your health and allow you to enjoy the feeling of taking deep breaths and the smell of fresh air. Regular walking can also help with managing any extra weight gain that resulted from kicking the smoking habit. (See Chapter 15 for help getting started with a walking program.)

Simply take a moment to truly acknowledge the power of your own convictions to create better health for yourself. You can be your best. Take each day one step at a time. Congratulate yourself for choosing health, not only for yourself, but also for your loved ones and everyone else who is around you.

Chapter 18

Drug Therapy for Cholesterol Management

Reducing your risk of cardiovascular disease, disability, and death requires that you make a commitment to support and enhance healthful living. Medications support this process. Drugs can be valuable tools to help you achieve optimal health. For some people, drug therapy to manage lipid levels is the best short-term action, until lifestyle changes have time to improve cardiovascular health. For others, drug therapy is the only way to address genetic tendencies toward unhealthy lipid levels.

Use of Drugs to Treat High Cholesterol

This chapter provides an overview of the various drugs frequently prescribed to manage lipids, such as statins, bile acid sequestrants, nicotinic acid, and fibrates, separately or in combination. As you read about side effects, keep in mind that pharmaceuticals can be very beneficial. Do not become alarmed by precautions and necessary safeguards—it's important to be informed to make intelligent choices.

According to federal government guidelines and American Heart Association recommendations, drug therapy should always be accompanied by health-enhancing lifestyle changes. In fact, studies show that drug therapy is more effective when used together with lifestyle changes to achieve healthy cholesterol levels and reduce the risk of heart attack and stroke. All therapies, therefore, need to be considered in the context of your lifestyle.

The combination of consuming a primarily plant-based diet, incorporating functional foods such as soy, soluble fiber, and plant stanols and sterols, participating regularly in physical activity, managing stress, quitting the cigarette habit, and following your prescriptive medication regime all work together to create better health.

When you incorporate a multipronged approach, you get results more quickly, you are able to reduce your medication levels sooner, and you will feel the improvements in your health more rapidly. Refer to the rest of this book for more detailed information on how to integrate these important lifestyle changes along with your drug therapy program.

Statins

For physicians, statins (known formally as HMG-CoA reductase inhibitors) are usually the drugs of choice for improving cholesterol levels. The primary goal of all lipid therapy is reduction of LDL cholesterol. Since statins lower LDL cholesterol more than any other type of drug, physicians typically consider statins first.

Statins accomplish this reduction of LDL by producing an enzyme, HMG-CoA reductase, that decreases the amount of cholesterol manufactured by the liver. Since the liver needs cholesterol, it removes more cholesterol from the bloodstream to replace what it has been inhibited from manufacturing.

In this manner, statins reduce LDL production and also boost the body's ability to remove excess LDL cholesterol circulating in the bloodstream. Use of statins also leads to slightly higher HDL cholesterol levels and lower triglycerides. The net results include lower LDL cholesterol and total cholesterol levels and a healthier overall lipid profile.

Statin Research Studies

Research studies show that using statins can reduce LDL cholesterol by as much as 20 to 40 percent. A large 1994 study called the Scandinavian Simvastatin Survival Study ("4S," for short) followed 4,400 patients who had both heart disease and high total cholesterol levels. The study found a 42-percent reduction in death among those taking statins, along with 37-percent reduction in nonfatal heart attacks and 37-percent reduction in bypass surgery or angioplasty. Deaths from other causes besides heart disease did not increase.

FACT

Preliminary evidence indicates that statin drugs can promote growth of new blood vessels in areas served by severely narrowed or blocked arteries. More research needs to be conducted, but these findings may indicate that statins can benefit people with heart disease in more ways than by simply reducing cholesterol levels.

The Cholesterol and Recurrent Events Study (or "CARE") in 1996 reaffirmed the benefits of statins in lowering cholesterol and reducing the risk of heart attack. In this study, researchers gave statin drugs to patients with an average cholesterol level of 209 mg/dL. The study noted that those who took the statins had a 24-percent reduction in heart attack or death, a 26-percent reduction in bypass surgery, and a 22-percent reduction in angioplasty. Female subjects who took statins were 45 percent less likely to have another heart attack.

Other large studies have shown that statin use decreased risk of heart attack, death, stroke, and peripheral arterial disease in both men and women, in middle-aged and older persons, and in people who had not yet had a heart attack as well as those who had survived a significant heart event. With results like these, physician confidence in the use of statins is high.

Statin Types and Usage

Types of statins include lovastatin, simvastatin, pravastatin, fluvastatin, and atorvastatin. These are marketed under the brand names Mevacor, Zocor, Pravachol, Lescol, and Lipitor, respectively. Since the body makes more cholesterol at night than during the day, patients are usually directed to take statins in a single dose at the evening meal or at bedtime.

Typically, statins impact cholesterol levels within four to six weeks. After about six to eight weeks, your health-care provider will retest your cholesterol levels to determine the effectiveness of the statin therapy and whether the dose requires adjustment.

Side Effects of Statins

Most people do not have serious side effects when taking statins. Some people may experience constipation, stomach pain, cramps, or gas. These symptoms are usually mild to moderate, however, and they go away over time. More serious side effects can result from an increase in liver enzymes that can lead to liver toxicity. Because of this risk, it's important to have your liver function tested periodically while you are on statin therapy. People with active chronic liver disease should not take statins.

Another serious side effect comes from statin myopathy. Muscle soreness, pain, and weakness may occur. In extreme cases, muscle cells can break down and release the protein myoglobin into the blood. Myoglobin in the urine can contribute to impaired kidney function, eventually leading to kidney failure. The risk of this occurring is increased when statins are taken in combination with any of the following drugs: gemfibrozil (brand name Lopid); erythromycin (Erythrocin); clarithromycin (Biaxin);

antifungals known as ketoconazole, itraconazole, nefazodone (Serzone); cyclosporine (Sandimmune or Neoral); and niacin.

Contact your health-care provider immediately if you experience any adverse side effects. Avoid consuming grapefruit juice, grapefruits, or tangelos (a hybrid grapefruit) when you are taking statins, as these fruits can impact how the drug is metabolized. Grapefruits contain a chemical that affects certain digestive enzymes as drugs are broken down in the intestinal tract and liver. Interestingly, this effect can occur even if you wait twenty-four hours to take the medication. Therefore, if you are taking statins, it is best to avoid grapefruit products entirely.

ALERT!

Results of a University of California, San Diego study, published in December 2003, suggest that some people may suffer amnesia after taking statins. Duke University scientists have found similar memory problems among patients on statins. While this may be a rare side effect, more research is required. Since cholesterol is essential to cell membrane structure, scientists suggest that reducing cholesterol may affect neurological functioning.

Bile Acid Sequestrants or Resins

Bile acid sequestrants, also referred to as bile acid resins, reduce LDL cholesterol by binding with cholesterol-rich bile acids in the intestines to facilitate their elimination from the body through the stool. Think back to the overview in Chapter 1 of the liver's role in the cholesterol manufacturing process. The liver uses cholesterol to manufacture bile acids, a digestive enzyme that breaks down fats. Bile acid sequestrants cause the body to eliminate bile acids in the intestines. Since the body needs bile acids to digest fats, the liver must manufacture more bile acids to replace those eliminated by the drug. The liver uses up its available cholesterol to make more acids, thus making less cholesterol available for release into the bloodstream. Bile acid sequestrants can reduce LDL cholesterol levels from 10 to 20 percent.

Research Studies on Bile Acid Sequestrants

In the Lipid Research Clinics Coronary Prevention Trial, researchers found a reduction in risk of coronary artery disease through the use of bile acid sequestrants. Bile acid resins, however, can raise triglycerides. Therefore, based on this study, people who have triglyceride levels of 200 mg/dL or higher should not take bile acid sequestrants.

Types of Bile Acid Sequestrants and Usage

Types of bile acid resins include cholestyramine (brand name Prevalite or Questran), and colestipol (Colestid). Cholestyramine and colestipol are often taken as powders that must be mixed with water or fruit juice and taken either once or twice a day with meals. Both drugs are also available as tablets. There is also a newer bile acid sequestrant, called colesevelam. Use of colesevelam has reduced LDL cholesterol by as much as 12 to 18 percent and is also easier to administer and better tolerated than some of the other products.

FACT

According to federal government guidelines, bile acid sequestrants should be considered as LDL-lowering therapy for women with elevated LDL cholesterol who are considering pregnancy, for people who only need modest reductions in LDL cholesterol to achieve target goals, and for combination therapy with statins in people with very high LDL cholesterol levels.

Side Effects of Bile Acid Sequestrants

The principle side effects with the use of bile acid resins have to do with digestion. This type of drug can cause a variety of gastrointestinal problems, such as constipation, bloating, fullness, nausea, abdominal pain, and gas. Drinking lots of water and eating high-fiber foods can help with these side effects. Physicians generally do not prescribe bile acid resins to people with a history of constipation problems.

Taking bile acids can also inhibit the absorption of certain nutrients from foods and of other medications. Physicians recommend that you take other prescription medications at least one hour before or at least four to six hours after the bile acid sequestrant. Be sure to discuss all these matters with your health-care provider if you are considering taking this type of medication.

Nicotinic Acid

Nicotinic acid, known as niacin or vitamin B_3, is being recommended more often as a way to reduce total blood cholesterol, LDL cholesterol, and triglyceride levels, and to elevate HDL levels.

Nicotinic acid raises HDL cholesterol and transforms small LDL into the less harmful, normal-sized LDL cholesterol. Niacin therapy moderately reduces LDL cholesterol levels. Among all the pharmaceutical choices, nicotinic acid is the most effective in raising HDL cholesterol. Niacin therapy is also the most effective medication for reducing levels of Lp(a).

QUESTION?

Can I just use over-the-counter niacin for my high cholesterol?
Self-treatment with niacin is *not* a safe option. Since dosage and timing are important, people should not attempt to self-medicate with over-the-counter B_3 vitamins. Treatment with this medication should only take place under the recommendation and supervision of a doctor.

Nicotinic Acid Research Studies

Studies demonstrate the power of niacin treatment on lipid disorders. Patients treated with immediate-release niacin have seen their HDL levels increase 15 to 35 percent, along with a 20- to 50-percent reduction in triglycerides, and a 10- to 20-percent reduction in LDL cholesterol. Studies also show that nicotinic acid can lower levels of Lp(a) up to 30 percent. Research, however, has not yet made it clear whether or not lowering Lp(a) by niacin therapy reduces the risk for coronary artery disease.

Types of Nicotinic Acid and Usage

Niacin formulations come in three categories: immediate release, short-term or intermediate release, and sustained or slow-acting release. If you are a candidate for niacin therapy, your physician will determine what formulation is most suitable for you. Most physicians start patients on a low dose and work up to a daily dose of 1.5 to 3 grams. This improves the body's acceptance of the drug.

Another important consideration among different products is the quality of the niacin and the amount that will be absorbed by the body. A challenge with many over-the-counter supplements is that they are prepared in forms that do not break down easily in the digestive system. They essentially pass through the body, without allowing for absorption of any nutrients. Supplements are not regulated by the FDA and are therefore not guaranteed to provide what is shown on the labels.

Niaspan, produced by KOS Pharmaceuticals, is specially formulated and packaged in a way that makes it clear how to regulate the levels of niacin in the bloodstream. Nicotinamide is another form of niacin; however, it is not effective in lowering cholesterol levels.

Side Effects of Nicotinic Acid

The challenge with niacin treatment is tolerability. Flushing or hot flashes and itching, the result of the opening of blood vessels, are the most common side effects. If you titrate the drugs appropriately, however, the side effects should decrease over time as your body becomes more tolerant of the therapy. Taking niacin during or after meals, or using aspirin or other additional medications recommended by your physician, can also decrease flushing.

FACT

According to federal government guidelines, nicotinic acid should be considered as a therapeutic option for higher-risk people. If the higher-risk person does not have high LDL cholesterol levels, it should be considered as a single agent. Nicotinic acid can also be used in combination therapy for higher-risk people with elevated levels of LDL cholesterol.

Other side effects include gastrointestinal upset such as nausea, indigestion, gas, vomiting, diarrhea, and even peptic ulcers. More serious risks include liver problems, gout, and high blood sugar. These risks increase as the dosage level is increased.

People who take high blood pressure medications also need to exercise caution with niacin therapy. Taking niacin can amplify the effects of blood pressure medications. People with diabetes typically do not receive niacin therapy because of its effect on blood sugar.

Fibrates

Physicians prescribe fibrates, or fibric acid derivatives, primarily to reduce triglycerides but also to increase HDL cholesterol. Fibrates, however, do not lower LDL cholesterol. Since LDL reduction is usually the primary target of therapy, fibrates are not typically physicians' drug of choice for individuals with elevated cholesterol levels. You should, however, evaluate the relevance of fibrate therapy to your individual case, since it is the drug of choice to reduce the most harmful small, dense LDL particles.

Fibrate therapy is a treatment option for people with coronary artery disease who have low LDL cholesterol but who still have unhealthy lipid levels. Physicians may prescribe fibrates along with statins for people who have both high levels of LDL cholesterol and unhealthy lipid levels. If you are considering drug therapy, be sure to ask your physician whether fibrates are an option.

Fibrate Research Studies

One study found that heart-disease patients with slightly elevated triglyceride levels and low HDL levels reduced their risk of a heart attack by taking fibrate therapy. Studies show that fibrates can reduce triglycerides by as much as 20 to 50 percent and can increase HDL cholesterol by 10 to 15 percent. According to federal government guidelines, physicians can prescribe fibrates to people with very high triglycerides to reduce risk of acute pancreatitis.

Types of Fibrates and Usage

Gemfibrozil and fenofibrate are types of fibrates, known by the brand names Lopid and Tricor. Clofibrate is the third fibrate available in the United States. People on fibrate therapy typically take a dose twice daily, usually thirty minutes before their morning and evening meals.

Fibrate Side Effects

Most people do not suffer any adverse side effects from fibrate therapy. Some people, however, do experience gastrointestinal problems or headache, dizziness, blurred vision, runny nose, fatigue, or flushing. For some people, fibrates increase the chances of developing gallstones. Tell your health-care provider right away about any side effects, particularly if you experience muscle or joint pain or weakness.

ALERT!

Taking fibrates can increase the effect of blood-thinning medications. If you are taking both fibrates and blood thinners, work closely with your physician to monitor the effect of the fibrates.

Combination Drug Therapy

Your physician may prescribe combination drug therapy, depending on the characteristics of your lipid profile and whether you already have heart disease. The target LDL is more aggressive for people with certain existing problems. For people with existing heart disease or diabetes, the goal is to attain an LDL level of less than 100 mg/dL. To achieve this low level, your physician may prescribe a combination of LDL- and triglyceride-lowering medications, or a drug to elevate HDL levels. If you have two or more risk factors, but you do not have coronary artery disease or its equivalent, then the LDL target goal is to achieve an LDL level of less than 130 mg/dL. This may also require combination drug therapy. For people who have one or no risk factors, but who do have elevated cholesterol levels, the target for LDL cholesterol is to achieve a level of less than 160 mg/dL. Such an individual may require only LDL-lowering drugs.

When you are put on therapeutic medications, your physician will regularly monitor your lipid levels to ascertain your progress. If you do not reach your goal after three months with a single drug, your doctor may recommend a second medicine to improve your progress. A combined drug approach may accelerate the lowering of your cholesterol. If you report particular side effects to your physician, he or she may also prescribe lower doses of a combination of medications to lessen the possibility of adverse effects.

Tips for Following Your Medication Program

Following your doctor's recommendations makes good sense. Your health-care provider is a trained professional who has taken time and effort to develop a program of therapy to support your well-being. Studies show that many patients do not follow medical advice. If you have taken the time to pursue a program of lipid-lowering medications, make the best of this support, and follow your medication program. The following tips can help you.

According to the American Heart Association, 10 percent of all hospital admissions are patients who did not take their medications according to the instructions. The average stay in American hospitals due to medical noncompliance is 4.2 days. More than half of all Americans with chronic diseases do not follow their physician's medication and lifestyle instructions.

One of the most important things that you can do to help you to stay on your medication program is to understand exactly what type of medication you are taking and why it is best for a person in your condition. This requires you to take some initiative to educate yourself about your lipid profile, your lipid goals, and your dosage schedule. Ask your health-care provider the following questions:

- What is my lipid profile and what is my goal of therapy?
- What type of medication (statin, nicotinic acid, fibrate) am I taking?
- Why is that medication best for a person in my condition?

- Are there any food/drug combinations that I should avoid?
- When should I take the medicine and should it be taken with, before, or after meals?
- What should I do if I forget to take a dose?
- What are the side effects of the medication?
- Who should I contact and how in case I have negative side effects?

Being consistent is essential to get the most out of your therapeutic program. Do not change your dosage amount, schedule, or quit taking prescription medications without consulting your physician. If you have a hard time with consistency, try some of the following tips:

- Take your medicine at the same time each day.
- Take your medicine when you perform a specific daily act, such as before you brush your teeth.
- Set your watch alarm as a pill reminder.
- Write yourself a note in a prominent place.
- Use a pill box that holds each day's prescription in its respective compartment.
- Write prescription renewal notes in your calendar to remind you before prescriptions run out.

If none of these tips help, consult with your pharmacist for more ideas. Work together with your health-care provider as a team. Be sure to observe your reactions to the medication. Take notes, and report everything back to your physician. Keep your follow-up appointments so you can discuss how things are going. Bring your observation notes to your appointment to remind you of things you may easily forget. Bring your prescription bottles as well. Follow your progress from visit to visit—record data in a cholesterol-monitoring log like the one in Appendix C. If you have questions, don't be afraid to ask them; communication is critical to getting the best health care.

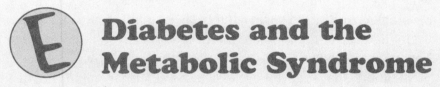

Chapter 19

Diabetes and the Metabolic Syndrome

People with diabetes are at higher risk for heart disease than nondiabetics. People who have a cluster of metabolic disorders, characterized as the metabolic syndrome, are also at greater risk for heart disease. The underlying condition—insulin resistance—is present in both conditions but in varying degrees of severity. This chapter provides an overview of the characteristics of these metabolic disorders as well as advice on restoring insulin sensitivity and reducing the associated risks for heart disease and death.

Metabolic Disorders

Metabolic disorders occur when a specific enzyme or cofactor is absent, or is present in insufficient quantities that result in the body's inability to receive particular nutrients. In other words, the body is unable to metabolize foods into nutrients for fuel or to build tissue. For people who have problems producing insulin, which is the key to the uptake of blood glucose (blood sugar), the body is unable to use the glucose that is circulating in the bloodstream for fuel. As a result, blood sugar levels become elevated.

If blood glucose levels are elevated because insulin is not available or insulin resistance is severe, the person is diagnosed with diabetes, which is a metabolic disorder. If, on the other hand, blood glucose levels are elevated because insulin sensitivity is impaired, and this impairment is present with other specific conditions, the person is considered to have a metabolic disorder, described as the "metabolic syndrome." Both of these conditions increase the risk of heart disease. Many people with diabetes, including children and adults, also have lipid disorders, and many also have hypertension. Both of these conditions increase the risk of heart disease. Therefore, people with diabetes not only need to manage their blood sugar, but it is also important for them to manage their blood pressure and cholesterol carefully.

Approximately 16 million Americans have diabetes. Roughly one-third of these people are unaware that they have diabetes. The incidence of diabetes increases with age; about 50 percent of people with diabetes are fifty or older.

What Is Diabetes?

When you eat foods that are rich in carbohydrates, such as breads, cereals, or grains, your body breaks it down into glucose. Also referred to as blood sugar, your body can use glucose for energy. In a normally functioning system, a healthy pancreas releases insulin into the bloodstream, and this insulin helps to remove the glucose from your bloodstream for your cells to use as fuel. In people who have diabetes, this process is dysfunctional. Either their bodies do not produce any insulin, or the insulin that they produce cannot be used.

Because their bodies cannot convert the sugar in the blood into energy, people with diabetes have high levels of glucose in their bloodstream. The kidneys of diabetic people need to work extra hard to filter the blood to remove the excess glucose. This causes frequent urination and excessive thirst from fluid loss.

The liver is also involved in the process of maintaining normal blood sugar levels. After you eat, the sugars from the food enter your bloodstream and are available as fuel, along with the triglycerides. If not all the sugar fuel is used, either due to poor processing based on low insulin or a reduced need for energy based on a low activity level, the liver removes the excess sugar from the bloodstream, much in the same manner as it removes excess cholesterol, and stores it in the liver as glycogen. If for some reason, you are unable to eat, the liver later can release this stored glucose into the bloodstream to provide an energy boost. This helps to keep your blood sugar levels in a more constant range.

FACT

Diabetes can lead to many dangerous conditions, particularly if untreated or incorrectly managed. These include heart disease, stroke, kidney disease and kidney failure, nerve damage, and gum disease. The disease also raises the risk threefold of dying from complications related to influenza or pneumonia. In America, diabetes is currently the sixth leading cause of death and is a leading cause of blindness and amputations.

Diabetes consists of two main types, both characterized by the body's inability to process available sugar into energy. The two major types are Type 1 and Type 2 diabetes. People with either type can experience elevated blood glucose levels.

Type 1 Diabetes

Type 1 diabetes is an auto-immune condition that occurs most often in children and adults younger than age thirty. It is also called juvenile-onset diabetes or insulin-dependent diabetes mellitus. This condition occurs when the body does not produce any insulin, so people with this type of diabetes take daily insulin injections. Approximately 5 to 10 percent of people with diabetes have Type 1. Young people with diabetes are not likely to have heart disease in their youth. As they age, however, their risk of heart disease is greater than the risk to those who do not have diabetes.

Type 2 Diabetes

Type 2 is the most common form of diabetes. It affects about 95 percent of people who have diabetes. This type of diabetes is referred to as maturity-onset diabetes, adult-onset diabetes, or non–insulin-dependent diabetes mellitus.

Type 2 diabetes is a metabolic disorder. In this case, the pancreas produces some insulin but not enough to allow the sugar to enter the body's cells. At the same time, muscle and tissue cells develop a resistance to the insulin. Therefore, even though sugar is flowing in the bloodstream, the body's tissues remain "hungry." Scientists still have been unable to identify the exact mechanism for why insulin resistance occurs, but it seems to have a relationship to excess body fat.

Your risk of heart disease increases regardless of whether you have Type 1 or Type 2 diabetes. People with Type 1 diabetes are unlikely to get heart disease when they are young, yet as they grow older, their risk becomes higher than the risk of their peers without diabetes.

The Relationship Between Diabetes and Heart Disease

When a person has diabetes, he or she is also more likely to develop heart disease. Depending on the diabetic's number of risk factors, the risk of heart disease may be even greater. For example, someone who has diabetes, high blood pressure, high cholesterol, who smokes, and who is completely inactive is at greater risk of heart disease than someone who only has diabetes. Therefore, controlling risk factors that you can change is extremely important to improve overall health.

Scientists believe that diabetes increases your risk of heart disease because persistent elevated levels of blood sugar damages arteries. If you recall how atherosclerotic plaque gets started (discussed in Chapter 2), you will remember that plaque begins to form on areas where the inside lining of the blood vessels is damaged. Scientists continue to research other mechanisms to explain why people with diabetes are at such an increased risk of heart disease.

Getting Tested for Diabetes

You can determine whether you have diabetes by having the levels of glucose in the bloodstream measured. Before you take a test for diabetes, it is recommended that you go without food or drink for at least nine to twelve hours.

ALERT!

"Pre-diabetes," or impaired fasting glucose, is a condition characterized by higher-than-normal blood glucose levels that are not high enough for diagnosis as Type 2 diabetes. The American Diabetes Association estimates that 16 million Americans have pre-diabetes. If you have this condition, work with your physician right away to start taking steps to lower your blood sugar levels.

A normal result for a fasting glucose test is between 65 and 109 mg/dL. A result that is lower than 65 mg/dL could indicate low blood sugar, also referred to as hypoglycemia. A result that is between 110 to 125 mg/dL could indicate an impaired fasting glucose level, also known as pre-diabetes. A result that is higher than 126 mg/dL could indicate diabetes. Consult with your physician for further evaluation if your test indicates that you have hypoglycemia, pre-diabetes, or diabetes.

Signs and Symptoms of Diabetes

People often disregard the symptoms of diabetes. However, studies indicate that if diabetes is detected early, the likelihood that complications will develop can be reduced. Therefore, it is important to be knowledgeable about the signs and symptoms of diabetes, particularly if you have a family history of this disease. The signs and symptoms of diabetes include the following:

- Frequent urination
- Excessive thirst
- Extreme hunger
- Unusual weight loss
- Increased fatigue
- Irritability
- Numbness or tingling in feet or legs
- Slow-healing cuts or bruises
- Blurry vision

If you are concerned that you may have diabetes, discuss it right away with your health-care provider.

FACT

Approximately 1 million people are diagnosed with diabetes every year. The percentage of American adults with diagnosed diabetes, including women with a history of gestational diabetes (diabetes during pregnancy), has soared more than 61 percent since 1991. The Centers for Disease Control expects this number to more than double by 2050. Minority racial and ethnic populations are particularly at risk of developing the disease.

Types of Tests

To test your blood glucose levels, you can either have a finger-prick fasting blood sugar test, or you can have a hemoglobin A1C test. The tests differ in that a finger-prick test provides a measure of your blood sugar at the moment of the test, while the hemoglobin A1C test shows how your blood sugar has been regulated over the past three-month period by analyzing the hemoglobin, instead of simply the sugar levels. In order to establish a diagnosis of diabetes, a hemoglobin A1C test is necessary.

The American Diabetes Association recommends that people with diabetes take the hemoglobin A1C test two to four times a year. The hemoglobin A1C test does not replace daily self-testing but rather provides a method to assess your success with blood sugar management over time. The FDA has approved a home test. Check with your healthcare provider to see whether it would be appropriate for you.

The Metabolic Syndrome

Experts have named a group of risk factors—excess weight, physical inactivity, and genetic factors—as likely to indicate the metabolic syndrome, a condition closely associated with the metabolic disorder referred to as insulin resistance or Type 2 diabetes. Because these risk factors often occur together, researchers have a difficult time teasing out the specific contributions of each factor to the overall increased risk of heart disease. While the metabolic syndrome is not a risk factor in and of itself, it is considered to enhance the level of risk, particularly when it is present with high cholesterol levels.

ALERT!

Experts describe abdominal obesity as the hallmark of the metabolic syndrome. To determine whether abdominal obesity is present, you need to measure the circumference of your waist. See Chapter 14 for guidelines on measuring for abdominal obesity.

Physicians identify metabolic syndrome when three or more of the following conditions are present:

- Abdominal obesity
- Triglyceride level higher than 140 mg/dL
- HDL cholesterol level of less than 40 mg/dL in men

- HDL cholesterol level of less than 50 mg/dL in women
- Blood pressure greater than or equal to 130/85 mmHg
- Fasting glucose greater than 109 mg/dL

Studies suggest that as many as 24 percent of Americans have the metabolic syndrome. In a study conducted at the Heart Disease Prevention Program at the University of California, Irvine, investigators found that the presence of the metabolic syndrome, in the absence of other risk factors, is associated with an increased risk of coronary artery disease, cardiovascular disease, and an increased risk of death. This increased risk of coronary artery disease and death from cardiovascular disease is present even if only one or two risk factors for the metabolic syndrome are present. Research into this area continues.

What You Can Do

If your doctor diagnoses you with diabetes or determines that you have the metabolic syndrome, it's even more important that you adopt healthy lifestyle habits. When you address the root causes of this condition—excess weight and a sedentary lifestyle—sensitivity to insulin is restored, and the risk factors are reduced. Lifestyle changes can make a huge difference. If you have diabetes, it can be successfully managed. If you are pre-diabetic, you can avoid becoming diabetic.

The Power of Healthful Eating

Physical activity and healthful eating need to go hand in hand to improve the factors associated with diabetes and the metabolic syndrome. Healthy nutrition should follow the guidelines discussed in Chapter 8, including eating a diet of primarily plant-based foods. Total dietary fat should represent between 25 to 35 percent of total calories, but it should be composed mostly of unsaturated vegetable fats. Researchers note that dietary fat, rather than calories, carbohydrates, or even sugar intake, seems to be a critical factor in Type 2 diabetes, although researchers have not yet been able to identify the exact mechanisms.

The Power of Exercise

Your exercise program to improve insulin sensitivity should include both heart-pumping cardiovascular activities and strength-training exercises to tone up your muscles. Regular exercise helps you maintain healthy blood sugar levels by burning fuels and by helping you to achieve and maintain a healthy weight and shed excess body fat. Improvements in glucose tolerance and insulin sensitivity are usually short-lived, however, and deteriorate within three days of your last workout. This factor makes regular aerobic exercise vital.

Diabetes increases a woman's risk of heart disease by three to seven times, compared to a two- to threefold increase in risk for men, according to the American Heart Association. While it is important for all people with diabetes to take extra good care of their health, this is even more necessary for women.

Cardiovascular or aerobic exercise, such as walking, is critically important for managing blood sugar levels and improving your body's ability to use insulin. Try to be active on at least three nonconsecutive days and up to five sessions per week. Ideally, your aerobic exercise session should last at least thirty minutes. It's not necessary to work at a high intensity. Take it easy, and progress gradually. If thirty minutes is too long, start with ten-minute bouts and accumulate thirty minutes in one day.

According to the position taken by the American College of Sports Medicine (ACSM) on exercise and Type 2 diabetes, resistance or weight training has the potential to improve muscle strength and endurance, enhance flexibility and body composition, decrease risk factors for cardiovascular disease, and result in improved glucose tolerance and insulin sensitivity. Strength training can also increase the resting metabolic rate to assist in weight control. Regular exercise that includes aerobics and strength training also provides important emotional health benefits, including reduced stress, heightened feelings of well-being, and enhanced quality of life.

Exercise Risks for People with Diabetes and Insulin Resistance

Before you begin your exercise program, be sure to consult with your health-care provider, as exercise affects blood sugar levels. Exercise helps to decrease blood glucose concentrations, potentially reducing or eliminating insulin doses, especially for those with Type 2 diabetes. You need to have a clear understanding of how activity and medications affect your blood glucose levels for your physical activity program to be both safe and effective.

ALERT!

According to the American Diabetes Association, you should not exercise if you have a fasting blood glucose of more than 300 mg/dL, foot problems, or nerve conditions such as peripheral neuropathy. You may, however, be able to successfully participate in non–weight-bearing activities such as swimming, water aerobics, or cycling.

Low Blood Sugar

The greatest exercise risk to people with diabetes is hypoglycemia, or low blood-sugar levels. Hypoglycemia can lead to a life-threatening loss of consciousness. People with Type 2 diabetes that is controlled by meal planning and exercise usually do not have problems with low blood sugar. However, people who take insulin or oral diabetes medicine, in particular sulfonylureas, may have low blood-sugar levels both during and after exercise.

The risk of developing low blood glucose is greatest after high-intensity or extended exercise. This reaction can take place even twelve or more hours after a workout. To help prevent hypoglycemia, you must time your medications carefully. The ACSM recommends injecting insulin at least one hour before exercise. In addition, you need to ensure adequate food intake and monitor blood glucose levels before and after exercise, as well as during longer exercise sessions or when trying a new activity.

The signs and symptoms of hypoglycemia include extreme fatigue, excessive sweating, headache, trembling, weakness, slurred speech, poor coordination, feeling faint, pale moist skin, full rapid pulse, and elevated blood pressure. If not dealt with, hypoglycemia can result in loss of consciousness or seizures.

ALERT!

If you begin to experience hypoglycemia, you need to consume a rapidly absorbed sugar source immediately, such as a half-cup of fruit juice or regular soda, two teaspoons of sugar or raisins, or six jelly beans or a piece of hard candy. To be on the safe side, always keep a source of rapidly acting carbohydrate easily available during exercise and tell others where this source is located.

Since exercise burns fuel, you need to monitor food intake carefully in relationship to increased activity. ADA advises individuals with diabetes to exercise from one to three hours after eating a meal. One hour of exercise generally requires 15 additional grams of carbohydrates, which you should consume before or after exercise, depending on your individual condition and needs. If exercise is vigorous or longer than one hour, an additional 15 to 30 grams of carbohydrates are recommended for each additional hour.

Dehydration

High blood-sugar levels can increase urination, contributing to dehydration. In addition, diabetic complications such as autonomic neuropathy, which affects the nerves serving internal organs and regulating blood pressure, blood glucose, and perspiration, may impair your sweating response, increasing the risk of heat-related illness.

Be sure to drink fluids before, during, and after exercise, especially in warmer environments. The American Diabetes Association recommends drinking at least a half liter of fluid two hours before exercise. Plain water is usually sufficient for sessions of one hour or less. For workouts lasting longer than one hour, water and extra carbohydrates are needed. People with diabetes will absorb beverages with a 6- to 8-percent carbohydrate solution, such as sports drinks, more easily than soft drinks or fruit juices, which are typically 13- to 14-percent carbohydrate solutions.

Problems Due to Poor Circulation

People with diabetes need to protect their feet when they exercise. If you have a more severe case of diabetes, you may also have nerve damage or circulatory disorders, such as peripheral vascular disease. This may cause impaired blood flow to the extremities (the hands and feet). Extra protection of your feet will help prevent bruising or injury.

Be sure to wear appropriate athletic footwear, and wash and dry your feet thoroughly after exercising and check for sores. Petroleum jelly may help to decrease friction on specific areas. If you have an open sore that is not healing, consult a health-care professional immediately. When not treated promptly, an infection can spread to the bone, resulting in amputation.

Avoid fitness equipment that may impair circulation, such as bands or buoyancy equipment on legs or feet in water exercise. Inadequate blood supply can cause you to be more prone to pain, aching, or cramping during exercise. Rest for about two minutes if cramping occurs during a workout.

While it may seem like there are a lot of precautions related to exercise, it is one of the best things you can do to help improve blood sugar levels and insulin sensitivity. With a regular activity program and improved nutritional habits, Type 2 diabetes can be avoided or controlled. Regular exercise and healthy eating habits are also keys to weight management. With time and consistency, you can lose excess weight, restore insulin sensitivity, reduce cholesterol and triglyceride levels, and may even make the use of further medications unnecessary.

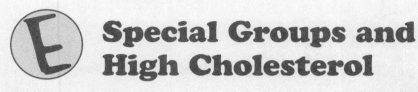

Chapter 20

Special Groups and High Cholesterol

While the same general principles related to healthy nutrition, regular physical activity, no smoking, and weight and stress management apply to all people, there are certain special considerations for people with particular needs. These people include children, teens, and older adults. Women also have needs and special considerations that are distinct from those of men.

High Cholesterol in Children and Adolescents

Recently, medical professionals have been paying greater attention to childhood cholesterol levels as concerns rise over the increasing incidence of Type 2 diabetes, inactivity, and overweight issues among kids. Since heart disease is a slow, progressive disease, more and more attention is being given to the significance of healthy habits since youth.

An Inherited Disorder

Children from certain families that include a parent or grandparent who had heart disease at an early age are genetically prone to have high cholesterol levels. If a male relative had a heart attack before age fifty-five or a female relative before age sixty-five, this places a child in a high-risk category.

Statistics reveal that approximately one in 500 children have inherited hypercholesterolemia. These children have a 50-percent risk of having heart disease before age fifty. If this condition is detected early, children can start incorporating healthy habits to greatly reduce their risk of having heart disease as adults.

Research shows that fatty streaks that represent the beginning of atherosclerotic plaque have been found in children as young as age three. Among children, girls tend to have higher total cholesterol and LDL levels than boys.

FACT

If you have a child with high cholesterol, take time to educate him or her about the value of healthy habits. Try not to portray the condition as a horrible disease. All kids and parents benefit from eating good foods and staying active. It's unnecessary for your child to feel stigmatized or to feel high levels of stress over the condition.

Guidelines for Blood Lipid Levels

The National Cholesterol Education Program's Expert Panel on Blood Cholesterol in Children and Adolescents recommends certain guidelines for cholesterol levels in children and adolescents age two to nineteen. According to these guidelines, total cholesterol is acceptable if it is less than 170 mg/dL. It is considered borderline if it is 170 to 199 mg/dL and high if it is 200 mg/dL or greater. LDL cholesterol should ideally be less than 110 mg/dL, with borderline levels ranging from 110 to 129 mg/dL. At levels of 130 or greater, LDL is considered high. The guidelines also recommend that HDL levels should be greater than or equal to 35 mg/dL, and that triglycerides should be less than or equal to 150 mg/dL.

American children have much higher blood cholesterol levels than children from other countries. The principle culprit is not genetics but poor nutrition, followed by lack of exercise. American kids typically eat a diet filled with fast, highly processed foods rich in saturated fats, trans-fats, and sugar.

Direct role modeling is one of the most powerful ways to improve lifestyle habits of kids and teens. Help your children to have a healthy and disease-free adulthood by incorporating healthy lifestyle habits for the whole family. Plan physical activities together such as hiking or bike-riding and keep healthy foods around the house.

Government treatment guidelines for children recommend lifestyle changes as the first line of therapeutic intervention. Improving eating habits, increasing physical activity, and managing weight can go a long way toward reducing elevated cholesterol levels. Certainly, these lifestyle habits are beneficial for all children, even those who are not from high-risk families.

Experts disagree about the role of cholesterol-lowering drugs for children. The American Heart Association and the federal government recommend that cholesterol-lowering drugs be recommended only for those children over ten years of age who have high LDL levels even after changes in diet. Other experts, however, remain concerned about the long-term effectiveness of drug therapy. Medical professionals uniformly recommend healthful lifestyle changes as being of paramount importance for children to enjoy good health.

Special Considerations for Teens

Teens, their parents, and health-care providers also need to be sensitive to cholesterol issues affecting today's youth. Studies show that between 15 and 20 percent of the population already has atherosclerotic plaque by the age twenty. About 10 percent of adolescents between the ages of twelve to nineteen have cholesterol levels that exceed 200 mg/dL. A study released in 2003 identified the presence of the metabolic syndrome among children between ages twelve to nineteen. (See Chapter 19 for more on the metabolic syndrome.) The study found that 8 to 12 percent of nonobese adolescents had the metabolic syndrome, compared to 34 to 41 percent of obese adolescents, placing this group at higher risk for heart disease.

The risk for adolescents is increased further by using oral contraceptives and cigarettes. In one study among females aged twelve to seventeen years, researchers found that the total cholesterol of oral contraceptive users was significantly higher than in nonusers. Birth control users who are also smokers are at even higher risk for heart disease.

Women with High Cholesterol

Heart disease is the number-one killer of women. In America, heart diseases kill nearly half a million women per year, more than the next seven causes of death, including all forms of cancer. The recommended levels of blood lipids are for the most part the same for women and men; however, women have some distinct differences that merit special consideration.

Silent Heart Disease

Researchers have discovered that women tend to experience heart attacks in a different way than men. Women in particular suffer from "silent heart disease," which often goes undiagnosed. A silent heart attack is a result of atherosclerotic buildup in coronary arteries that causes death of so little heart tissue that it may be symptom-free or easily confused with feelings of indigestion or anxiety. (One way to tell that it is not indigestion is that antacids do not make the pain go away.)

According to one study, 35 percent of women, compared to 28 percent of men, experienced silent heart attacks. According to the American Heart Association, clinicians often attribute chest pain in women to other causes and misinterpret the fact that they have heart disease. As more and more studies are conducted on women subjects, more information about the differences in the development of heart disease in men and women is becoming available.

Other Concerns for Women

Pregnancy is a time in life when a woman's lipid profile tends to change. Pregnant women typically have an increase in blood cholesterol levels. This is not cause for undue alarm, unless otherwise noted by your health-care provider.

As mentioned previously, oral contraception can increase levels of blood cholesterol as well as blood pressure. Therefore, if you are taking birth control pills, it is even more important to engage in other health-enhancing practices. Smokers, in particular, have a higher risk of heart disease and stroke if they also take birth control pills.

FACT

Women may have a greater tendency to have atypical chest pain or to complain of abdominal pain, difficulty breathing, nausea, and unexplained fatigue. Also, although women are often known for urging their husbands or children to see the doctor, they tend to avoid or delay seeking medical care for themselves.

Testing and Research

One more confounding factor in the diagnosis and treatment of heart disease in women is that diagnostic tests and procedures are not as accurate for women as they are for men. For example, an exercise stress test has a higher likelihood of showing a false positive or a false negative for women subjects. More expensive diagnostic tests tend to be more precise. Discuss all your options thoroughly with your health-care provider.

In February 2004, the American Heart Association announced new guidelines for preventing heart disease and stroke in women based on a

THE EVERYTHING LOW CHOLESTEROL BOOK

woman's individual cardiovascular health. This represents significant prog-ress in using research based on how a woman develops cardiovascular dis-ease and in creating recommendations for treating women on a continuum based on individual risk levels, rather than a "one size fits all" approach.

The Age Factor: Cholesterol and Menopause

A woman's risk of heart disease increases approximately ten to fifteen years later than the average man's. This disparity is reflected in guide-lines that state an age of forty-five or above is a risk factor for a man; for a woman, on the other hand, age does not become a risk factor until she is fifty-five. The reasons for this difference are not fully understood. Some of it is thought to be due to the protective effects of estrogen. A woman's heart disease risk rises when she becomes postmenopausal, regardless of whether menopause occurred naturally or as the result of surgery.

Here's a story from Kay, age fifty-four and a professional nurse. It shows how cholesterol levels can be affected by a hysterectomy and the consequential immediate menopause.

> For many years during routine cholesterol screening I was lucky to run in the 160 to 180 range without dietary adjustments. I am genetically slender and never had to worry about my weight.
>
> Suddenly, after I had a hysterectomy in my forties, my cholesterol started to rise, with the old dietary habits. My weight did not go up. I tried three brands of cholesterol medication which all caused my liver enzymes to elevate.
>
> Then it came down to dietary changes and exercise. I was concerned because I knew that I could not take medications and had to rely on better nutrition and exercise. These changes have made me feel better and stronger, but keep my cholesterol in the low 200s, where it had been 230 on the previous examination. I will keep up with both of these programs for the rest of my life.

By the time a woman reaches the age of seventy-five or older, her risk of heart attack is approximately the same as that of a man's. Women age seventy-five and above actually have a higher risk of death by stroke than men. The reasons for this are not clear. Some researchers suggest that it may simply be due to the fact that atherosclerosis is a slow, progressive disease and more women live longer than men. More research on women's health issues is needed to bring further light to these questions.

Treatment of postmenopausal women with hormone replacement therapy has been theorized to reduce the heart disease risk in women; however, studies demonstrated that this hypothesis was incorrect. Medical experts no longer recommend estrogen treatment to prevent heart disease.

Another aspect of menopause that may contribute to a woman's higher risk of heart disease is the tendency to gain weight, particularly around the abdominal area. Abdominal fat that creates an apple-shaped physique is known to be a sign for increased risk of heart disease. While healthy habits are valuable throughout life, postmenopausal women should pay particular care to healthy nutrition and exercise habits, as well as to effective weight management.

Older Adults with High Cholesterol

Most deaths from heart disease occur in the older adult population. Men aged sixty-five and above and women aged seventy-five and above are classified as older adults for the purpose of discussing heart disease. Cholesterol levels, even in older age, have predictive power for the increased risk of heart disease. Furthermore, studies have shown that reducing LDL cholesterol levels also reduces the risk of death from heart disease. Therefore, maintaining healthy lifestyle habits is still valuable, even in older age.

In older age, high blood pressure affects more women than men. Up until age fifty-five, more men than women have hypertension. Between the ages of fifty-five and seventy-four, the percentage of women with high blood pressure increases. By age seventy-five, a higher percentage of women have high blood pressure than men.

One study among older adults with an average age of seventy-two showed that eating fatty fish at least once a week reduced the risk of heart attack by as much as 44 percent. Clearly, life extension can even occur at older ages. Quality of life is also important and can be maintained through healthy nutrition, regular physical activity, and weight management. Even studies of people over the age of ninety showed that strength training with weights could bring improvements.

A lifetime of healthy habits is always the ideal situation. But few of us live ideal lives. We can all make daily life more pleasurable by enhancing health, which includes maintaining healthy lipid levels. It is never too late to take steps to improve the quality of daily living.

Appendix A

Resources

Health Resources

American Cancer Society
1599 Clifton Road
Atlanta, GA 30329
(800) ACS -2345
✑*www.cancer.org*

**American College of Obstetrics
and Gynecologists (ACOG)**
409 12th Street, SW
Washington, D.C. 20023-2188
(800) 673-8444 or (202) 863-2518
✑*www.acog.com*

American Diabetes Association
ATTN: National Call Center
1701 North Beauregard Street
Alexandria, VA 22311
(800) 342-2383
✑*www.diabetes.org*

American Heart Association
National Center
7272 Greenville Avenue
Dallas, TX 75231
(800) 242-8721
✑*www.americanheart.org*

American Lung Association
1740 Broadway
New York, NY 10019
(800) LUNG-USA
✑*www.lungusa.org*

American Red Cross
National Headquarters
2025 E Street, N.W.
Washington, D.C., 20006
(202) 303-4462
✑*www.redcross.org*

Centers for Disease Control and Prevention (CDC)
1600 Clifton Rd.
Atlanta, GA 30333
Public Inquiries
(404) 639-3534 or (800) 311-3435
www.cdc.gov

CDC Office on Smoking and Health
Mail Stop K-50
4770 Buford Highway, NE
Atlanta, GA 30341-3724
(800) 232-1311 or (770) 488-5705
www.cdc.gov/tobacco

National Cancer Institute
Bldg. 31, Room 10A31
31 Center Drive, MSC 2580
Bethesda, MD 20892-2580
(800) 4-CANCER
TTY Tel: (800) 332-8815
www.cancer.gov

National Heart, Lung, and Blood Institute
Information Center
The National Cholesterol Education Program
P.O. Box 30105
Bethesda, MD 20824-0105
(301) 251-1222
www.nhlbi.nih.gov

National Institute of Diabetes and Digestive and Kidney Diseases (NIDDK)
NIDDK, NIH, Building 31, Room 9A04
31 Center Drive, MSC 2560
Bethesda, MD 20892-2560
www.niddk.nih.gov

National Institutes of Health
Bethesda, MD 20892
(301) 496-4000

Stanford Prevention Resource Center
Stanford University School of Medicine
Hoover Pavilion, Room N229
211 Quarry Road
Stanford, CA 94305-5705
(650) 723-6254
http://prevention.stanford.edu

Food and Nutrition Resources

American Dietetic Association
1200 S. Riverside Plaza Suite 2000
Chicago, IL 60606-6995
(800) 877-1600 or (312) 899-0040
www.eatright.org

Consumer Nutrition Information Line of the American Dietetic Association
To find a registered dietitian contact the association by phone or e-mail:
(800) 366-1655
hotline@eatright.org

Center for Science in the Public Interest
Publishes the *Nutrition Action Newsletter*
1875 Connecticut Ave., NW
Suite 300
Washington, D.C. 20009
(202) 332-9110
Fax: (202) 265-4954
E-mail: *cspi@cspinet.org*
www.cspinet.org

Cooper Concepts, Inc.
12200 Preston Road
Dallas, TX 75230
(800) 393-2221
www.coopercomplete.com

Food and Nutrition Information Center
10301 Baltimore Ave.
Beltsville, MD 20705-2351
(301) 504-5719
www.nal.usda.gov/fnic/

Horizon Organic Dairy
P.O. Box 17577
Boulder, CO 80308-7577
Consumer Hotline: (888) 494-3020 or
(303) 530-2711
www.horizonorganic.com

The National Directory of Farmers Markets
Online Market Locator
www.ams.usda.gov

Organic Trade Association
P.O. Box 547
Greenfield MA 01301
(413) 774-7511
E-mail: *info@ota.com*
www.ota.com

Prather Ranch
For organic, grass-fed beef
Macdoel, CA
(877) 570-2333
E-mail: *sales@PratherRanch.com*
www.pratherranch.com

Revival Soy
1031 E. Mountain Street, Building 302
Kernersville, NC 27284
(800) 738-4825 or (336) 722-2337
E-mail: *customercare@revivalsoy.com*
www.revivalsoy.com

Trader Joe's
Online Store Locator
www.traderjoes.com

U.S. Department of Agriculture (USDA)
14th & Independence Ave., SW
Washington, D.C. 20250
(202) 720-2791
Fax: (202) 720-2166
www.usda.gov

U.S. Department of Health and Human Services
200 Independence Avenue, S.W.
Washington, D.C. 20201
(877) 696-6775
www.dhhs.gov

U.S. Food and Drug Administration (FDA)
5600 Fishers Lane
Rockville, MD 20857
(888) 463-6332
www.fda.gov

Weight-Control Information Network
One Win Way
Bethesda, MD 20892-3665
(877) 946-4627
Fax: (202) 828-1028
E-mail: *win@info.niddk.nih.gov*
www.niddk.nih.gov/health/nutrit/
pubs/health.htm

Whole Foods Market, Inc.
Research and Support Team
700 Lavaca Street, Suite 500
Austin, TX 78701
Corporate office: (512) 477-4455
www.wholefoods.com

Exercise Resources

American College of Sports Medicine
P.O. Box 1440
Indianapolis, IN 46206-1440
(317) 637-9200
www.acsm.org

Aerobics and Fitness Association of America (AFAA)
15250 Ventura Blvd., Suite 200
Sherman Oaks, CA 91403
(818) 905-0040 or (800) 446-2322
www.afaa.com

American Council on Exercise
P.O. Box 910449
San Diego, CA 92191-0449
(858) 535-8227
Fax: (858) 535-1778
www.acefitness.org

American Senior Fitness Association
(800) 243-1478
www.seniorfitness.net

Aquatic Exercise Association (AEA)
3439 Technology Drive, Unit 6
Nokomis, FL 34275
(888) AEA-WAVE
www.aeawave.com

Cooper Institute for Aerobics Research
12330 Preston Road
Dallas, TX 75230
(800) 365-7050
www.cooperinst.org

IDEA Health & Fitness Source
6190 Cornerstone Court E., Suite 204
San Diego, CA 92121
(858) 535-8979
www.ideafit.com

International Council for Active Aging
3307 Trutch Street
Vancouver, BC V6L-2T3
(604) 734-4466
(866) 335-9777 (North America only)
Fax: (604) 708-4464
www.icaa.cc

International Health, Racquet and Sportsclub Association (IHRSA)
263 Summer Street
Boston, MA 02210
(800) 228-4772
www.ihrsa.org

Medical Fitness Association (MFA)
915 Elmswood Avenue
Evanston, IL 60202
(847) 475-2332
www.medicalfitness.org

National Strength and Conditioning Association
P.O. Box 9908
Colorado Springs, CO 80932-9908
(800) 815-6826 or (719) 632-6722
Fax: (719) 632-6367
http://nsca-lift.org

President's Council on Physical Fitness and Sports
701 Pennsylvania Avenue, NW
Suite 250
Washington, D.C. 20004
(202) 272-3421
www.fitness.gov

YMCA of the USA
101 N. Wacker Drive
Chicago, IL 60606
(888) 333-9622 or (800) 872-9622
Fax: (312) 977-0031
www.ymca.net

Disabled Sports Organizations

Disabled Sports, USA (DSUSA)
451 Hungerford Drive, #100
Rockville, MD 20850
(301) 217-0960
www.dsusa.org

The National Center on Physical Activity and Disability
Department of Disability and Human Development
University of Illinois at Chicago
1640 West Roosevelt Rd.
Chicago, IL 60608-6904
(800) 900-8086 (voice and TTY)
Fax: (312) 355-4058
E-mail: *ncpad@uic.edu*
www.ncpad.org

Rehabilitation Institute of Chicago
Center for Health and Fitness
710 N. Lake Shore Drive
Chicago, IL 60611
(312) 908-4292
Fax: (312) 908-1051
www.rehabchicago.org

Product Resources for Cholesterol Testing

Berkeley HeartLab, Inc.
839 Mitten Road
Burlingame, CA 94010-1318
(650) 697-4500
For locator information on physicians who offer more advanced lipid testing, call (866) 871-4408 or (800) HEART-89.
E-mail: *info@bhlinc.com*
www.berkeleyheartlab.com

Cholestech Corporation
3347 Investment Blvd.
Hayward, CA 94545
(800) 733-0404
www.cholestech.com

Lifestream Technologies, Inc.
Post Falls Office
510 Clearwater Loop, Suite 101
Post Falls, ID 83854
(877) 457-9409 or (208) 457-9409
www.lifestreamtech.com

Product Resources for Exercise

Fitness Wholesale
Fitness equipment and accessories
895-A Hampshire Road
Stow, OH 44224
(888) 396-7337 or (330) 929-7227
Fax: (330) 929-7250
E-mail: *fw@fitnesswholesale.com*
www.fitnesswholesale.com

Junonia
Fitness apparel for plus-sized women
800 Transfer Road, Suite 8
St. Paul, MN 55114
Tel: (800) 671-0175
www.junonia.com

M. Rose Sportswear Group, Inc.
Fitness apparel for women
1255 Activity Drive, Suite B
Vista, CA 92083-8517
(877) 866-7673 or (760) 734-4090
Fax: (760) 734-4220
E-mail: *mrose@mrosesportswear.com*
www.mrosesportswear.com

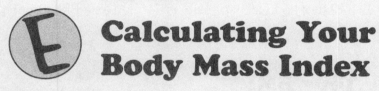

Appendix B

Calculating Your Body Mass Index

The body mass index (BMI) is a measure that reduces the relationship between weight and height to one number. When you compare your BMI value to charted ranges, you get an approximation of body fatness, rather than a precise measure. The figure is not equal to a measurement of body fat percentage.

The value of knowing your BMI is that it provides a rough estimate of whether your body size indicates a need to manage your weight more effectively.

To find your BMI, use the formula below, or check the Body Mass Index Chart for an approximate value. To understand what your BMI means, check the BMI categories for men and women. Overweight is defined as a BMI of 25 to 29.9; obesity is defined as a BMI equal to or more than 30.

Calculate Your BMI

To calculate your BMI, you must know your weight in pounds (measured with underwear but no shoes) and your height in inches. Follow this simple three-step method:

1. Multiply your weight by 703.
2. Divide the result by your height.
3. Divide the result again by your height to get your BMI.

For example: If you are five-foot-seven (or 67 inches tall) and weigh 170 pounds, you would do the following:

1. Multiply 170×703 to get 119,510.
2. Divide 119,510 by 67 to get 1,785.
3. Divide 1,785 by 67 to get 26.6.

In this example, the BMI is 26.6; this BMI falls in the overweight category.

Body Mass Index Chart

For a less precise answer without the math, here is a chart for men and women that gives the body mass index (BMI) for various heights (in inches) and weights (in pounds, with underwear but no shoes). Find your height, read across the row to your weight, then read up the column to find your approximate BMI score.

BMI Score	21	22	23	24	25	26	27	28	29	30	31
4'10"	100	105	110	115	119	124	129	134	138	143	148
5'0"	107	112	118	123	128	133	138	143	148	153	158
5'1"	111	116	122	127	132	137	143	148	153	158	164
5'3"	118	124	130	135	141	146	152	158	163	169	175
5'5"	126	132	138	144	150	156	162	168	174	180	186
5'7"	134	140	146	153	159	166	172	178	185	191	198
5'9"	142	149	155	162	169	176	182	189	196	203	209
6'0"	150	157	165	172	179	186	193	200	208	215	222
6'1"	159	166	174	182	189	197	204	212	219	227	235
6'3"	168	176	184	192	200	208	216	224	232	240	248

The Body Mass Index Chart

What Does Your BMI Mean?

BMI ranges from 18.5 to 24.9.
Normal weight: Good for you! Try not to gain weight.

BMI ranges from 25 to 29.9.
Overweight: Try not to gain weight, especially if your waist measurement is high. You need to manage your weight if you have two or more risk factors for heart disease and are overweight, or have a high waist measurement.

BMI is 30 or greater.
Obese: You need to manage your weight. Lose weight slowly—about half a pound to two pounds a week. See your doctor or a registered dietitian if you need help.

Source: *Clinical Guidelines on the Identification, Evaluation, and Treatment of Overweight and Obesity in Adults*; National Heart, Lung, and Blood Institute, in cooperation with the National Institute of Diabetes and Digestive and Kidney Diseases, National Institutes of Health, June 1998.

Appendix C

Chart Your Progress

Track Your Numbers— Your Cholesterol Monitoring Log

Photocopy the log on the next page and bring it with you when you visit the doctor. It will help you track your progress as you work your way to a more heart-healthy lifestyle.

Food Log

Photocopy the log on the next page to record what you eat in a typical week. As you increase your awareness of your eating habits, you can start to move toward eating more healthfully. Compare your typical consumption with the recommendations you learned in Chapters 8 and 9. Use the notes section to record any emotions you may have related to your eating, such as anger or sadness, or physical feelings such as fatigue or headaches. This may increase your awareness of eating that is unrelated to your true physical needs for food or that is related to underlying physical conditions. You can share this log with your health-care provider.

Date   Notes:

Medication

Dose

Lipid Goal

Lipid Profile Test Results:

Total Cholesterol

Total HDL

Total LDL

Triglycerides

Glucose

Liver Function Test

Other:

Blood Pressure

Weight

Body Composition or BMI

Goals

Met physical activity goal of 30 minutes most days of the week?

If NO, what improvements to make?

Met dietary goals of adding whole grains, fruits, vegetables, beans, poultry, fish, and low and/or nonfat dairy products to replace processed and fast foods and fatty dairy products and meats?

If NO, what improvements to make?

Regularly performed relaxation exercises or form of stress management?

If NO, what improvements to make?

Weekly Food Log _____ to_____

	Sunday	Monday
Breakfast		
Lunch		
Dinner		
Snacks		
Fluids		
Notes		

	Tuesday	Wednesday
Breakfast		
Lunch		
Dinner		
Snacks		
Fluids		
Notes		

	Thursday	Friday
Breakfast		
Lunch		
Dinner		
Snacks		
Fluids		
Notes		

	Saturday	NOTES:
Breakfast		
Lunch		
Dinner		
Snacks		
Fluids		
Notes		

Index

Recipes Index

THE EVERYTHING SERIES!

BUSINESS & PERSONAL FINANCE

Everything® Budgeting Book
Everything® Business Planning Book
Everything® Coaching and Mentoring Book
Everything® Fundraising Book
Everything® Get Out of Debt Book
Everything® Grant Writing Book
Everything® Homebuying Book, 2nd Ed.
Everything® Homeselling Book
Everything® Home-Based Business Book
Everything® Investing Book
Everything® Landlording Book
Everything® Leadership Book
Everything® Managing People Book
Everything® Negotiating Book
Everything® Online Business Book
Everything® Personal Finance Book
Everything® Personal Finance in Your 20s & 30s Book
Everything® Project Management Book
Everything® Real Estate Investing Book
Everything® Robert's Rules Book, $7.95
Everything® Selling Book
Everything® Start Your Own Business Book
Everything® Time Management Book
Everything® Wills & Estate Planning Book

COOKING

Everything® Barbecue Cookbook
Everything® Bartender's Book, $9.95
Everything® Chinese Cookbook
Everything® Chocolate Cookbook
Everything® College Cookbook
Everything® Cookbook
Everything® Dessert Cookbook
Everything® Diabetes Cookbook
Everything® Easy Gourmet Cookbook
Everything® Fondue Cookbook
Everything® Grilling Cookbook

Everything® Healthy Meals in Minutes Cookbook
Everything® Holiday Cookbook
Everything® Indian Cookbook
Everything® Low-Carb Cookbook
Everything® Low-Fat High-Flavor Cookbook
Everything® Low-Salt Cookbook
Everything® Meals for a Month Cookbook
Everything® Mediterranean Cookbook
Everything® Mexican Cookbook
Everything® One-Pot Cookbook
Everything® Pasta Cookbook
Everything® Quick Meals Cookbook
Everything® Slow Cooker Cookbook
Everything® Soup Cookbook
Everything® Thai Cookbook
Everything® Vegetarian Cookbook
Everything® Wine Book

HEALTH

Everything® Alzheimer's Book
Everything® Anti-Aging Book
Everything® Diabetes Book
Everything® Hypnosis Book
Everything® Low Cholesterol Book
Everything® Massage Book
Everything® Menopause Book
Everything® Nutrition Book
Everything® Reflexology Book
Everything® Stress Management Book

HISTORY

Everything® American Government Book
Everything® American History Book
Everything® Civil War Book
Everything® Irish History & Heritage Book
Everything® Middle East Book

HOBBIES & GAMES

Everything® Blackjack Strategy Book
Everything® Brain Strain Book, $9.95
Everything® Bridge Book
Everything® Candlemaking Book
Everything® Card Games Book
Everything® Cartooning Book
Everything® Casino Gambling Book, 2nd Ed.
Everything® Chess Basics Book
Everything® Crossword and Puzzle Book
Everything® Crossword Challenge Book
Everything® Cryptograms Book, $9.95
Everything® Digital Photography Book
Everything® Drawing Book
Everything® Easy Crosswords Book
Everything® Family Tree Book
Everything® Games Book, 2nd Ed.
Everything® Knitting Book
Everything® Knots Book
Everything® Motorcycle Book
Everything® Online Genealogy Book
Everything® Photography Book
Everything® Poker Strategy Book
Everything® Pool & Billiards Book
Everything® Quilting Book
Everything® Scrapbooking Book
Everything® Sewing Book
Everything® Woodworking Book
Everything® Word Games Challenge Book

HOME IMPROVEMENT

Everything® Feng Shui Book
Everything® Feng Shui Decluttering Book, $9.95
Everything® Fix-It Book
Everything® Homebuilding Book
Everything® Landscaping Book
Everything® Lawn Care Book
Everything® Organize Your Home Book

All Everything® books are priced at $12.95 or $14.95, unless otherwise stated. Prices subject to change without notice.